D0845657

UNITED STATES
HOLIDAYS AND OBSERVANCES

UNITED STATES HOLIDAYS AND OBSERVANCES

*By Date, Jurisdiction, and Subject,
Fully Indexed*

Steve Rajtar

McFarland & Company, Inc., Publishers
Jefferson, North Carolina, and London

Library of Congress Cataloguing-in-Publication Data

Rajtar, Steve, 1951–
United States holidays and observances : by date, jurisdiction, and
subject, fully indexed / Steve Rajtar.
p.   cm.
Includes indexes.

ISBN 0-7864-1446-4 (illustrated case binding : 55# alkaline paper)

1. Holidays — United States.   2. Special days — United States.   I. Title.
GT4803.R35   2003   394.26973 — dc21   2002154293

British Library cataloguing data are available

Cover photograph: ©2002 Comstock

Manufactured in the United States of America

*McFarland & Company, Inc., Publishers
Box 611, Jefferson, North Carolina 28640
www.mcfarlandpub.com*

To Gayle, Jason, Karen, Kelly and Will,
who make every day special

Contents

Preface: Every Day's a Holiday

Every day of the year, somewhere in the United States, a holiday is being observed by individuals, governments or organizations.

This book lists and describes those holidays, date by date. If it is a holiday statutorily designated by the Federal government or by the state or equivalent jurisdiction, it is listed here.

What is meant by "the United States"?

The United States is composed of 50 states, plus other areas that enjoy at least limited U.S. citizenship or rights. The non-state jurisdictions that are included in this book are:

> American Samoa
> District of Columbia
> Guam
> Northern Mariana Islands
> Puerto Rico
> U.S. Virgin Islands

The U.S. government also has its own federal law, which applies throughout the country. A holiday might be federal, or state (or territorial), or both.

The United States is a member state of the United Nations. The U.N. has numerous days designated for various observations, and many of them are celebrated in the United States to varying degrees. Often, instead of being officially recognized by the federal or state governments, the U.N. observations are carried out by groups of citizens who may or may not be a part of an international organization.

The United Nations designates longer periods of time for focusing on important issues, and so declares the "Year of the ..." or "Decade of ...". Since they are recognized by Americans (albeit not because their governments say so), they are in this book, listed under January 1.

For the near future, the United Nations has designated the following:

Decade to Roll Back Malaria in Developing Countries, Particularly in Africa (2001–10)

International Decade for a Culture of Peace and Non-violence for the Children of the World (2001–10)

International Decade of the World's Indigenous People (1994–2004)

International Year of Freshwater (2003)

International Year of Microcredit (2005)

Second International Decade for the Eradication of Colonialism (2001–10)

United Nations Decade for the Eradication of Poverty (1997–2006)

United Nations Decade for Human Rights Education (1995–2004)

United Nations Literacy Decade: Education for All (2003–12)

Thanks to these observances, every day of the year has a number of commemorations in effect. Add to them the federal holidays and those of the other 56 jurisdictions, and you have a plethora of days to celebrate.

Which holidays are not included?

There are days, weeks, and months too numerous to mention that have been designated by cities, counties, business organizations, and others. They may be one-time events or they might be declared annually, but they are not recognized by the United Nations, the federal government or the other 56 jurisdictions covered in this book, so they are not included.

What is a holiday?

The definition of "holiday" varies from state to state. If a day is a holiday, certain statutory rules go into effect, which may include some of these and more:

Government employees are not required to work, or must be paid at a higher rate.

Schools are closed.

Contracts entered into on such date are void or voidable.

The day is not counted in determining how many business days have passed (such as when one is given a certain number of days to respond to a lawsuit).

Often, a jurisdiction has different classes of holidays, and may designate some as "commemorative days," "days of remembrance," "special days," "days of honor," "memorial days," "days of commemoration," or "observances." That normally means that the special day does not entitle employees or students to stay home, but it does focus honor, concern, or funds on something that is determined to be important.

In this book, no distinction is made among the various classes of holidays and observances. The character of the observance can only be determined by studying the statutes of the jurisdiction. This book is a listing of all observances designated by statute as of the beginning of 2002. Expect more to be added as people, events, diseases, and other matters are brought to the attention of legislators. Expect many more jurisdictions to fix September 11 as a day to remember the victims and heroes of the terrorist attacks which occurred in New York City in 2001, as did the U.S. Congress when they designated it "Patriot Day."

Do observances occurring on weekends count as holidays?

Maybe. In some states, they are officially designated as holidays. In some, business transacted on Saturdays or Sundays is not legally valid. Legal notices given then are nullities. It all depends on what the laws provide.

Even if Saturdays or Sundays are not officially designated as holidays, they are often specially dealt with in the respective statutes in order to set them apart from Mondays and Tuesdays. In this book, they are listed only where the jurisdiction has officially declared them to be holidays. Please keep in mind that even if they are not listed here, there are likely to be some rules in any particular jurisdiction that makes them different from other days.

What about religious holidays?

They are included here only if they have been designated as holidays or observances by the legislatures. Christmas has been so designated in nearly each one; Yom Kippur, Good Friday and a few others have been designated in a few. Easter has not been designated as a holiday, even though two days before and the day after may be, since Easter by definition already occurs on a Sunday, which is special in itself.

Many religions have their own days which are observed by substantial numbers of Americans. However, if those days have not received a legislature's official designation by being written into government statutes, they do not appear here.

What is a "week"?

For most of us, a week begins on Sunday and ends the following Saturday. Some of the holidays designated as "weeks" are specified as being as short as five days or as long as eleven. Some that are designated as "days" are really seven days long.

There is a problem of definition where a statute designates a period of observance as "the first week of January." If January 1 is a Sunday, it's clear that the first week is January 1–7. If January 1 is a Monday, does "the first week" start then and extend through the following Sunday, or does it run from January 7 through the 13th?

It varies from state to state and from year to year. Sometimes a state may go with one choice, and sometimes with another, depending on what may also be on its calendar for that year. Unlike holidays such as Independence Day and Veterans' Day, which are fixed on July 4 and November 11 regardless of the day of the week, designations such as "the first week" leave some room for interpretation, and one should consult the official state calendar for the year in question.

Another matter of variance concerns the actual day of observance, which may vary from the official day stated in the statute. In some states, if certain holidays fall on a weekend they are celebrated on the following Monday. Sometimes, however, a holiday falling on a Saturday is instead observed on the previous Friday. To be sure, you have to consult the jurisdiction's official calendar for the year you are interested in.

Which jurisdictions have the most and which the fewest designated observances?

Massachusetts has 152 designated periods of observance. Those days, weeks and months add up to 848 days a year, many of them overlapping, so that the state's residents sometimes have many things to celebrate simultaneously. Puerto Rico is not far behind, with 142 observances totaling 638 days a year.

On the other end of the spectrum are American Samoa and the District of Columbia with 11 individual days each. The state with the fewest is Idaho, with 12.

The day on the 2003 calendar with the greatest number of separate observances is May 16, with 29. The only days with zero are August 13, December 22 and December 23. To each of those numbers, add the United Nations observances listed above. Because of observances with dates that vary from year to year, calendar dates will fluctuate in their numbers of special topics being observed.

What does this tell us?

The people honored, the events commemorated and the causes promoted say much about the history of each jurisdiction and its priorities. Although the legal effect of designating a day or week or month in the official statutes varies, it is consistently a statement that the matter is important. It is interesting to see the variation in what is perceived as important as one travels from area to area within the United States.

JANUARY

Observances with Variable Dates

First Week in January

Ohio Braille Literacy Week (OH) — This is in honor of Louis Braille, the inventor of the Braille system used, in modified form, for printing, writing, and musical notation for the blind. He was born near Paris on January 4, 1809, and became blind from an accident at the age of three or four. He had picked up a leather awl which slipped and pierced one eye, which developed an infection that eliminated the sight in both eyes. In school, he and other blind students were taught to read raised letters pressed into paper with bent wires, but it was not possible for them to write using the same complex method. In 1821 the school was visited by Charles Barbier, who had invented "night writing" for the use by soldiers in trenches, using combinations of twelve raised dots, but the system proved to be too complicated and was rejected by the army. Braille modified the concept to develop a writing system using six dots, and in 1827 the first book in Braille was published. Braille became a teacher in that school, but his writing system met resistance from many and was little used when he died from tuberculosis in 1852. However, in 1868 four blind men, including Dr. Thomas Armitage, formed the British and Foreign Society for Improving the Embossed Literature of the Blind, and promoted Braille's system into worldwide acceptance and use.

First Monday in January

Gubernatorial Inauguration Day (GU) — Since 1971 this has been the day every four years that the governor and lieutenant governor have been inaugurated. Ceremonies are arranged by the Transition Committee and the incumbent governor. In years when the legislature is also inaugurated, its ceremony is coordinated to avoid a scheduling conflict.

Week including January 11

Eugenio Maria de Hostos Week (PR) — Hostos was born on January 11, 1839, and was educated in Puerto Rico and Spain, becoming active in republican politics as a university student. Leaving Spain in 1869 when it refused to grant independence to Puerto Rico, he went to the U.S. and became the editor of the Cuban independence journal *La Revolucion*. After the Spanish-American War, he advocated autonomy for the island, but the U.S. rejected that and established territorial rule.

Second Sunday in January

Volunteer Fireman's Day (NJ) — This day celebrates the volunteer firemen of New Jersey. Many are members of the North Jersey Volunteer Firemen's Association, founded in 1928, serving the men and women who serve in the counties of Bergen, Essex, Hudson, Morris and Passaic. That and other organizations provide training and support for those who risk their lives to fight fires.

Friday Preceding the Third Monday in January

Lee-Jackson Day (VA) — This day honors Robert Edward Lee (1807–1870) and Thomas Jonathan (Stonewall) Jackson (1824–1863), defenders of causes. Thomas Jonathan Jackson is the second most revered of all Confederate commanders (after Robert E. Lee), and, like Lee, graduated from West Point and fought in the Mexican War. His nicknames while he taught at Virginia Military Institute were "Tom Fool Jackson" and "Old Blue Light," but they were replaced by "Stonewall" by Gen. Barnard Bee at the first Battle of Bull Run. The name was applied both to Jackson and to his 1st Brigade, who distinguished themselves in battle. After several defeats in western Virginia, he came back with victories at Front Royal, 1st Winchester, Cross Keys and Port Republic. His greatest day was when he led his troops around the Union right flank at Chancellorsville to rout the 11th Corps, but he was wounded by his own men while returning to his own lines that same evening, and after the amputation of his arm, he died eight days later on May 10, 1863.

Third Week in January

Jaycee Week (MA) — This week celebrates the United States Junior Chamber, which gives young people between the ages of 21 and 39 the tools they need to develop business and management skills, and connect with others in and beyond their communities.

Third Sunday in January

Volunteer First Aid and Rescue Squad Day (NJ) — In New Jersey, many communities are served by groups of volunteers formed to help people. They are part of the New Jersey State First Aid Council, which brings members of the squads together in order to discuss methods of betterment of ambulance service, reduction of the loss of life, development of better service through education, and fostering of a spirit of harmony and friendship among the squads. On this day the squads, and the individuals who comprise them, are honored for their service to their communities.

Third Monday in January

Martin Luther King, Jr. Day (DE, KS, ME, MI, MT, SC, SD, TN, TX, VA) [**Anniversary of the Birth of Martin Luther King, Jr.** (WA), **Birthday of Dr. Martin Luther King** (CO), **Birthday of Martin Luther King, Jr.** (Fed, GA, NE), **Dr. Martin Luther King, Jr.'s Birthday** (AR, DC, IA, LA, MD, MS, RI), **Dr. Martin Luther King, Jr. Day** (CA, HI, NY, PA, UT), **Martin Luther King Day** (CT, MO, ND, OH), **Martin Luther King, Jr. Civil Rights Day** (NH), **Martin Luther King, Jr./Civil Rights Day** (AZ), **Martin Luther King, Jr.– Idaho Human Rights Day** (ID), **Martin Luther King, Jr., Wyoming Equality Day** (WY), **Martin Luther King, Jr.'s Birthday** (AL, AK, IL, IN, KY, NV, NM, NC, OK, OR, VI, VT), **Martin Luther King's Birthday** (MN, NJ, PR, WV)] — This day is dedicated to the remembrance of Dr. Martin Luther King, Jr. (1927–1968) and to the observance and appreciation of the various ethnic minorities who have contributed so much to the state and nation. His 1963 march on Washington, D.C., and his "I Have a Dream" speech placed civil rights and racial segregation in the forefront of national issues. He was killed by James Earl Ray in Memphis, Tennessee, on April 4, 1968. In Utah, this day formerly was known as Human Rights Day. In Connecticut, the last preceding school day is to include an observance of Martin Luther King's selfless devotion to the advancement of equality and the preservation of human rights. Effective with the celebration of this day in 2003, events in Rhode Island are governed by the 13-member Martin Luther King, Jr. State Holiday Commission, which will plan, supervise and administer the celebration in conjunction with the federal Martin Luther King Day Commission and the Martin Luther King Center for Non-Violent Social Change.

Robert E. Lee's Birthday (AL, AR, MS) — At the outbreak of the Civil War, Pres. Lincoln offered Lee the command of the Union army, but Lee instead offered his services to Confederate Pres. Jefferson Davis, who named Lee to replace Gen. Joe Johnston who was wounded after the Battle of Bull Run. The Army of Northern Virginia, under Lee's command, defeated every Union general who opposed him, until U.S. Grant was victorious at the Battle of Attrition. Lee came back with a victory at the Battle of Chancellorsville in May 1863, but he was defeated at Gettysburg after a failed attack known as Pickett's Charge. Later, Lee surrendered to Grant at Appomattox Court House on April 9, 1865, effectively ending the war. After the war, Lee served as president of Washington University (now known as Washington and Lee University) in Lexington, Virginia, until he died on October 12, 1870. His civil rights, which had been suspended after the war, were reinstated posthumously by Pres. Gerald Ford in 1975.

Wednesday During the Third Week in January

Jaycee Day (MA) — On this day, attention is drawn to the activities of the United States Junior Chamber, which was founded in St. Louis, Missouri, by Henry Glessenbier and his friends in 1910. Called the Herculaneum Dance Club, they were inspired in 1915 by Col. H.N. Morgan to shift their focus from the preservation of conservative dance styles to civic issues in which they could become involved. Their group became the Young Men's Progressive Civic Association, and in 1916 they were called the Junior Citizens (JCs or Jaycees). Two years later they were renamed as the St. Louis Junior Chamber of Commerce. After World War II, Glessenbier contacted other similar groups and 29 of them formed the United States Junior Chamber of Commerce.

Third Friday in January

Arbor Day (FL) — The first official Arbor Day celebration was held on March 12, 1874, proclaimed by Nebraska governor Robert W. Furnas. It became a legal holiday in that state in 1885, setting April 22 as the date of observance, commemorating the birthday of J. Sterling Morton, the newspaperman and Nebraska pioneer who first proposed it. It is held on various dates throughout the U.S. to coincide with the best tree-planting weather.

Fourth Week in January

Child Nutrition Week (MA) — This is a week to remind those concerned with the nutrition of children, including parents, teachers, school administrators, and cafeteria managers, that child nutrition employees work hard the year-round. In this state, the programs to thank these individuals for their hard work are administered by the Massachusetts Department of Education's Nutrition Programs and Services.

First Week Following the Last Sunday in January

Educational Week Pro Tourism in Puerto Rico (PR) — During this week Puerto Rico celebrates outstanding individuals and organizations involved with tourism and hospitality, such as the Caribbean Hotel Association. It and other tourism-based organizations are dedicated to excellence in hospitality, marketing and a growing tourism industry.

OBSERVANCES WITH FIXED DATES

January 1

Asian and Pacific Decade of Disabled Persons (U.N.) — This decade was proclaimed for 1993–2002 to strengthen regional cooperation in achieving the goals of the World Programme of Action concerning the disabled in Asia and the Pacific.

Decade to Roll Back Malaria in Developing Countries, Particularly in Africa (U.N.) —

The period from 2001 through 2010 is being used to combat one of the world's most deadly diseases, which kills approximately one million people a year in Africa. Goals include providing personal and community protective measures, such as insecticide-treated blankets, to at least 60 percent of those at risk for the disease, and providing at least 60 percent of the pregnant women who are at risk with chemoprophylaxis or presumptive intermittent treatment. The United

Nations hopes that at least 60 percent of those suffering from malaria will be able to have prompt access to correct, affordable and appropriate treatment within 24 hours of the onset of symptoms.

Eye Care Month (PR) — This month is celebrated by the College of Optometrists of Puerto Rico, the Puerto Rico Ophthalmologic Association and the Puerto Rico Eye Care Association.

International Decade for a Culture of Peace and Non-violence for the Children of the World (U.N.) — Established in November of 2000, the decade of 2001–10 was declared to strengthen the global movement for a culture of peace, and the U.N. invited its member nations to place greater emphasis on promoting a culture of peace and non-violence. The General Assembly designated UNESCO, the United Nations Educational, Scientific and Cultural Organization, as the lead agency for this decade. Religious bodies and groups, artists, educational institutions and the media were invited to support the decade to benefit all of the world's children.

International Decade of the World's Indigenous People (U.N.) — The goal of this decade (1994–2004), proclaimed by the United Nations General Assembly in 1990, is to strengthen international cooperation for solving problems faced by indigenous people. The focus is on areas such as human rights, the environment, development, education and health. The theme of "Indigenous People: Partnership in Action" is to be coordinated by the High Commissioner for Human Rights.

International Year of Ecotourism (U.N.) — During 2002, emphasis is on the promotion of development and the protection of the environment, integrating further development of the tourist industry, especially in developing nations.

International Year of Freshwater (U.N.) — The United Nations in 2000 proclaimed 2003 as a period to take advantage of the opportunity to increase awareness of the importance of freshwater, and to promote action at all levels.

International Year of Microcredit (U.N.) — The year of 2005 is observed to give impetus to worldwide microcredit programs, making credit and related services for self-employment and income-generating activities available to an increasing number of individuals living in poverty. Attention is focused on the role of microcredit in poverty eradication and its contribution to social development.

International Year of Mountains (U.N.) — In 2002, members of the United Nations are encouraged to promote conservation and sustainable development in mountain areas. Awareness of mountain ecosystems is to be increased, as is their importance in providing crucial goods and services, such as water supply and food security. The cultural heritage of mountain communities is to be defended.

New Year's Day (Fed, AL, AK, AS, AZ, AR, CA, CO, CT, DC, FL, GA, GU, HI, IL, IN, IA, KS, KY, LA, ME, MD, MI, MN, MS, MO, MT, NE, NV, NH, NJ, NM, NY, NC, ND, CM, OH, OK, OR, PA, PR, RI, SC, SD, TN, TX, VI, UT, VT, VA, WA, WV, WI, WY) [**New Years Day** (DE, ID)] — Celebration of the arrival of the new year dates back to Babylon in about 2000 B.C., where it was held beginning with the first new moon after the vernal equinox in spring. In 153 B.C. the Roman senate declared the new year to be January 1, but it was not fixed on that date until the introduction of the Julian calendar in 46 B.C. The Catholic Church opposed the celebration for several centuries, and it has been considered a holiday by most Western nations only since about 1600. In the U.S., there are traditional New Year foods, including black-eyed peas with either hog jowls or ham, cabbage, and rice, that are supposed to bring good luck for the rest of the year.

Second Industrial Development Decade for Africa (U.N.) — This decade (1993–2002) focuses on strengthening working relationships among the United Nations Industrial Development Organization, the World Trade Organization, and other multilateral institutions. The goal is to provide technical assistance to African countries to enhance their capacity to overcome technical barriers to trade in industrial and other products.

Second International Decade for the Eradication of Colonialism (U.N.) — On the 40th anniversary of the adoption of the Declaration on the Granting of Independence to Colonial Countries and Peoples, the General Assembly of the United Nations declared 2001–10 as a decade to work toward eradication of colonialism. It calls upon colonial nations to take steps to enable the peoples they administer to exercise their right to self-determination, including independence.

Third Decade to Combat Racism and Racial Discrimination (U.N.) — The General

Assembly of the United Nations is calling upon nations in 1993–2003 to combat new forms of racism, such as xenophobia and related intolerance; discrimination based on culture, nationality, religion or language; and racism resulting from official doctrines of racial superiority or exclusivity, such as ethnic cleansing.

United Nations Decade for Human Rights Education (U.N.)—This decade (1995–2004) was proclaimed in recognition that human rights education should be a lifelong process by which people learn respect for the dignity of others. The United Nations calls upon governments to direct education toward the full development of the human personality and the strengthening of respect for human rights and fundamental freedoms. During this decade, the Plan of Action is to be implemented by the United Nations High Commissioner for Human Rights.

United Nations Decade for the Eradication of Poverty (U.N.)—This decade was proclaimed for 1997–2006 by the United Nations General Assembly with a target of halving, by 2015, the proportion of people living on less than one dollar a day, and those who are suffering from hunger. Through decisive national action and strengthened international cooperation, the goal is to eradicate absolute poverty and reducing overall poverty substantially throughout the world.

United Nations Literacy Decade: Education for All (U.N.)—From 2003 through 2012, the message is that literacy is at the heart of basic education for all. Attention is placed on the notion that creating literate environments is essential to eradicating poverty, achieving gender equity and ensuring sustainable development.

United Nations Year for Cultural Heritage (U.N.)—The year of 2002 is a time to consider the tangible and intangible cultural heritage of the world to be a common ground for promoting mutual understanding and enrichment among cultures and civilizations.

January 5

Dr. George Washington Carver Recognition Day (RI)—Carver was a botanist, chemist and educator, born on January 5, 1864, near Diamond Grove, Missouri. The identity of his father is not known, but is presumed to be a slave from a neighboring farm. While an infant, he and his mother were kidnapped by Confederate night-raiders. Although his owner, Moses Carver, was able to recover George after the end of the Civil War in exchange for a race horse, his mother was never found. George was then raised by the Carvers, and acquired an early interest in nature. He was the first black student at Simpson College; he then transferred to Iowa Agricultural College (now known as Iowa State University) to study science. Included in his accomplishments are his discovery of more than 300 industrial uses for peanuts, plus hundreds more for sweet potatoes, pecans and soybeans. He developed a cropping rotation method which revolutionized Southern agriculture. He produced textile dyes of 500 different shades, replacing dyes which had previously been imported from Europe. From 1897 until his death on January 5, 1943, Carver served as a member of the faculty of Booker T. Washington's Tuskegee Normal and Industrial Institute for Negroes. Carver did not patent or profit from most of his work, instead opting to share it with everyone for the common good.

George W. Norris Day (NE)—This celebrates the accomplishments of George W. Norris, which include (1) establishment of a nonpartisan unicameral legislative body for the state; (2) establishment of the Tennessee Valley Authority; (3) development of electricity in the rural areas of the nation; (4) passage of the 20th Amendment to the U.S. Constitution, commonly known as the Lame-Duck Amendment; and (5) passage of the Norris–La Guardia Act, which outlawed yellow-dog contracts and was a great boon to working men and women throughout the nation.

State Constitution Day (NH)—The New Hampshire State Constitution was established on October 31, 1783, with an effective date of June 2, 1784.

January 6

Haym Salomon Day (NY)—Haym Salomon was born in Poland in 1740. After participating in that country's struggle for independence, he came to New York in 1772. A personal friend of George Washington, Salomon proposed to him an American revolution against England based on an idea borrowed from the Talmud—"One nation united under one God with freedom and liberty for every citizen." Salomon offered his personal fortune of 600,000 pounds sterling, which would translate to several million dollars in today's economy. For the cause of American independence, he raised an additional 3.5 million pounds sterling in France, obtained Gen. Lafayette and his arsenal to help in the fight, and recruited every able-bodied Jewish man in the colonies to join the army. When the British hired German mercenaries to fight on their side, Salomon was able to have many of them switch to the colonists' side by offering them more money. Salomon's money and efforts made the American Revolution possible, but he personally died bankrupt in 1785.

Sam Rayburn Day (TX) — Samuel Taliafero Rayburn was born in Roane County, Tennessee, on January 6, 1882, and moved to Fannin County, Texas, at the age of five. He attended East Texas Normal College and taught for a while, then entered politics. He was elected to the Texas House of Representatives in 1906 while he was attending law school at the University of Texas at Austin, and from 1910 to 1912 was Speaker of the State House of Representatives. At the conclusion of that term, he ran for and won a seat in the U.S. House of Representatives, and was reelected 24 times. He served as the U.S. Speaker of the House from 1940 to 1947, from 1949 to 1953, and from 1955 until he died on November 16, 1961. Rayburn was the Democratic Majority Leader of five Congresses and Democratic Minority Leader of two. Three times, he chaired the Democratic National Convention.

Three Kings Day (PR, VI) — This is the 12th of the "Twelve Days of Christmas," celebrated around the world. This day is called "Epiphany," "The Adoration of the Magi," and "The Manifestation of God," commemorating the arrival of Caspar, Melchior and Balthasar, who followed a bright star to Bethlehem and brought with them gifts of gold, frankincense and myrrh. In the Virgin Islands, this is a holiday only on the island of St. Croix. It is celebrated there to emphasize and maintain the Hispanic heritage and culture existing in the Virgin Islands, especially on that island.

January 8

Anniversary of the Battle of New Orleans (MA) [**Battle of New Orleans** (LA)] — This is in memory of the services of the soldiers and sailors of the War of 1812, and the lessons to be learned from the successes and failures of our armies in that war. The series of battles itself was fought by about 4,000 militiamen, pirates and sailors led by Gen. Andrew Jackson. Fighting behind barricades, they prevented 8,000 British soldiers from taking New Orleans on several days from December 1814 through January 8, 1815. From their mud and cotton-bale protection, they were able to pick off the attackers crossing through a quarter mile of open field on the Chalmette Plantation. The 11,000 to 14,450 British suffered about 2,000 casualties, while the Americans had eight killed and 13 wounded. After British commander Maj. Gen. Sir Edward Pakenham was killed by a shell which severed an artery in his leg, his successor pulled the survivors off the field in a general retreat. Jackson became a national hero, and this day was celebrated as a holiday by the time the Civil War began. This is also known as Jackson Day and Old Hickory's Day.

January 9

Commonwealth Day (CM) — The Commonwealth of North Marianas has a political union with the U.S., with federal funds administered by the U.S. Department of the Interior, Office of Territorial and International Affairs. Beginning in 1947, the area became a Trust Territory, recognized by the United Nations and administered first by the United States Navy, and later by the Department of the Interior. Since January of 1978, under a Covenant Agreement, the nation is self-governing, with a locally-elected governor, lieutenant governor and legislature. On November 4, 1986, residents of the Northern Marianas were granted U.S. citizenship, and in 1990 the Security Council of the United Nations voted to dissolve the Trusteeship.

Day to Commemorate Felisa Rincon Vda. de Gautier's Birthday (PR) — This celebration commemorates the former female mayor of Puerto Rico's capital city, San Juan Bautista. She was born in 1897 and assisted Luis Munoz in establishing the Popular Democratic Party during the 1930s. She is remembered for holding weekly open houses at her official residence and flying snow to San Juan for children's Christmas parties. The League of American Women in 1953 honored her with its Woman of the Year Award. She died in 1994.

January 11

Birthday of Eugenio Maria de Hostos (PR) — This day celebrates the life of Eugenio

Maria de Hostos (1839–1903), a noted Puerto Rican educator, philosopher, sociologist, writer and patriot. Educated in Spain, he advocated an Antilles federation including Puerto Rico, Cuba and the Dominican Republic. He devoted his life to seeking the political independence of Puerto Rico and Cuba, and founded the first normal school in Puerto Rico. As a professor at the University of Chile, he was a key factor in women being admitted to the school. As a rationalist, he believed that "to be civilized and to be moral is the same thing."

January 13

Stephen Foster Memorial Day (Fed) — Born in Lawrenceville, Pennsylvania, on July 4, 1826, Stephen Collins Foster received his early musical training from German immigrant Henry Kleber, and became one of the most famous musical composers of the U.S. Much of his work celebrates the black portion of the population at a time when slavery was an important and controversial issue. His folksy songs include *Massa's in de Cold Cold Ground, O Susanna, Laura Lee, I Would Not Die in Summer Time, My Old Kentucky Home, Suwanee River* and *Old Folks at Home.* Foster also composed instrumental music, including the *Social Orchestra*, a collection of 73 arrangements for flute, piano, violin and other instruments. He was not well known to the public during his lifetime, as he did not perform music professionally. While he was alive, he earned $15,091.08 in royalties for his songs. He died in New York City on January 13, 1864.

January 14

Albert Schweitzer's Reverence for Life Day (MA) — Schweitzer was born on January 14, 1875, in Kayserburg, Alsace, Germany. After studying science, theology and music, he decided to become a medical missionary, so he studied medicine at the University of Strassbourg from 1905 until 1913. In 1913, largely with money he himself raised, he founded a hospital in Lambarene, Gabon (then French Equatorial Africa), which served thousands of natives. Consistent with his philosophy of a "reverence for life," he used the $33,000 from his 1952 Nobel Peace Prize to expand the hospital and establish a leper colony. During 1955, Queen Elizabeth II awarded

him the Order of Merit, the highest British civilian award. Schweitzer's writings include a biography of Johann Sebastian Bach (1905), *On the Edge of the Primeval Forest* (1920), *More from the Primeval Forest* (1925), *From My African Notebook* (1936), and *Reverence for Life*. He died on September 4, 1965.

January 15

Birthday of Martin Luther King, Jr. (FL) [**Dr. Martin Luther King, Jr.'s Birthday** (WI), **Martin Luther King, Jr. Day** (MA)] — Martin Luther King, Jr. was born on January 15, 1929, in Atlanta, Georgia. His grandfather was a Baptist preacher, and his father was the pastor of Ebenezer Baptist Church in Atlanta. The younger King was educated at Crozier Theological Seminary and Boston University. He became acquainted with the philosophy of Mahatma Gandhi, and on a trip to India in 1959 he met with some of Gandhi's followers, becoming convinced that nonviolent resistance was the most potent weapon available to oppressed people seeking freedom. King led a black bus boycott in Montgomery, Alabama, and gained a national reputation for the advocation of civil rights. Initially, his birthday was celebrated on January 15, but later, to bring it into conformity with most federal holidays, it was changed to the third Monday of January. Three states still have it on their books as January 15, although their actual celebration coincides with the third Monday.

January 16

Temperance and Good Citizenship Day (WA) — For this day, the Washington Superintendent of Public Instructions will prepare and publish for circulation among teachers of the state a program which embodies topics promoting temperance and good citizenship.

January 17

Robert E. Lee's Birthday (NC) — Robert E. Lee was born on January 19, 1807, in Stratford, Virginia. His father was known as "Light Horse Harry Lee," a Revolutionary War hero. He graduated second in his class at West Point, earning no demerits for discipline infractions during his years there. He was granted a commission as an engineer, and helped build the waterfront in St. Louis and coastal forts in Savannah and Brunswick, Georgia. He married Mary Custis, a granddaughter of George and Martha Washington.

January 19

Confederate Heroes Day (TX) — This day was chosen to honor Jefferson Davis, Robert E. Lee and other Confederate heroes, especially the men who also had an effect on the history of Texas, who believed that their cause was just. These include Lee, who fought in the Mexican War and was serving as second in command of troops in Texas before the Civil War. Another was Gen. Albert Sidney Johnson, a Texan who lost his life at the Battle of Shiloh on April 6–7, 1862.

Robert E. Lee Day (KY, LA, TN) [**Birthday of Robert E. Lee** (FL, GA)] — General Robert Edward Lee, commander of the Confederate army during the Civil War, was born on January 19, 1807. His first military action after graduation from West Point was in 1845, in the war with Mexico. Under Gen. Winfield Scott he was in charge of mapping out terrain and dividing the line of advance for troops, and once he led the troops into battle. He met and worked with later key players in the Civil War, including James Longstreet, U.S. Grant, George Pickett and Thomas J. Jackson. Following the Mexican War, Lee went back to his profession as an army engineer. He and wife Mary moved into the Custis mansion, now surrounded by Arlington National Cemetery.

Virginia and American History Month (VA) — This period is a special tribute to the founders, builders and preservers of the commonwealth and the nation. It continues through February 22.

January 20

Inauguration Day (DC, LA) — Despite the celebration of the swearing-in of the new U.S. President being a national event, it is officially designated to be a holiday only in the District of Columbia and Baton Rouge, Louisiana.

January 26

General Douglas MacArthur Day (AR) — Born in 1880, Douglas MacArthur rose to the rank of army general, and was one of the most controversial individuals to hold that rank. From 1930 to 1935 he served as the U.S. Army Chief of Staff. In 1942 he became the Supreme Commander of Allied Forces in the Southwest Pacific. He held that position until 1945, and then again starting in 1950. After a confrontation with Pres. Harry Truman, he was relieved of his command. He died on April 5, 1964.

Washington Army and Air National Guard Day (WA) — When this became a day of recognition in 1991, nearly 9,000 dedicated men and women were serving the state of Washington and the U.S. on a voluntary basis. They are involved with domestic matters, such as providing aid after the eruption of Mount St. Helens in 1980, and those abroad, including service in Kosovo and Macedonia in 2000.

January 28

Birthday of Armando Sanchez Martinez (PR) — This day has been designated by the Puerto Rican legislature to honor this semi-famous native.

Christa McAuliffe Day (IL) — This day commemorates space exploration and the role played by Christa McAuliffe, who was to be the first civilian in space. In an effort to rekindle interest in what had become routine space shuttle missions, the leaders of NASA wanted an ordinary citizen to communicate the excitement of travel in space, so they chose this social studies teacher from Concord High School in Concord, New Hampshire. She called her trip aboard the *Challenger* the "ultimate field trip." Unfortunately, the mission ended in tragedy on January 28, 1986, when the shuttle exploded shortly after being launched, killing all aboard.

January 30

Franklin D. Roosevelt Day (KY, TN) — Roosevelt was born on January 30, 1882, and died on April 12, 1945. The only man elected to four terms as president, he is best known as leading the country out of the Great Depression and during World War II. In Tennessee he is particularly remembered as the father of the Civilian Conservation Corps.

Pennsylvanians with Disabilities Day

(PA)—This day was chosen to recognize disabled citizens of the state because it is the birthday of one of America's most distinguished physically disabled individuals, Franklin Delano Roosevelt. He was stricken with polio in 1921, but recovered partial use of legs and led the U.S. through the Great Depression and World War II.

FEBRUARY

OBSERVANCES WITH VARIABLE DATES

First Week Following the Last Sunday in January

Educational Week Pro Tourism in Puerto Rico (PR)— During this week, Puerto Rico celebrates outstanding individuals and organizations involved with tourism and hospitality, such as the Caribbean Hotel Association. It and other tourism-based organizations are dedicated to excellence in hospitality, marketing and a growing tourism industry.

First Week in February

Home Education Week (GA)— The state of Georgia recognizes that in the first two centuries of this country, the majority of pre-college children received their education at home, and that the country in those days enjoyed an extremely high literacy rate on its way to becoming the most educated nation on earth. It also recognizes the critical importance of the fundamental right of parents to direct the upbringing and type of education for their children. This is an opportunity to recognize home educators and home-instructed students for their efforts to improve the quality of education.

Week of Little League Baseball of Puerto Rico (PR)— This is a week to celebrate the island's extremely popular baseball program for youth, and their successes in international play.

First Sunday in February

Four Chaplains Sunday (ND)— This is in honor of the four chaplains who sacrificed their own lives to save the lives of other servicemen on the USS *Dorchester*, a U.S. Army troop transport ship that was sunk off the coast of Greenland on February 3, 1943.

Tadeusz Kosciuszko Day (MA)— This is in recognition of 170,000 Polish-Americans living in Massachusetts, and their contribution to the growth and development of the state and nation. It commemorates Polish general and national hero Tadeusz Andrzej Bonawentura Kosciuszko (2/4/1746–10/15/1817). With the money he was paid for his services during the American Revolution, he purchased slaves and set them free.

First Tuesday in February

Firefighter Appreciation Day (GA)— On this day, citizens are invited to remember the past firefighters who died while serving our communities, or who have dedicated their lives to protecting our safety.

First Thursday in February

Girls and Women in Sports Day (GA)— This is a day to celebrate the participation of females in sports and athletics. It is also a day to commemorate the enactment of federal Title IX in 1971, opening new opportunities for women and girls to participate in an area which previously had been more limited for them. This day is sponsored by Girl Scouts of the U.S.A., the National Association for Girls and Women in Sports, the Women's Sports Foundation, the YWCA of the U.S.A., and Girls Incorporated. On this day, the Georgia Women's Intersport Network sponsors awards to recognize outstanding high school female athletes and coaches in the state.

First Saturday in February

Gasparilla Day (FL) — This is an annual re-enactment of the Jose Gaspar invasion, based on a fictitious legend dating back to 1904. As the legend goes, Gaspar and "Ye Mystic Krewe" invaded the shores of downtown Tampa and took over the city. An entourage of boats accompanies the "Jose Gaspar," a replica of a pirate ship permanently anchored in Tampa Bay, shooting cannon as they approach Harbor Island. When they leave their boat, they board a decorative float, and a parade commences. Other aspects of the celebration include an art show, distance run, and illuminated night parade.

Week Including February 8

Boy Scout Week (MA) — This is held to commemorate the February 8, 1910, incorporation of the Boy Scouts of America. It was formed by William D. Boyce, a Chicago publisher who had discovered Scouting in London during the previous year. While he was lost in a fog, a boy assisted him in finding his destination. Boyce was surprised and impressed when the boy declined to accept any payment for his services, on the grounds that a Scout could not accept money for performing a "good turn." Boyce sought further information at the headquarters of British Scouting, which had been established by Robert S.S. Baden-Powell in 1907. Boyce returned to the U.S. with Scouting uniforms, literature and insignia, and, in conjunction with other men who had similar ideas, started the organization which is today the largest organization for boys in the U.S.

Second Week in February

Midwives Week (VI) — During this week, the Virgin Islands recognize and appreciate the services performed by its midwives. The profession is described in the Bible, and midwives assisted at births on the *Mayflower*.

Traffic Safety Week (MA) — This is a time for all citizens to focus on the consequences of traffic law violations and the numbers of drivers, bike riders and pedestrians who are injured on our roads. Educational programs are held, with the goal of reducing accidents.

First Monday Following February 4

Mrs. Rosa L. Parks Day (MI) — This is a celebration of a woman of great courage, vision, love and faith, who for decades resided in Michigan and continues to serve the state and her country by actively laboring to achieve equality for all. Parks was born in Tuskegee, Alabama, on February 4, 1913. A seamstress, she became famous when, on December 1, 1955, she refused to give up her seat on a bus to a white man. She was tired of the treatment she and other African Americans received. She was arrested and tried and fined $14, and the Montgomery, Alabama, bus system was boycotted by blacks for 381 days. Finally, the U.S. Supreme Court ruled in November 1956 that segregation on transportation is unconstitutional. Because of harassment she received in Alabama, Parks and her family moved to Detroit, Michigan, in 1957. In later years she participated in civil rights marches, has been honored for her work, and with her husband established in 1987 the Rosa and Raymond Parks Institute of Self Development in Detroit.

40 Days Before Easter (As early as February 8 or as late as March 15)

Mardi Gras Day (LA) [**Mardi Gras** (AL, MS)] — This is also known as Shrovetide, which in early England included various sports, especially soccer, plays and masques. The commencement of celebrations in New Orleans is usually considered to have taken place in 1857, with the formation of "The Mystick Krewe of Comus." That organization staged a parade with two floats, one carrying a king and one showing Satan in a blazing hell. In Alabama this is a holiday in

Mobile and Baldwin Counties. In Louisiana it is celebrated in some parishes and all municipalities. In Mississippi it may be declared a holiday by the governing authorities of any municipality or county to replace any holiday as a legal holiday (other than Robert E. Lee's Birthday or Dr. Martin Luther King, Jr.'s Birthday).

Shrove Tuesday (FL) — This is a holiday in counties where associations are organized for the purpose of celebrating Mardi Gras. The name "shrove" may come from "shrive," or "to confess." In early England, people were supposed to go to their confessors the week prior to Lent and confess their sins. It is celebrated on the Tuesday before Ash Wednesday, which begins a 40-day period of Lent, for the faithful to fast and make other sacrifices. The English have a custom of eating pancakes on this day, originally resulting from the need to use up eggs and fat, which were prohibited from being eaten during Lent.

Second Tuesday in February

Hispanic Culture Day (NM) — This day is in recognition of the many contributions, sacrifices and accomplishments of Hispanic people from throughout the world that have built New Mexico into a beautiful and dynamic mosaic of cultural diversity. Spanish influence began with the Conquistadors arriving with Coronado in the early 1540s, and the Catholic missionaries, who by 1680 had constructed about 80 missions throughout the state. The natives resisted the influx of the Spaniards, killed many, and threw out the rest. They returned twelve years later to recolonize the region, this time with tolerance of the practice of native religion along with their Catholicism. The early Hispanics are credited with many aspects of the culture of New Mexico, including the introduction of cattle, sheep and horses, the wheel, and the usage of metal for weapons, tools and art. The Spanish influence is also evident in the state's architecture, art, clothing and place names.

Second Wednesday in February

Youth to Work Day (CT) — This was established to allow an adult to bring a youth to work for the purpose of exposing such youth to the workplace. It emphasizes the limitless choices open to youth, and encourages children to believe in themselves, work hard, and make their dreams a reality. It also challenges youth to challenge stereotypes for gender roles in the workplace.

Second Friday in February

African-American Day (NM) — This day recognizes the many contributions and sacrifices African-Americans have made to ensure the rights of all Americans, so that they may be free and equal citizens and full participants in the governing of New Mexico and the U.S.

Friday Following the Second Monday in February

Arbor Day (OK) — The first official Arbor Day celebration, held on April 22, 1885, in Nebraska City, Nebraska, included a grand parade and a speech by J. Sterling Morton, the man who had first proposed the observance in 1872. Students assembled by grade, and each tree planted was labeled with the grade and the time planted; those who planted the tree were expected to care for it.

Week Including February 18

Luis Munoz-Marin Week (PR) — Luis Munoz Marin was born in San Juan, Puerto Rico, on February 18, 1898, and was educated at Georgetown University in Washington, D.C. He returned to Puerto Rico in 1920 and was a founder of the Popular Democratic Party in 1938. He initially supported Puerto Rican independence, and then found commonwealth status more economically viable. He worked with the governor appointed by the U.S. to work for improved housing, industrial and farming conditions. He also pushed for the redistribution of land from large owners to small farmers, and the poor approved his slogan of "Bread, land and liberty." His "Operation Bootstrap" encouraged mainland businesses to invest in Puerto Rican interests. He was the island's first elected governor in 1949, and was reelected three times, despite being denounced by the Catholic Church for his teaching of birth control. Rather than run for a fifth term as governor, he returned to his seat in the Senate. He died in San Juan on April 30, 1980.

Third Week in February

Rotary Week (PR)— This week celebrates the Rotary Clubs of Puerto Rico. The one in San Juan is the oldest existing Rotary Club in all of Latin America, having been founded in 1918. One milestone for that club occurred in 1987 when it inducted five of the world's first women Rotarians. The Puerto Rican clubs are part of Rotary International, an organization of business and professional leaders united to provide humanitarian service, encourage high ethical standards in all vocations, and help build goodwill and peace in the world. It is present in more than 160 countries and has about 1.2 million members. The first Rotary Club was founded in Chicago on February 23, 1905, by attorney Paul P. Harris.

Third Monday in February

Daisy Gatson Bates Day (AR)— This day honors the mentor of the "Little Rock Nine" of the 1957 Central High crisis. She was born in Huttig, Arkansas, in about 1914 and attended that city's segregated public schools, experiencing firsthand poor conditions for black children. In 1941 she married and moved to Little Rock. Her husband started a newspaper which stressed the need for improvement in conditions for blacks, which resulted in many white businesses withdrawing their advertisements.

In 1954 she led the NAACP's protest against the Little Rock school system's slow plan for integration. She personally brought black students into the white schools, including nine at Central High School on September 25, 1957, with National Guard units and 1,000 paratroopers to help enforce integration. She remained active in civil rights programs, and later the street running parallel to Central High was renamed in her honor.

Washington's Birthday (Fed, CT, DC, FL, GA, ID, IA, KS, KY, LA, ME, MD, MI, MS, NV, NH, NJ, NY, NC, RI, VT, WV) [**George Washington Day** (PR, VA), **George Washington's Birthday** (AL, AR, IN, ND), **George Washington's Birthday/President's Day** (SC), **Washington Day** (TN), **Washington's and Lincoln's Birthdays** (MN, WY), **Washington's Day** (MA)]— George Washington was born on February 22 (or February 11, under the old-style cal-endar that was in effect during the first portion of his life) in 1732. After serving in the British army he became the Commander in Chief of the Continental Army. He was the first president of the United States (1789–97), and the first holiday observance of his birthday took place in 1796, during the last year of his second term. Washington, known as the "Father of His Country," died on December 14, 1799.

Presidents' Day (AK, DE, HI, OK, PA, TX, WA, WI) [**President's Day** (GU, NE, CM), **Presidents Day** (IL, OR, VI), **Lincoln/ Washington President's Day** (AZ), **Lincoln's and Washington's Birthdays** (MT, SD), **Washington-Lincoln Day** (CO, OH), **Washington and Lincoln Day** (UT), **Washington and Lincoln's Birthday (Presidents' Day)** (NM)]— This day began as the commemoration of the birthday of George Washington, which was considered a bona fide national holiday by the early 19th century. In 1968 federal legislation shifted the Washington's Birthday celebration from February 22 to the third Monday in February, when it became popularly known as "President's Day" to also celebrate the birth of Abraham Lincoln (February 12) and other men who have become president of the U.S.

Thomas Jefferson's Birthday (AL)— Thomas Jefferson was born on April 13, 1743, but perhaps it is just convenient to celebrate it on the same day with Washington and Lincoln. Jefferson is known for being the chief author of the Declaration of Independence. Following the Revolutionary War, he worked in Virginia to revise his state's laws to bring them into conformity with the freedoms embraced by the new U.S. Constitution.

Jefferson served as the third U.S. President, and in 1815 sold his personal library to the Congress to rebuild the Library of Congress, which had been destroyed by fire during 1814. During his retirement years at his estate of Monticello, he founded, designed and directed the building of the University of Virginia. Thomas Jefferson died on July 4, 1826.

Third Tuesday in February

Election Day (PA)— It is curious that in the laws of the state, this day is set aside for local elections, but municipal elections usually instead find themselves being scheduled in May.

Third Wednesday in February

Retired Teachers Day (CT)— This day honors the retired teachers of Connecticut and their contributions to education.

Third Saturday in February

Purple Heart Day (SC)— This day is to honor the decoration itself and the men and women who have received it. George Washington created the award as the "Badge of Military Merit" in 1782 to help raise his soldiers' morale. It originally consisted of a piece of dark blue cloth with a purple silk heart edged in lace and braid. It was presented to three soldiers during the Revolutionary War, signifying any singularly meritorious action on the recipients' parts.

Last Week in February

Homeless Awareness Week (MA)— The Massachusetts Coalition for the Homeless was founded in 1981, the first such state-wide advocacy organization for homeless people in the U.S. This is a time for the Coalition, and other groups concerned about the homeless, to bring important issues to the attention of everyone. The number of homeless families in Massachusetts has been increasing in recent years, with nearly 3,000 homeless children in over 1,300 families receiving shelter by the state's Emergency Assistance Family Shelter Program. It estimates that for each in a shelter there is one more family which must fend for itself because it cannot qualify for assistance. As a result, in 2000 the Coalition established the Welfare Solidarity Project to help such families, and this week is utilized as a time to spread the word about this and other programs designed to help the homeless.

OBSERVANCES WITH FIXED DATES

February 1

American Heart Month (Fed)— The citizens of the U.S. are urged to recognize the nationwide problem of heart and blood vessel diseases, and to support all essential programs required to solve the problems.

American History Month (GA, IL, ME, MA, NH, NM, RI, VT)— The states recognize the importance of the understanding of the history of our nation, and promote its study. This is an annual opportunity for people to be reminded of the unselfish and devoted service, along with heroic sacrifices, of those who contributed so much to the glorious history of their states and the nation.

Georgia History Month (GA)— This is a special tribute to the founders, builders and preservers of the state. On February 12 the anniversary of the landing of James Edward Oglethorpe and colonists at Savannah in 1733 is celebrated. It is also known as Oglethorpe Day. Educational programs celebrating the rich history of Georgia are put on by the Georgia Historical Society, chartered in 1839 by the Georgia General Assembly.

Missouri Lifelong Learning Month (MO)— During this month, public awareness is focused on the importance of ongoing education throughout each person's lifetime.

Month of Trio Music (PR)— This is a celebration of the musical contributions of the trios. Trio music has been one of the more popular forms on the island, with some of the more popular trios over the years including Trio Los Panchos, Trio Borinquen, Trio Los Hispanos, Trio Los Condes, Trio Los Voces and Trio Montemar.

National Freedom Day (Fed)— This is a commemoration of Abraham Lincoln's February 1, 1865, signing of the resolution adopted by the Senate and House of Representatives that proposed the 13th Amendment to the U.S. Constitution, abolishing slavery.

Ohio Township Day (OH)— This day recognizes township officials and employees in the Ohio Township Association, which was formed in 1928. It includes over 5,200 active members who are clerks and trustees from the approximately 1,310 townships of the state, plus over 4,000 associate members. When Ohio became a state in 1803, the previously-surveyed townships, some being five miles square and some six, were the basic unit of local government. They are responsible for roads, police and fire protection, cemeteries, parks and recreation, zoning, waste disposal, and other functions necessary for their residents.

February 2

Guadalupe-Hidalgo Treaty Day (NM)—This day is in recognition and commemoration of the day in 1848 on which the Treaty of Peace, Friendship, Limits and Settlement, commonly known as the Treaty of Guadalupe-Hidalgo, was executed between the U.S. and the Mexican Republic. The treaty ended the Mexican War, with California, New Mexico and Arizona being ceded to the U.S. The U.S. paid $15 million to Mexico, assumed the claims which American citizens had against Mexico, and offered U.S. citizenship to Mexicans who resided in the area.

February 3

Four Chaplains Day (MN)—This day honors Army chaplains George L. Fox (Protestant), Alexander D. Goode (Jewish), Clark V. Poling (Protestant) and John P. Washington (Roman Catholic), who sacrificed their lives to save the lives of other service personnel. This occurred on February 3, 1943, during the sinking off the coast of Greenland of the USS *Dorchester*, an Army troop transport ship.

February 4

American Indian Day (NM)—This is in recognition of the many contributions of the American Indians to the economic and cultural heritage of all the citizens of the U.S.

USO Appreciation Day (MA)—This marks the anniversary of the 1941 founding of the United Service Organizations, which provides social, educational, recreational and religious services for U.S. military service personnel. The President of the United States is its honorary chairman, and it operates 122 centers around the world, including five mobile canteens. They serve over 5,000,000 men and women each year. It was formed in response to a request from Pres. Franklin Roosevelt to have a single organization coordinate civilian war efforts rather than the six organizations who were previously involved autonomously — Salvation Army, YMCA, YWCA, National Catholic Community Services, National Travelers Aid Association and the National Jewish Welfare Board.

February 6

Alzheimer's Disease Day (FL)—This is a day to focus the public's awareness on the most common form of dementia among senior citizens, seriously affecting their ability to carry out their daily activities. It is estimated that four million Americans suffer from Alzheimer's, usually beginning after age 60. It is named for a German doctor, Alois Alzheimer, who in 1906 noticed changes in the tissue of the brain of a woman who had died of an unusual mental illness. The abnormal clumps and tangled bundles of fibers he found are now considered hallmarks of the disease. Educational programs on this day are designed to publicize the opportunities for early diagnosis to allow patients and their families to prepare for the future.

Ernest Gruening Day (AK)—This is a celebration of a lifetime of service to the Territory and State of Alaska and the U.S. by Ernest Gruening. He was born on February 6, 1887, in New York City. After working at newspapers in Boston, he became editor of the *Nation*. He directed Robert La Follette's unsuccessful campaign for the presidency of the U.S. in 1924. Later in the 1920s he founded the Portland, Maine, *Evening News*, edited *These United States*, and authored *Mexico and Its Heritage*. While working at the U.S. Department of the Interior, he directed the division dealing with territories and island possessions, and then headed the Puerto Rico Reconstruction Administration. He was appointed as Alaska's territorial governor and lobbied for statehood. When statehood arrived, he became one of its first U.S. Senators. After opposing the Vietnam War, he was defeated in a bid for reelection in 1968. His books include *The State of Alaska*, *The Battle for Alaska Statehood* and the autobiographical *Many Battles*. Gruening died on June 26, 1974.

February 10

Law Enforcement Officer Appreciation Day (GA)—This is a day to say "thank you" to the men and women who protect citizens' civil liberties, constitutional rights, lives and property.

February 12

Lincoln's Birthday (FL, IL, IA, KS, KY, MD, MI, NJ, NY, OH, OR, VT, WV) [Abraham Lincoln's Birthday (AR, IN), **Abraham Lincoln Day** (TN), **Lincoln Day** (CA, CT, MA, MO)]—Abraham Lincoln was born in Hardin County, Kentucky, on February 12, 1809, lived for a time in Indiana, and then moved to Illinois. He gained a national reputation during the 1858 debates with Stephen A. Douglas, despite Douglas' victory in the race for U.S. Senator. Lincoln won the presidency in 1860 and, despite being a Republican, rallied most of the northern Democrats to the Union cause during the Civil War. One of his most memorable acts was the Emancipation Proclamation, which on January 1, 1863, declared forever free the slaves who were located within the Confederate states. Lincoln was reelected in 1864 and was assassinated by John Wilkes Booth at Ford's Theatre in Washington, DC, on April 14, 1865. This day was first celebrated as a holiday in 1866, one year after Lincoln died. In Ohio this is a school holiday, held on a day different than Washington-Lincoln Day, which is celebrated outside of the schools. In Oregon it is solely a school holiday.

February 14

Admission of Oregon into the Union (OR)—This is a school holiday in Oregon, commemorating its entry into the union as the 33rd state in 1859. In anticipation of Congressional approval, Oregon residents voted in June of 1857 to hold a constitutional convention, and drafted a governing document modeled on those of Iowa, Indiana and Michigan. They strongly opposed slavery, but also overwhelmingly voted against allowing freed slaves to live in Oregon. They elected officials pursuant to their new constitution and waited for Congress to act, which they finally did on February 14, 1859, with Pres. Buchanan signing the law that conferred statehood.

February 15

Maine Memorial Day and **Spanish War Memorial Day** (MA)—Also known as Battleship Day, this is the anniversary of the sinking of the U.S. battleship *Maine* in Havana harbor, beginning the Spanish-American War. Leading up to this event, the Cuban revolutionaries fought to liberate themselves from Spain, and the U.S. sentiments were generally in favor of liberation.

War nearly began when Spain seized the filibuster ship *Virginius* and executed most of the crew, including many American citizens. In 1897 the island received limited autonomy, but the Cubans wanted full independence. Riots occurred in January of 1898, and Pres. McKinley sent the *Maine* to protect American citizens. Things seemed to become calmer, but on the evening of February 15 an explosion obliterated the forward third of the ship and the remainder quickly sank, killing 266. After the U.S. Navy concluded that a mine struck the ship, it blockaded Cuba, and war was formally declared in April. Major campaigns of the war included Santiago (Chile), Puerto Rico and Manila (Philippines), and the war was over by the middle of August 1898.

Susan B. Anthony Day (CO) [**Susan B. Anthony's Birthday** (FL, IL)]—This celebrates the birth of Susan B. Anthony on February 15, 1820, in Adams, Massachusetts. Raised by a father who believed that toys and music were distractions from the important lessons of self-discipline, principled convictions, and belief in one's own self-worth, she became very independent. Much of her schooling was at home, taught by a woman, then she attended a private female academy. At the age of 29 she became involved in the causes of the abolition of slavery and temperance, and later crusaded for women's rights and suffrage. After the Civil War she focused on women's right to vote and led the suffrage movement until 1900.

February 16

Elizabeth Peratrovich Day (AK)—The past Grand President of the Alaska Native Sisterhood is honored for her courageous and unceasing efforts to eliminate discrimination and bring civil rights to Alaska. Elizabeth Wanamaker Peratrovich (7/4/1911–12/1/1958) was born in Petersburg, Alaska, with a Tlingit name of Kaaxgal.aat. She attended the Western College of Education in Bellingham, Washington, where she married Roy Peratrovich. They moved to Klawock and then to Juneau, where they were appalled at the blatant discrimination against Native Alaskan peoples. She provided crucial testimony which helped result in the enactment of the Anti-Discrimination Act.

Lithuanian Independence Day (MA, NY, PA, RI)—This commemorates the day in 1918 when the Declaration of Independence was promulgated, resulting in the establishment of Lithuania as a sovereign nation.

February 17

Juan Boria Memorial Day (PR)—Juan Boria was born in 1906 in Jaime Towers. During his youth he worked with his father, who was by profession a carpenter. He graduated from the University of Puerto Rico with a major in Industrial Arts, a subject he taught in the island's public schools. Boria is known for his translation of the poetry of black (Afro-Antillean) Puerto Rican poets, including Fortunato Viscarrondo and Luis Pales Matos. For his work he received an honorary doctorate in Arts and Humanities from the University of the Sacred Heart in Santurce. He was a well-known personality in Puerto Rico, appearing on television and radio, and a municipal theater was named after him. Boria died on May 29, 1995, in Cupay, Puerto Rico.

February 18

Day in Commemoration of the Birthday of Don Luis Munoz-Marin (PR)—This day honors his life and work as landmarks of noble civic action and creative precedent in Puerto Rico. He was born on February 18, 1898, and died on April 30, 1980. He served as the first governor of the Commonwealth of Puerto Rico.

February 19

A Day of Remembrance: Japanese American Evacuation (CA)—State law provides that citizens should reflect upon that day of February 19, 1942, when Executive Order No. 0966 was issued to place over 11,000 persons of Japanese ancestry, most of whom were citizens of the U.S., in American concentration camps during World War II. This observance also commemorates February 19, 1976, when Executive Order No. 9066 was rescinded.

Iwo Jima Day (MA)—This commemorates the extreme heroism and courage of the men and women of the armed forces of the U.S. who participated in the successful assault on the island of Iwo Jima, where extraordinary valor was common virtue. This marks the beginning of the invasion of the island by U.S. Marines. This is a day to remember the six men who raised the famous flag in 1945—Mike Strank (died March 1, 1945, when he was hit by a mortar shell on Iwo Jima), Harlon Block (died March 1, 1945, in a mortar blast on Iwo Jima), Franklin Sousley (died in battle on March 21, 1945, on Iwo Jima), Ira Hayes (died in Arizona on January 24, 1955), Rene Gagnon (died in Manchester, New Hampshire, on October 12, 1979), and John Bradley (died on January 11, 1994, in Antigo, Wisconsin).

State of Texas Anniversary Remembrance (STAR) Day (TX)—This commemorates the day in Austin in 1846 that Texas joined the union and James Pinckney Henderson became the state's first governor, replacing the republic president Anson Jones. The acronym "STAR" was chosen because Texas is known as the "Lone Star State." The star was adopted as its national emblem soon after independence was declared from Mexico to represent sovereignty and fellowship.

February 20

Homeless Unity Day (MA)—This is a day to promote awareness of the problem of a large number of homeless individuals, and a time to encourage people to become involved in working toward providing appropriate homes for the needy.

February 21

International Mother Language Day (U.N.)—This day was declared by UNESCO around the world to recognize the sacrifices of martyrs who died to establish the rightful place of Bangladesh. After the British left India in 1947, Pakistan was formed of two Muslim-majority areas. The eastern portion, now known as Bangladesh, spoke Bengali. The western portion, now known as Pakistan, included the central government, which adopted Urdu as the state language for the entire country. In the eastern portion a movement was started for the recognition of Bengali, reaching a violent peak on February 21, 1952. A student strike attempting to convince legislators to recognize Bengali brought several arrests on the Dhaka University campus, and at one point the police opened fire, killing seven people who were identified, and perhaps others who were not. In 1956 the Pakistan Constitution recognized both Bengali and Urdu, and fifteen years later the War of Liberation separated the two portions of Pakistan into two separate, independent nations. Since 1972, the Bangladesh Constitution has recognized Bengali as the official language. In addition to a day to remember the Bangladesh language martyrs, it is a time to raise awareness among all peoples of the value of languages, which should be conserved as a shared heritage of humanity.

Police Day (PR)— This day honors all active, retired or deceased members of the Police of Puerto Rico. This includes the Inline Skating Unit, established on March 22, 1999. It was thought by many as a joke and waste of valuable resources, but has turned out to be a very efficient tool in fighting crime. The skates call more attention to the officers and give them access to areas which are impossible to reach by patrol cars and motorcycles. Each officer is also able to patrol a larger area than those on foot, so that a team of two officers on inline skates can replace six on foot patrol.

February 22

Washington's Birthday (AS, OH, OR)— Held on the actual date of Washington's birth in 1732, this day celebrates his accomplishments as a military officer in the British army (during the French and Indian War), and in the American army (in the Revolutionary War), and his political career, which included service in the Virginia House of Burgesses, the First and Second Continental Congresses, the Constitutional Convention, and as the first President of the U.S. In Ohio this is celebrated in schools on a day which may be other than Washington-Lincoln Day, which is celebrated outside of the schools. In Oregon it is solely a school holiday.

February 23

Iwo Jima Day (CT)— This commemorates the raising of the American flag over the battlefield during heavy fighting on Mt. Suribachi on Iwo Jima. The famous flag-raising photo of six men won Joseph Rosenthal a Pulitzer Prize. Based on it, the largest cast bronze statue up to that time was erected in Arlington National Cemetery to honor those men and all U.S. Marines.

February 25

George Rogers Clark Day (IN)— This commemorates the capture of Fort Sackville from British Lt. Governor Henry Hamilton and his soldiers by Lt. Col. George Rogers Clark and his frontiersmen at the end of a three-day battle on February 25, 1779. Clark and his men marched from Kaskaskia on the Mississippi to the site in Vincennes, Indiana, where there is now a national historical park. The attack on the fort was performed with such accurate gunfire, the British were not even able to open their gunports. This celebration is also known as Vincennes Day.

February 28

Gulf War Veterans Day (CT)— This day recognizes the service and sacrifice of the sons and daughters of Connecticut who served in the military service of the U.S. in the Persian Gulf War. Although the war itself against Iraq and its allies lasted only 42 days, a total of over 600,000 American troops served between August 2, 1990, and July 31, 1991. Many still suffer the effects of exposure to chemicals and require the same services that have been available to veterans of other wars.

Kelevala Day (MA)— This day is in commemoration of the Knights and Ladies of Kelevala, an organization dedicated to spreading an awareness of the cultural achievement of the Finnish people and Americans of Finnish heritage, and of their contribution to the development of Massachusetts and the U.S. In Finland this is a national holiday dedicated to the epic poem *Kelevala*.

Parade Day (FL)— This is a holiday in Hillsborough County, opening the Florida Strawberry Festival in Plant City, an annual event to celebrate this fruit crop of this section of Central Florida, which stretches over approximately 11 days.

Roman Baldorioty de Castro Day (PR)— Baldorioty was born in Guaynabo, Puerto Rico, in 1822, and was educated in Madrid and Paris. After returning to Puerto Rico in 1853, he became a teacher at the School of Commerce, Agriculture, and Maritime Studies in San Juan. From 1860 to 1865 he served as a delegate to the Spanish parliament. He fought for the abolition of slavery. He founded the magazine *Asuntos de Puerto Rico* and the newspapers *El Derecho* and

La Cronica. He founded the Autonomist Party in 1887 and is considered to be the father of Puerto Rican autonomy. In a crackdown on political dissenters, he was accused of publishing seditious propaganda and was jailed in the El Morro Castle. He became sick while imprisoned and died soon after in Ponce in 1889.

MARCH

Observances with Variable Dates

40 Days Before Easter (As early as February 8 or as late as March 15)

Mardi Gras Day (LA) [**Mardi Gras** (AL, MS)]—This is also known as Shrovetide, which in early England included various sports, especially soccer, plays and masques. The commencement of celebrations in New Orleans is usually considered to have taken place in 1857, with the formation of "The Mystick Krewe of Comus." That organization staged a parade with two floats, one carrying a king and one showing Satan in a blazing hell. In Alabama this is a holiday in Mobile and Baldwin Counties. In Louisiana it is celebrated in some parishes and all municipalities. In Mississippi it may be declared a holiday by the governing authorities of any municipality or county to replace any holiday as a legal holiday (other than Robert E. Lee's Birthday or Dr. Martin Luther King, Jr.'s Birthday).

Shrove Tuesday (FL)—This is a holiday in counties where associations are organized for the purpose of celebrating Mardi Gras. The name "shrove" may come from "shrive," or "to confess." In early England, people were supposed to go to their confessors the week prior to Lent and confess their sins. It is celebrated on the Tuesday before Ash Wednesday, which begins a 40-day period of Lent, for the faithful to fast and make other sacrifices. The English have a custom of eating pancakes on this day, originally resulting from the need to use up eggs and fat, which were prohibited from being eaten during Lent.

First Week in March

Save Your Vision Week (Fed)—This was established to convince the people of the U.S. of the importance of vision to the welfare of themselves and the country. A goal is to educate the public about the need for regular eye examinations, beginning with early vision screening for children. Another is to stress the need for protective eyewear when one is participating in sports or certain occupations.

First Monday in March

Casimir Pulaski Day (IN) [**Casimir Pulaski's Birthday** (IL)]—This commemorates the birth of Casimir Pulaski and his contribution to American independence. Known as the "Father of American Cavalry," he was born in Warka, Poland, on March 4, 1747. His family was rich, and his father was one of the founding members of the Confederation of Bar, beginning in 1768, who took up arms against Russia, which controlled Poland at the time. upon his father's death, Casimir took over the burden of military command. His brilliant taking and holding of Jasna Gora at Czestochowa earned him an impressive reputation, but soon after he was implicated in a plot to kill the king and was forced into exile. In Paris, Benjamin Franklin enlisted him to help in the American Revolution, and he soon joined George Washington's army. After a dashing charge at Brandywine that allowed the American army to escape from the British, he was rewarded with a commission as brigadier general and the command of all American cavalry. In 1779 he and his troops broke the British siege of Charleston, South Carolina, and he was then sent to Savannah in a joint campaign with French allies. Seeing the French attack failing, Pulaski galloped into the battle to rally the men and was hit by cannon shot, from which he died two days later. He was buried at sea.

Chamorro Week (GU) — This is a week to examine and reflect upon Guam's beautiful but fast disappearing culture, and to review and assess the trials and tribulations behind the creation and development of Guam's civil government and political system. It is also an opportunity for the people of Guam to renew their commitment to the ideals of a free political system. This observance lasts for eight days.

Guam Discovery Day (GU) — This day commemorates the discovery of Guam by Europeans. The people of Guam are encouraged on this day to fly their flags at home and at other appropriate places. The actual historical day of discovery was March 6, 1521, when the island was sighted by Ferdinand Magellan.

First Tuesday in March

Arkansas Teachers' Day (AR) — This is a day to celebrate and thank the teachers of Arkansas, as the Arkansas Department of Education recognizes that education is the key to the state's future. The Department's goals are to provide a positive focus on education in Arkansas, and to encourage all public school students to do their very best in their schoolwork. It was an Arkansas teacher, Mattye Whyte Woodridge, who began corresponding with educational and political leaders in 1944 to promote the idea of a National Teacher Day (now celebrated by many educators in early May). One she wrote to was Eleanor Roosevelt, who persuaded Congress to proclaim such a day in 1953.

Town Meeting Day (VT) — This is the anniversary of Vermont's admission to the union as the 14th state in 1791. Each year, residents meet in about 40 towns across the state. Any issue is open to debate and vote. Such votes do not carry the weight of law, and they do not compel public officials to change any policy. They have been, however, noted as a measure of public opinion on major policy questions. It is more than a tradition — it is an opportunity for every citizen to speak his or her mind in a public forum, in a society where the individual is often overlooked.

Week Including March 8

National Women's History Week (RI) — This week focuses on the historical accomplishments of Rhode Island women.

Second Week in March

Rhode Island School Bus Safety Week (RI) — This is a period to stress the taking of important steps in making school buses safer, both through advances in the construction and maintenance of the buses themselves, and in the training and supervision of their drivers.

Women in History Week (OR) — This week commemorates the lives, history and achievements of women in history, including Frances E. Willard and women in Oregon history. Willard was born in 1838 in Churchville, New York, grew up in Oberlin, Ohio, and in Janesville, Wisconsin. She taught school in Illinois and was invited by a group of Chicago women to join the Woman's Crusade to fight liquor. She believed that women could gain political power through participation in the temperance crusade against the drinking of alcohol. She served as president of the Women's Christian Temperance Union and aligned that organization with the Prohibition Party, the longest-lived minor political party in the history of the U.S. Willard wrote *Women and Temperance* in 1883 and *Glimpses of Fifty Years* in 1889, and strongly supported women's voting rights. She died on February 18, 1898, and is one of the two Illinois residents honored with statues in Statuary Hall in the U.S. Capitol.

Women's History Week (NJ) — This time is in recognition of the significant and diverse contributions of women to the development of both the State of New Jersey and the U.S.

Second Wednesday in March

Social Workers' Day (RI)—This is a day to thank the more than 150,000 members of the National Association of Social Workers, and other similar organizations, for their essential services to needy families and individuals. Emphasis is placed on professional growth and development of social workers, maintaining professional standards, and the advancement of sound social policies.

Second Friday in March

Arbor Day (NM)—New Mexico citizens are encouraged to plant forest trees for the benefit and adornment of public and private grounds, places and ways. This includes the state tree, the pinon.

Week Including March 15

Arbor Week (NC)—During this week, school children and other residents of North Carolina are encouraged to plant trees and shrubs on public or private land. These include pines, the state tree.

Maine Cultural Heritage Week (ME)—This is a time to recall Maine's lengthy and important traditions in all the arts, including literature, the performing arts and the plastic arts, and to acknowledge the many contributions made by Maine's citizens to folk arts and crafts.

3 Days Before Easter (As early as March 19 and as late as April 22)

Holy Thursday (VI)—This is also known as "Maundy Thursday," and commemorates the institution of the Eucharist. "Maundy" comes from the Latin word for "commandment." In the New Testament the events of Holy Thursday include Jesus' washing of the feet of others and the Last Supper. Afterwards, Jesus was betrayed by Judas and arrested for sentencing by Pontius Pilate.

2 Days Before Easter (As early as March 20 and as late as April 23)

Good Friday (AS, AR, CA, DE, FL, GU, HI, IL, IN, LA, MD, NJ, NC, ND, CM, PA, PR, TN, VI, WI)—Christians commemorate this day as the one on which Christ was crucified on the cross and died. The origin of the term "Good" is unclear, and may be derived from the word "God's" or a meaning which connoted mourning. In Florida it is a holiday in a judicial circuit only if its chief judge so designates it. In Wisconsin it is only a holiday between 11 A.M. and 3 P.M.

Third Week in March

Employ the Older Worker Week (MA)—This week is an opportunity to remind the public that the general population, and the workforce, is aging, with 65 no longer an automatic event of retirement. This is a time to plan for helping workers maintain their skills throughout their working lives. It is also a time to remind employers that senior citizen status does not mean that a worker is incapable of performing in the workplace—instead, experience and maturity can make the older worker a valuable asset.

Third Sunday in March

Youth Day (OK)—On this day, the people of Oklahoma recognize and celebrate the accomplishments of their young people in sports, academics, and other facets of life.

Third Monday in March

Arbor Day (AR)—This is a day for Arkansas residents, especially school children, to plant trees, shrubs and other plants, including the state tree, the pine.

Third Thursday in March

Vietnam Veterans Day (OK)—This day honors those veterans who served in Vietnam, Cambodia or Laos during the Vietnam Conflict. The observance was set on the third Thursday of the month in Oklahoma in 1998.

Third Friday in March

School Energy Conservation Day in Ohio (OH)—This day promotes public awareness in the schools of the need to conserve energy resources through reductions in their use, as well as through their reuse and recycling.

Third Saturday in March

Save the Florida Panther Day (FL) — This is an opportunity for the public to learn about *felis concolor coryi*, the official state animal and one of the most endangered species on the planet. Efforts are made to preserve its habitat and ensure the survival of ecosystems for numerous other endangered animals and plants. It is estimated that only about 50 to 70 survive in the wild, and to keep the species going, the 26,000 acre Florida Panther National Wildlife Refuge was set aside in 1989 in Collier County. On Save the Panther Day, programs are held to raise awareness and funds to support recovery efforts.

Week Including March 22

Racial Equality Week (PR) — This period highlights the life and works of those persons in Puerto Rico and the rest of the world who have contributed to the progress in the field of human rights, social equality and the disappearance of racism. Slavery became a way of life in Puerto Rico after the early Spaniards turned from a search for gold to the growing of sugar cane, and found that there were not enough Taino Indians to work the fields. The Spanish brought in natives from Africa, and by 1530 the African slaves outnumbered all other people on the island. This day celebrates the elimination of slavery in Puerto Rico.

Monday Following Easter (As early as March 23 and as late as April 26)

Easter Monday (VI) — Although this holiday is largely an opportunity to merely continue (and recover from) the festivities of the previous day, there is a celebration in this country which was established in 1878. It is the Egg Roll, which was moved to the White House grounds to stop the damage the festivities were doing to the land around the Capitol. Although it is not memorialized in the laws of the District of Columbia, it gets more media attention than the official day of observance in the Virgin Islands.

Monday After Easter (MD) — This is a holiday for school children in Maryland, allowing for an extended celebration of this festival.

Fourth Week in March

Wildflower Week (GA) — Wildflowers are celebrated throughout the U.S., and there is a National Wildflower Research Center which maintains a huge collection of native North American Plants. Located in Austin, Texas, it also provides information on the best wildflower viewing sites throughout the U.S. In Georgia, the numerous species of wildflowers include bloodroot, green and gold, violets (common blue, birdfoot, downy yellow, early blue and southern wood), little brown jug, Carolina allspice, and small pussytoes.

Last Full Week in March

Arbor Week (OK) — This is a period during which Oklahoma residents are supposed to realize the role which trees and shrubs play in their lives, and their value to the maintenance of a clean, beautiful environment.

Delaware Head Start Week (DE) — Administrators, staff and volunteers at all Head Start Programs and Early Childhood Assistance Programs in the state are called upon to arrange special programs for observance. Head Start works with state residents to plan parent meetings and parent involvement activities.

Last Week in March

Practical Nursing Education Week (MA) — During this week, focus is laid on the educational opportunities for Licensed Practical Nurses, who care for the sick, injured, convalescent and disabled under the supervision of registered nurses and physicians. Most of them provide bedside care and take vital signs of patients, such as pulse, respiration, blood pressure and temperature. They also give injections, feed patients, treat bedsores, apply heat and cold, and perform routine laboratory tests. All states require a high school diploma and the completion of an approved nursing program, which usually lasts about one year.

Sunday Following Easter (As early as March 29 and as late as May 2)

Gold Star Mother's Day (NH) — This day recognizes and honors all mothers who have lost sons or daughters while on duty in the U.S. Armed Forces. Gold Star Mothers groups exist to assist veterans, especially those who were wounded or incapacitated during hostilities, and perpetuate the memory of those whose lives were sacrificed in war.

Last Monday in March

Seward's Day (AK) — This commemorates the U.S. purchase of Alaska from Russia in 1867 for $7,200,000, with Secretary of State Seward signing the treaty with Russia on March 30, 1867. Many thought that price was outrageously high and called the action "Seward's Folly," after the Secretary of State who arranged the transaction. Many thought the price was too high because there was nothing in the vast wasteland that would interest them, and because the Russians were anxious to leave. The Russians had suffered great losses at the hands of natives, and the cost of maintaining such a remote outpost was great, so they were happy to rid themselves of it. The opinions of the doubters were changed in 1897 when gold was discovered along the Klondike River, drawing many fortune-seekers to the area.

Last Friday in March

Arbor Day (KS) — This day is celebrated by students and other state residents planting cottonwoods, which are the state tree, and other trees, shrubs and vines, in an effort to beautify and help preserve the ecology of Kansas.

Last Saturday in March and the Following Sunday

Farmers' Appreciation Days (GU) — These days have been proclaimed in commemoration of the accomplishments of the farmers of Guam.

OBSERVANCES WITH FIXED DATES

March 1

Alzheimer's Awareness Month (MO) — The purpose of this observance is to increase awareness of Alzheimer's disease and related dementias.

Environmental Education Month (KY) — State agencies involved in environmental education are encouraged to work with schools and communities to promote the environment and its preservation. Environmental education focuses on citizenship, and studies have shown that students from schools with integrated environmental lessons score higher on standardized tests.

Hepatitis C Awareness Month (NJ) — New Jersey agencies are encouraged to implement educational programs for the general public and health care professionals dealing with the prevalence, prevention and screening of hepatitis C. Special focus is placed on targeting high-risk state residents, and the treatment of the disease, which can result in cirrhosis and hepatocellular carcinoma.

Irish-American Heritage Month (MA) — This month recognizes the significant contributions Irish-Americans have made to the Commonwealth of Massachusetts and the U.S. Nine of the signers of the Declaration of Independence had Irish ancestors, as have 19 of the U.S. Presidents. More than 44 million Americans claim Irish heritage.

Ohio Statehood Day (OH) — This day is in recognition of the date in 1803 when Ohio became the 17th state. The "Father of Ohio Statehood," Thomas Worthington, was born in 1773. He served as the sixth governor of the state and was Ohio's first U.S. Senator. Worthington died in 1827 and is remembered at Adena, his 5,000-acre estate at Chillicothe, the first state capital, which contains artifacts and furnishings from the earliest days of Ohio's existence as a state.

State Day (NE) — This day honors Nebraska's pioneers, natural resources, history and the event of the admission of Nebraska as the 37th state in 1867.

Women's History Month (MD) — Beginning in 1911 in Europe, women's place in history has been recognized and celebrated. About that time, women's suffrage was an important topic, but it waned during the 1920s; during the Great

Depression and World War II, women's rights were no longer considered an important issue. In the 1960s, interest in women's rights and history again became popular. By the 1970s, the feeling was that the traditionally-taught histories were incomplete, and that we needed a stronger focus on the contributions of women and minorities. Colleges instituted courses on the subject, and states and women's organizations began to promote projects to celebrate women throughout the nation's history. The purpose of this month is to increase consciousness and knowledge of women's history.

March 2

Advent of American Citizenship in Puerto Rico (PR) — Although Puerto Rico is not a state, its residents have been U.S. citizens since 1917, and have been drafted into the U.S. Armed Forces since that time. Puerto Ricans had been granted limited autonomy by Spain in 1897. After the U.S. defeated Spain in the Spanish-American War, and the island was occupied by U.S. forces for the residents' protection, many Puerto Ricans worked for statehood. In 1904 the U.S. Supreme Court confirmed that they were not aliens, but instead were entitled to the protection of the Constitution. Under the Foraker Act, people there were considered to be "citizens of Puerto Rico" until 1917, when the Jones Act gave them statutory citizenship (although less than equal civil rights). The island remains a commonwealth, a locally self-governing unincorporated territory of the U.S.

Texas Flag Day and **Texas Independence Day** (TX) — These celebrations commemorate Texas' declaration of independence from Mexico on March 2, 1836. Drafted by a committee consisting of Edward Conrad, James Gaines, George C. Childress, Bailey Hardeman and Collin McKinney, it was signed by 60 delegates from all over Texas, including Sam Houston, who voted unanimously for independence. Its language in many ways parallels the 1776 Declaration of Independence of the United States. Nine years later, the Republic of Texas was annexed to the U.S. by joint resolution of the U.S. Congress.

Texas Week (TX) — This week is set aside to exalt and extol the highest and best cultural and spiritual values of Texas. This day is also the anniversary of the birth in 1793 of Sam Hous-

ton, the chief military figure in Texas' fight for independence from Spain. The week includes Alamo Day, celebrated on March 6, to commemorate the deaths of about 150 volunteers who held off an overwhelming force of Mexican soldiers for almost two weeks. James Bowie, Davy Crockett and others perished when the Alamo mission was attacked, and only 15 women, children and servants were allowed to live.

March 4

Mayor's Day (IL) — This is a holiday only in the City of Chicago School District 299, and commemorates past Chief Executive Officers of the city, in particular mayors Richard J. Daley and Harold Washington. Daley was born on May 15, 1902, and served six terms as Chicago's 39th mayor, from 1955 until he died on December 20, 1976. Washington, born on April 15, 1922, was the city's 42nd mayor, serving from 1983 until he died in office early in his second term on November 25, 1987.

Pulaski Day (NY) — This is the birthday of Count Casimir Pulaski, born in 1747. A Polish cavalry general, his assistance was important to the colonists during the American Revolution. He died on October 11, 1779.

March 5

Anniversary of Boston Massacre (MA) — During the Boston Massacre, Crispus Attucks, an African-American, and Samuel Maverick, James Caldwell, Samuel Gray and Patrick Carr met heroic deaths as the first martyrs in the cause of American independence. The conflict arose as a result of the American colonists' resentment of the British troops being quartered in the city. On Friday, March 2, 1770, a fight between Boston ropemakers and three British soldiers took place, and tensions were still hot the following Monday when a soldier entered a pub to look for work and met the group of angry Colonial seamen. Later that day, a group of about 30 to 50, who were called upon to stage a demonstration, began taunting the sole British soldier standing guard outside the custom house, and seven other soldiers came out to protect him. When they opened fire, the five men died.

Crispus Attucks Day (NJ) — This day honors the first American patriot to give his life in our country's war of freedom. Attucks was born to a black man and a Natick or Nantucket Indian female, and as a slave in Framingham was known to be a skilled buyer and seller of cattle. After fleeing his master, he worked as a ropemaker and sailor, which made him vulnerable to impressment into the British navy. He also lost work at times when British soldiers took part-time jobs in off-duty hours. After the confrontation which left Attucks and four others dead, he was buried in the Park Street Cemetery, despite his being a mulatto. In the trial of the soldiers, in which they were defended by John Adams (who later became the second President), Attucks was alleged to have struck the first blow, and to have been the leader of the group who taunted the custom house guard. Attucks became a folk hero, known as "the first to defy, the first to die."

March 7

Arbor Day (CA) — After being first proposed in 1872 by J. Sterling Morton and officially approved by the Nebraska legislature in 1885, it has spread throughout the U.S. and is also observed in many other countries.

Arkansas Agriculture Recognition Day (AR) — This observance celebrates the state's largest industry, with diverse geography producing diverse agriculture. Approximately 45,000 farms cover 14 million acres, generating more than $5 billion annually. Fruits, grain, vegetables, fish, fiber, pork, poultry, cattle and numerous other products are produced, and are publicly displayed on this day.

March 8

International Women's Day (PR) — The purpose of this day is to exhort all Puerto Rican people to pay homage of admiration to all women in the commonwealth. This day is celebrated around the world, focusing on the movement for women's rights and achievement of universal suffrage for women. The observance became popular between 1913 and 1917 when women held rallies to protest World War I and express solidarity with their sisters.

Lucy Stone Day (MA) — Lucy Stone was born near West Brookfield, Massachusetts, on August 13, 1818. She graduated from Oberlin College in 1847 and that same year began lecturing on women's rights. In 1850 she organized the first national women's rights convention in Worcester, Massachusetts. She also spoke out against slavery and, as a matter of principle, continued to go by her birth surname of Stone rather than adopt her husband's name. She founded the *Women's Journal*, which was the official publication of the American Woman Suffrage Association (which Stone helped to organize) and the National American Woman Suffrage Association. She died in 1893, and the editing duties of the *Journal* were taken over by her daughter, Alice Stone Blackwell. The Lucy Stone League, formed in 1921, continued her battle for women's rights.

United Nations Day for Women's Rights and International Peace (U.N.) — Beginning in 1975, the International Women's Year, the United Nations has observed a week to recognize and support women's rights. Member nations are encouraged to celebrate, in accordance with their historical and national traditions and customs, in an effort to create conditions for the elimination of discrimination against women. It is also observed to facilitate the full and equal participation by women in social development. The United Nations has continued this observance by holding world conferences on women in Mexico City (1975), Copenhagen (1980), and Nairobi (1985). Women's rights were proclaimed as human rights at the U.N. International Conference on Human Rights in Vienna in 1993. In many socialist countries, this is the counterpart to the U.S. Mother's Day.

March 11

Irish-American History and Heritage Week (NJ) — This commemorates the Irish men and women who came to New Jersey while it was a British colony, seeking political and religious freedom and economic opportunity. They are remembered for building canals, bridges and railroads, and their years of toil as servants in the sweatshops of the cities. The observance ends on St. Patrick's Day, March 17.

March 14

Charter Day (PA) — This is an observation of the anniversary of the execution of the Royal Charter by King Charles II on March 14, 1681, thereby creating the corporate legal existence of Pennsylvania. To provide a measure of religious freedom, the Charter guaranteed to inhabitants of the colony the freedom from religious persecution, provided that they believed in and acknowledged "One almighty God, the Creator, Upholder and Ruler of the World." All residents could serve the government, legislatively and executively, provided they believed in Jesus Christ and swore allegiance to the King of England. To celebrate the granting of this charter to William Penn, the state legislature designated this as "Charter Day."

Slovak Independence Day (MA)— This commemorates the promulgation on March 14, 1939, of the Declaration of Slovak National Independence, which established the Slovak Republic as a sovereign nation-state. Neighboring Bohemia and Moravia were occupied by Germany, and the Czech state became (at least temporarily) extinct.

March 15

Andrew Jackson Day (TN)— Born in Waxhaw on the border of North and South Carolina on March 15, 1767, to a family of Irish immigrants, Jackson was a prisoner of the British during the Revolutionary War, in which the rest of his family died. He worked in a law office in Salisbury, North Carolina, and became a public prosecutor in an area which is now part of Tennessee. Between 1788 and 1795 he traveled the 200 miles between Nashville and Jonesboro 22 times, and experiences during attacks by Indians led to his later days as an Indian fighter. After serving in the U.S. Senate and the Supreme Court of Tennessee, he became active in the Tennessee militia. He was ordered to Natchez with 2,000 men to protect New Orleans during 1812, but the British did not advance. Jackson then commanded his troops against the Indians, winning at Talluschatches, Talladega and Horseshoe Bend. In 1814 he led his troops against the British in the Florida Panhandle and in the Battle of New Orleans. After the War of 1812 ended, he continued fighting Indians during the First Seminole War. Jackson ran for president in 1824 and received a plurality of the electoral votes but was defeated by John Quincy Adams, who was chosen by the House of Representatives. Jackson defeated Adams in 1828 and Henry Clay in 1832,

and his terms as president were known for the introduction of the spoils system (where party members were rewarded with government posts), and the depositing of federal funds in Democratic-designated banks (instead of the Bank of America). He died at The Hermitage near Nashville on June 8, 1845.

Peter Francisco Day (MA, RI)— This holiday is in honor of the heroic contribution by Peter Francisco toward the success of the American Revolution. He was found without any family or home in Virginia at the age of five, presumably separated from his Portuguese immigrant parents, and later fought in the Revolutionary War. This day calls attention to the heroism in our nation's many wars of American soldiers of Portuguese ancestry.

Statehood Day (ME)— This commemorates the admission of Maine into the Union, and the ideals and wisdom of those men and women who have formed Maine's history and traditions. Also known as Admission Day, it marks Maine's becoming the 23rd state in 1820. It followed 35 years of efforts of residents to separate themselves from Massachusetts, as they resented being ruled from faraway Boston. During the War of 1812, Massachusetts indicated an unwillingness to provide protection for the area, and coastal merchants joined the movement for separation. Finally, in 1819, Massachusetts gave permission for the District of Maine to petition for statehood, which was granted the following year. Under the Missouri Compromise, Maine entered the Union as a free state, while Missouri the following year came in as a slave state.

March 16

National Poison Prevention Week (Fed)— The people of the U.S. are encouraged to learn of the dangers of accidental poisoning, and to take preventive measures. This week of observance, to promote safety, was established by the U.S. Congress in 1961. It is set for March 16–22, regardless of the day of the week on which it begins.

Robert Goddard Day (MA)— Born on October 5, 1882, in Maple Hill, Massachusetts, Goddard taught physics at Clark University beginning in 1908. Four years later, he began exploring mathematically the practicality of using rocket power to reach high altitudes and escape velocity. He developed the first liquid-propellant rocket engine in 1920–25, with the first rocket launch using such a propulsion system taking place at Auburn (near Worcester), Massachusetts, on March 16, 1926. He was the first to develop gyro stabilization apparatus and deflector vanes, and served as the Director of Research of the Navy Department, Bureau of Aeronautics during World War II. Goddard died on August 10, 1945.

March 17

Evacuation Day (MA)—This commemorates the first major American military victory in the Revolutionary War, the evacuation of Boston by the British. The British had been essentially under siege within the city for about seven months as of March 1, 1776. Using a British cannon captured earlier from Ft. Ticonderoga by a contingent led by Col. Henry Knox, General Washington fortified Dorchester Heights. During the movement, the armies lobbed shells at each other, with the colonists escalating the action on March 4, distracting the attention of the Redcoats, led by Gen. Howe. When he awoke on March 5, Howe found that there were heavy guns aimed at his soldiers and down at the British fleet. Rather than repeat the heavy casualties of the Battle of Bunker Hill, the British troops and supplies hastily left Boston on the morning of March 17, never to return. This was a major psychological victory for Washington and the colonists.

St. Patrick's Day (CT)—This honors the Irish people, their culture and the contributions they have made to the state and country. Hundreds of thousands emigrated to the U.S. in the 1840s and 1850s following the Irish Potato Famine. They faced a hard life here, with no federal aid, inadequate health care, and squalid tenements for large families. They eventually became active in the local political process, and were the mainstay of the Democratic big city political machines of the Gilded Age. Worldwide, people have been celebrating St. Patrick for almost 1600 years. He was born as Maewyn between 372 and 390 A.D. to Roman parents. When Irish King Niall attacked England, Maewyn was taken back to Ireland as a slave and was given the job of herding pigs and sheep. After six years he escaped back to England, only to find that the Romans had been defeated and chased off the island. After traveling through Europe, he returned to Ireland when he was about 60 years old to preach Christianity, using a three-leafed clover as an aid to teach about the Trinity. Also called Patricius, he served as the Archbishop of Armagh. A legend holds that he himself scared all of the snakes out of Ireland and into the sea, where they drowned. He died in 461. The first St. Patrick's Day parade took place in New York City on March 17, 1762, featuring Irish soldiers serving in the English army.

March 18

Grandparents' and Grandchildren's Day (MI)—The first Grandparents Day observance was the result of the work of Marian McQuade of West Virginia, who had 15 children and 40 grandchildren. She wanted to recognize and honor grandparents for their knowledge and guidance as senior citizens. Because they often are free to love and guide and befriend the young without having to take responsibility for them every day, they can often reach out past pride and fear of failure, and close the space between generations.

South Carolina Day (SC)—This day was selected because it is also the birthday of John C. Calhoun. He was born on March 18, 1782, in Abbeville, South Carolina. He attended law school in Litchfield, Connecticut, and practiced law in South Carolina. Entering Congress in 1811, he and Henry Clay urged war with England to redeem the honor of the U.S. He served as Vice President under both John Quincy Adams and Andrew Jackson, and fought against high tariffs that were hurting Southern farmers. A proponent of slavery, while in the Senate he engineered a "gag rule," which prevented Senators from even discussing that issue.

In 1844, while serving as Secretary of State, he arranged for Texas to be annexed to increase the territory open for slavery. Two years later he was again in the Senate, and led the fight against the Wilmot Proviso, which would have excluded slavery from Texas and other territories obtained as a result of the Mexican War. In 1850 Calhoun was still fighting for rights of slave owners, despite being nearly too sick to speak. He died on March 31, 1850, and in 1957 the Senate named him as one of the five greatest Senators of all time.

March 21

Bahai New Year's Day (HI) — The Bahai calendar consists of 19 months of 19 days each, with a couple of extra days between the 18th and 19th months. Plus, they have adopted the custom of Iran of celebrating the New Year at the Spring equinox. Rather than midnight as in most of the U.S., the day begins at sunset, so the celebration begins in early evening.

Bird Appreciation Day (MO) — This day is to be observed by cities, elementary and secondary schools, state agencies and civic organizations to enhance the knowledge and appreciation of birds found in Missouri.

Bird Day (PA) — Citizens are urged to engage in the special study of birds in order to become more aware of the beauty and usefulness of the birds frequenting the Commonwealth of Pennsylvania.

International Day for the Elimination of Racial Discrimination (U.N.) — The date of March 21 was selected by the U.N. General Assembly to remember the day in 1960 when police opened fire and killed 69 people participating in a peaceful anti-apartheid demonstration in Sharpville, South Africa. The international community is urged to redouble its efforts to eliminate all forms of racial discrimination.

Week of Solidarity with the Peoples Struggling Against Racism and Racial Discrimination (U.N.) — Since 1979, this week to fight racism and discrimination has been observed by the nations who are members of the United Nations. The dates of this observance are fixed as March 21–27.

March 22

Emancipation Day (PR) — Also known as Abolition Day, this celebrates the end of the struggle for the abolition of slavery in Puerto Rico, spearheaded by Jose Julian Acosta, Francisco Mariano Quinones, Julio L. de Vizcarrondo, Ramon Emeterio Betances and Segundo Ruiz Belvis. The Spanish National Assembly finally ended slavery on March 22, 1873. Owners were compensated in the amount of 35,000,000 pesetas per slave. The slaves were required to continue working for three more years.

World Day for Water (U.N.) — Established in 1992, this day proclaimed by the United Nations General Assembly aims at promoting awareness of the extent to which water resource development contributes to economic productivity and social well-being.

March 23

Commonwealth Cleanup Week (KY) — Citizens of Kentucky are supposed to clean and display the natural beauty of the commonwealth, with a goal of considering the ways in which Kentucky's beauty enriches their daily living and underpins their economic vitality. It was estimated in 2002 that there were 1,884 illegal dumps in the state, and Kentucky residents are encouraged to clean them up using the guidelines of the Kentucky Natural Resources and Environmental Protection Cabinet. The dates for this observance are set for March 23–29.

Puerto Rican Boxers' Day (PR) — This day is in remembrance of the birthday of Sixto Escobar, the first Puerto Rican bantamweight world boxing champion. Escobar was born on March 23, 1913, in Barcelona, Puerto Rico, and became a professional boxer at the age of 17. He was managed by Lew Brix and held the NBA Bantamweight Title in 1934–35, regained it later in 1935 and unified it with the World Bantamweight Title in 1936. He held it until late in 1937, and then regained it in early 1938 and kept it until late in 1939. Escobar's last professional fight was a loss to Harry Jeffra on December 2, 1940, bringing his professional record to 42 wins, 18 losses and four draws. He died on November 17, 1979.

World Meteorological Day (U.N.) — This commemorates the 1950 establishment of the World Meteorological Organization to facilitate an international system of coordinating weather data and observation. The 185 member nations of the U.N. enjoy free and unrestricted flow of weather data from observation equipment, including drifting ocean buoys, automated aircraft systems, polar-orbiting satellites above the Antarctic, observation ships, and Stevenson screens at Ayers Rock in the Australian Outback.

March 24

Covenant Day (CM) — Fourteen islands in Micronesia comprise the Commonwealth of the Northern Mariana Islands, with Saipan as the largest and most populous. During World War

II, through fierce fighting, some of the islands were captured by the U.S. Following the war, they became part of the United Nations Trust Territory of the Pacific Islands. During the 1960s the islands' residents considered whether to petition for independence or become affiliated with the U.S. In 1978 the residents voted to establish strong ties with the U.S., and Congress ratified the Covenant to Establish a Commonwealth of the Northern Mariana Islands in Political Union with the United States of America. Under the Covenant, which is celebrated on this day, residents adopted local government and also hold U.S. citizenship.

March 25

Greek Independence Day (MA, NC) — This commemorates March 25, 1821, when the Greek flag was first raised in revolt against the Ottoman Empire. The Ottomans had seized control of Greece at the beginning of the 15th century. In 1821 the Greeks began a revolution with the aid of the French, British and Russians. On this day in 1821, Bishop Germanos of Patras raised the Greek flag at the monastery in Agia Lavras, attempting to inspire the locals to take up arms against the Ottomans. Germanos chose this date because it was the day in the Orthodox calendar celebrating the visitation of the archangel Gabriel, announcing the upcoming birth of Jesus. The bishop wanted to announce the birth of a new spirit in Greece.

Greek-American Day (CT) — This is in honor of Americans of Greek ancestry, their culture and the great contribution they have made to this country.

Maryland Day (MD) — This is a commemoration of the landing of Lord Baltimore and the first 140 or so colonists on St. Clement's Island in 1634. Those colonists came to the colony aboard two ships, the *Ark* and the *Dove*, after boarding on the English Isle of Wight. This celebration began in Maryland schools in 1903, and it was made an official state holiday in 1916. The colony was founded by Cecil Calvert, the second Lord Baltimore, under a charter granted on June 20, 1632, by British King Charles I. They wanted to establish a colony where Roman Catholics, as well as everyone else, could practice their religion. The king gave the colony to the Calvert family as a gift, on the conditions that the king

was paid an annual rent of two arrowheads, and that the colony be named after his wife, Queen Henrietta Maria. As a result, it was called "Mary-Land," or Maryland.

March 26

Prince Jonah Kuhio Kalanianaole Day (HI) — This day commemorates Prince Jonah Kuhio Kalanianaole, who was born on Kauai in 1871 to the high chief D. Kahalepouli and Princess Kekaulike. A cousin of Queen Liliuokalani, he was named by her to be an heir to the throne and was bestowed the title of "prince." After being educated in California and at the Royal Agricultural College in England, at the age of 24 he joined in the Royalist uprising against the new republic in January of 1895, and was captured and convicted of "misprison of treason." He later worked with the industrialists who overthrew the monarchy, believing that cooperation would bring political power that could help his people more than resistance would. He ran for the office of territorial delegate to the U.S. Congress, won, and was reelected ten times. During his tenure, he focused on the development of Pearl Harbor and Honolulu Harbor, regular mail delivery, and the "back to the farm" movement. He died on January 7, 1922. This day of observance is also known as Regatta Day.

March 27

Italian American War Veterans of the United States, Inc. Day (MA) — This is the anniversary of the founding of the Italian American War Veterans of the United States, Inc., and recognizes the distinguished patriotic services rendered by that organization. It also commemorates the services and sacrifices of the men of Italian ancestry who fought in defense of the U.S.

Pascua Florida Week (FL) — The Governor of Florida is authorized to proclaim this week with a call to schools and citizens to recognize the patriotic occasion. It remembers the first sighting of the Florida peninsula by Juan Ponce de Leon on or about April 2, 1513. De Leon named the new land "La Florida" in honor of "Pascua Florida," the Spanish Feast of the Flowers at Eastertime. This observance continues through April 2.

March 28

Edmund S. Muskie Day (ME) — This honors Edmund Sixtus Muskie, whose distinguished career as a political leader of Maine and the U.S. marks him as one of the state's outstanding citizens. Born in Rumford, Maine, on March 28, 1914, he was a leading voice on domestic issues during his 22 years in the U.S. Senate, known as "Mr. Clean" for his efforts to curb air and water pollution as part of his hard-line environmental stances. He ran for president in 1972, but lost the Democratic nomination to George McGovern. During 1980–81 he served as Secretary of State in the cabinet of Pres. Jimmy Carter. He died on March 26, 1996.

March 29

Delaware Swedish Colonial Day (DE) — This day commemorates the landing of Swedes upon the soil of Delaware in 1638. The ship *Kalmar Nyckel* landed at Minquas Kill; the colonists negotiated for land with members of the Lenni Lenape tribe and constructed a fort. Sweden maintained the colony for 17 years, and then the territory was claimed by the Dutch. Until the late 1700s, the Swedish Missionary Society maintained ties by sending missionaries to the Lutheran churches constructed by the Swedish colonists.

Iowa State Flag Day (IA) — The Iowa flag has three vertical stripes of blue, white and red, similar to the flag of France. On the white stripe is a bald eagle carrying a blue streamer bearing the words "Our liberties we prize and our rights we will maintain." Beneath that is the name of the state in large red letters. The flag was designed by Dixie Cornell Gebhart and was adopted by the legislature in 1921, almost 75 years after Iowa became a state. The need for a flag was prompted by the urgings of Iowa National Guardsmen stationed along the Mexican border during World War I, who saw units from other states with banners to rally around.

Statewide Cleanup Day (KY) — Each year, thousands of Kentucky residents participate in this cleanup event by removing thousands of bags of trash from roadsides, illegal dumps and waterways. Cash prizes are awarded to outstanding group projects by the Kentucky Natural Resources and Environmental Protection Cabinet.

Viet Nam War Veterans Day (IL) [**Vietnam Veterans Day** (MA)] — This honors and remembers the men and women of this nation who served so valiantly in the cause of freedom. This marks the day in 1973 that the final U.S. troops withdrew from the country.

March 31

Dr. Cesar Estrada Chavez Day (AZ) [**Cesar Chavez Day** (CA, RI)] — This is a celebration of the anniversary of the birth of Cesar Estrada Chavez, as a tribute to his unselfish commitment to the principles of social justice and respect for human dignity. Born on March 31, 1927, he was a migrant farm worker from age 10. In 1952 he became active with the Community Service Organization which helped fight racial and economic discrimination against Chicano residents, but he wanted more. In the early 1960s he founded the National Farm Workers Association; and using principles of non-violence, with strikes and boycotts, he focused attention on the plight of migrant farm workers and garnered support to have his organization be the first successful farm workers' union in U.S. history. He remained president of United Farm Workers of America, AFL-CIO, until his death on April 23, 1993.

Thomas Mundy Peterson Day (NJ) — Born in 1824, Thomas Mundy Peterson became the first African-American to cast a vote in a U.S. election following the passage of the 15th Amendment to the U.S. Constitution. On March 31, 1870, in the city of Perth Amboy, New Jersey, he participated in a municipal charter referendum just one day after the 15th Amendment was adopted. The vote he cast was in favor of a revised city charter in the 1713 city hall of Perth Amboy, which itself is historical because it is the oldest municipal building in continuous use in the U.S. That building was also the site of the first state ratification of the first ten amendments to the U.S. Constitution, known as the Bill of Rights, in November of 1789. Peterson had a reputation as an honorable and good citizen, and in 1884 the citizens of Perth Amboy awarded him a gold medal in honor of his historic vote. School No. 1, which had opened in 1871, was renamed after Peterson, who had served as the school's first janitor. He died in 1904.

Transfer Day (VI) — This commemorates the transfer of St. Thomas, St. Croix and St.

John from Denmark to the United States, a week before the outbreak of World War I in 1917. They had been sold for $25,000,000 to the U.S. by Denmark in 1916 (after about 49 years of the U.S. attempting to purchase them), following years of a lack of self-government and dire economic straits. The U.S. sent marines to occupy the islands and prevent a German takeover, and improve the strategic defense of the Panama Canal. Since the islands were acquired for military purposes rather than expansion, the natives were not initially granted citizenship and the islands were administered by the Department of the Navy.

APRIL

Observances with Variable Dates

Date Varies

Day of Homage to Old Age (PR) — The Governor is to set a day in April to observe activities relating to senior citizens.

3 Days Before Easter (As early as March 19 and as late as April 22)

Holy Thursday (VI) — This is also known as "Maundy Thursday," and commemorates the institution of the Eucharist. "Maundy" comes from the Latin word for "commandment." In the New Testament the events of Holy Thursday include Jesus' washing of the feet of others and the Last Supper. Afterwards, Jesus was betrayed by Judas and arrested for sentencing by Pontius Pilate.

2 Days Before Easter (As early as March 20 and as late as April 23)

Good Friday (AS, AR, CA, DE, FL, GU, HI, IL, IN, LA, MD, NJ, NC, ND, CM, PA, PR, TN, VI, WI) — Christians commemorate this day as the one on which Christ was crucified on the cross and died. The origin of the term "Good" is unclear, and may be derived from the word "God's" or a meaning which connoted mourning. In Florida it is a holiday in a judicial circuit only if its chief judge so designates it. In Wisconsin it is only a holiday between 11 A.M. and 3 P.M.

Monday Following Easter (As early as March 23 and as late as April 26)

Easter Monday (VI) — Although this holiday is largely an opportunity to merely continue (and recover from) the festivities of the previous day, there is a celebration in this country which was established in 1878. It is the Egg Roll, which was moved to the White House grounds to stop the damage the festivities were doing to the land around the Capitol. Although it is not memorialized in the laws of the District of Columbia, it gets more media attention than the official day of observance in the Virgin Islands.

Monday After Easter (MD) — This is a holiday for school children in Maryland, allowing for an extended celebration of this festival.

Sunday Following Easter (As early as March 29 and as late as May 2)

Gold Star Mother's Day (NH) — This day recognizes and honors all mothers who have lost sons or daughters while on duty in the U.S. Armed Forces. Gold Star Mothers groups exist to assist veterans, especially those who were wounded or incapacitated during hostilities, and perpetuate the memory of those whose lives were sacrificed in war.

First Week in April

Earth Week (MA) — The purpose of this week is to call to the attention of all citizens the desirability of protecting our natural environment from pollution or destruction. In 1973 this was instituted to replace Earth Day.

First Full Week in April

Arbor Week (OR) — This week is dedicated to the preservation and perpetuation of forests and the growing of timber, and of the environment. Citizens are encouraged to plant, protect and preserve trees and shrubs, and foster greater understanding and means for preserving and improving the environment. They are encouraged to plant the state tree, the Douglas fir, and others on public and private lands.

First Sunday in April

Veterans of World War I Hospital Day (MA) — This is an opportunity to recognize the services which have been provided by health care professionals to veterans of World War I. Those who participated in that war fell victim to the use of poisonous gases and were exposed to deadly diseases, sometimes requiring medical attention or even hospitalization for the rest of their lives.

First Wednesday in April

Arbor Day (MD) — On this day, residents of Maryland are encouraged to plant shrubs and trees, including the state tree, the white oak.

Retired Teachers' Day (RI) — In 1998 the Rhode Island legislature concluded that the state's retired teachers span monumental changes, ranging from the Great Depression, World War II, and the social turmoil, coupled with tremendous technological advances in the last three decades of the 20th century. Retired teachers, who take pride in stressing civic responsibility and promoting individual, family and community values, and who have worked to provide a brighter

future for all Americans, are to be commended on this day for their lifetime contributions.

First Friday in April

Arbor Day (MO) — On this day, citizens in Missouri are encouraged to plant trees, shrubs and flowers. Each planting is to benefit the air, water, soil, wildlife and human habitation.

Student Government Day (MA) — Each of the governor, lieutenant governor, state secretary, state treasurer, state auditor and attorney general may select a high school senior who will be permitted to occupy the official's chair and office, in order to observe the processes of government. Students throughout the state elect a student senate of 40 and a student house of representatives of 240.

Second Sunday in April

Aunt's and Uncle's Day (MA) — After mothers, and then fathers, and then grandparents received days of recognition, the next closest relatives naturally were given theirs. This day is observed to show appreciation for the guidance and love shown by aunts and uncles, often blossoming into full-time relationships when parents are unable to care for their children.

Day of the Child (PR) — This is an opportunity to celebrate the joy that children bring into our lives, and to educate the public about issues which must be faced to provide children with the best start toward adulthood.

Second Tuesday in April

Children's Day (FL) — Organizations and citizens are encouraged to acknowledge Florida's children as the resource giving it the greatest hope of future excellence, and to reaffirm their commitment to help Florida's children develop their qualities, strengths and potential, resulting in greater productive capacity and enlightened citizenship.

Second Wednesday in April

Arbor Day (WA) — Observance of this day is coordinated by the Washington Arbor Day Council, a group of public and private organizations and agencies dedicated to the promotion of tree planting and preservation in Washington State. It includes the Tree Remembrance Program, where one may donate money to have a tree planted in memory of someone special, and awards for groups and individuals who demonstrate excellence in various planting efforts or events.

Second Friday in April

Arbor Day (VA) — Trees and other plants are to be planted on this day in Virginia, as part of the nationwide program first proposed by J. Sterling Morton in 1872. According to Morton:
> A collection of inanimate marbles may, for a few years, preserve the name, and entry, and exit on this stage in life's short play. But how much more enduring are the animate trees of our own planting? They grow and self-perpetuate themselves, and shed yearly blessings on our race. Trees are the monuments I would have, and in them I would find my most acceptable epitaph.

Second Saturday of April and the Following Sunday

White Cane Safety Days (GU) — Residents of Guam are called upon to observe the laws relative to the rights of visually handicapped persons, and to take precautions necessary for the safety of disabled persons. Emphasis is placed on the need to be aware of the presence of disabled persons and to keep safe and functional for them streets, highways, sidewalks, walkways, public buildings, public facilities, and other public places, places of public accommodation, amusement and resort. Residents are encouraged to offer assistance to disabled persons upon appropriate occasions.

Second Full Week in April

Landscape Architecture Week in Virginia (VA) — This time has been selected to recognize the importance of the profession of landscape architecture, which encourages environmental stewardship, promotes energy conservation, enhances the preservation of the commonwealth's historical heritage, and ensures that the place known as Virginia is preserved through wise de-

sign, management, and maintenance of its landscapes.

Licensed Practical Nurse Week (MA) — This week celebrates the services performed by Licensed Practical Nurses, also known as Licensed Vocational Nurses, who provide care under the direction of physicians and registered nurses. The LPNs help patients with dressing, bathing and personal hygiene, and care for their other physical and emotional needs. Included are the LPNs who work 40-hour weeks in hospitals and nursing homes, and also those who provide round-the-clock care for patients who require it.

Friday of the Second Week in April

Librarian's Day (PR) — This is a day to celebrate librarians and their role of making books and information available to students and the general public.

Week of April 19

Child Care Worker Appreciation Week (OH) — This is a commemoration of those child care workers who lost their lives in the bombing of the Oklahoma City federal building on April 19, 1995, and focuses public attention on child care workers in Ohio.

Third Full Week in April

National Organ and Tissue Donor Awareness Week (NJ) — This is a time to bring to the public's attention that every 18 minutes a new name is added to the list of more than 57,000 Americans who are waiting for organ transplants. It is also a time to encourage organ and tissue donation to reduce the number of people per day (ten) who die because suitable organs are not available. Educational programs stress that one person can save up to 50 lives with donations of bone marrow, bone, cartilage, skin, corneas, tendons, and vital organs, including the heart, lungs, kidneys, liver and pancreas.

Sunday of the Third Week in April

Vaccination Day (PR) — On this day, the public is urged to consider the need for the vaccination of children against a variety of diseases which, without vaccination, could be deadly. This begins National Infants Immunization Week, sponsored by the Centers for Disease Control and Prevention.

Week Including Third Monday in April

Jose de Diego Week (PR) — Jose de Diego was born in Aguadilla, Puerto Rico, on April 16, 1866. He was a brilliant orator and major poet, but is most known for his advocacy for independence. He was a founder of the Autonomist Party in 1887, and of the Unionist Party in 1904. He sought the establishment of a confederation of Spanish-speaking islands of the Caribbean, including the Dominican Republic. He served as president of the House of Delegates (1907–17) and speaker of the House of Representatives (1917–18). He is known as Puerto Rico's finest love poet, his works including *A Laura* and *Postuma*. He founded the Antillian Academy of Language, begun at the Municipal Theater of San Juan on April 23, 1916. He died on July 17, 1921, while reciting his own poetry.

Third Monday in April

Jose de Diego Day (PR) — This celebrates Jose de Diego, born April 16, 1866, and educated in Spain. In 1892 he completed his law degree and became involved in Puerto Rico in the Assembly of the Autonomist Party in Mayaguez, pushing for a merger with the National Autonomist Party. He became the sub-secretary of Justice, and then the president of the Chamber of Delegates. In 1917 he became the first president of the House of Representatives. He was a leader of the movement for independence from Spain and founded the Antillean Academy of Language.

Patriot's Day (ME) — On this day is commemorated the 1775 beginning of the American Revolution, with skirmishes between British Redcoats and Concord and Lexington Minutemen. The battle is annually reenacted at Lexington Green, followed by a march to Concord for a memorial service for those who died in the battle.

Third Wednesday in April

Cooperative Dialogue Day (PR) — This is a day to encourage all peoples to come together on important issues, although they may strongly disagree, and enter into dialogue in a cooperative manner to produce solutions which will be beneficial to all involved.

Third Saturday in April

Combat Veterans' Day (RI) — This day of remembrance was introduced to the state legislature on January 26, 2000. It recognizes those members of the U.S. Armed Services who served in military combat.

Dogwood Day (VA) — This day celebrates the state tree of Virginia, the American dogwood. It was adopted by the legislature in 1956 because it is well-distributed throughout Virginia, and has beauty which is symbolic of the many attractive features of the state. It blooms in early Spring with a tiny cluster of flowers surrounded by four white leaves that appear to be petals.

Week Including April 21 and 24

Texas Conservation and Beautification Week (TX) — During this week, citizens should be made aware that they should preserve for posterity the environment because, "The heavens declare the glory of God and the firmament showeth His handiwork."

Week Including April 25

Arbor Week (IA) — Citizens are encouraged to give serious thought to, and appreciation of, the contribution of trees to the beauty and economic welfare of Iowa.

Fourth Sunday in April

Children and Youth Sunday (GU) — This is a special day on which the people of Guam consider the needs and accomplishments of the children and youth of their island.

Friends Day (CT) — Honored and recognized today are the enduring value of friendship and the fundamental need, common to each member of our society, for a friend.

Fourth Friday in April

Arbor Day (MI) — This is a day for school children and others to plant trees, shrubs and other plants in Michigan, improving both public and private lands.

Workers' Memorial Day (MA, RI) — This day is in remembrance of the courage and integrity of American workers. The AFL-CIO reports that annually more than 60,000 workers die from job injuries and illnesses, and six million more are injured. The first Workers' Memorial Day was observed in 1989, and today hundreds of communities recognize the workers who have been killed or injured on the job. Internationally, they are remembered on the International Day of Mourning.

Last Week in April

Earth Week (GU) — In Guam, this is a week to review and assess environmental progress. It is also to determine what further steps must be taken to continue an island-wide effort of education on environmental problems, renewing the commitment of every citizen to the restoration and protection of the quality of the environment.

Golf Week (SC) — This week recognizes (1) the economic impact of the golf industry in South Carolina, (2) the importance of the state's junior golfers, and (3) the importance of turfgrass research.

Puerto Rico Land Week (PR) — During this week, agricultural and cattle expositions, and exhibits of ornamental and medicinal plants are held. The objective is to rouse public interest in the value of our land and the other national resources of Puerto Rico, and stimulate and extol the fellow feeling and devotion of Puerto Ricans toward their conservation and enrichment.

Secretaries Week (MA, VI) — This is a time to acknowledge the services performed by those who serve as secretaries, often being the ones who keep businesses successful.

Sunday of Puerto Rico Land Week

Land Day (PR) — This is an opportunity to celebrate the land comprising the island of Puerto Rico and its products. Included are the white sand beaches, rain forest, caves and canyons. The land's products include sugar cane, pineapples, coffee, bananas and plantains.

Wednesday of Secretaries Week

Secretaries Day (MA) — This is an opportu-nity for executives, professional business persons, and others who have clerical assistants to show their appreciation for necessary and valuable services performed by their hard-working secretaries.

Week Including Last Friday in April

Rothrock Memorial Conservation Week (PA) — This week focusing on conservation of forestry areas is named after Dr. Joseph Trimble Rothrock, known as the "Father of Forestry in Pennsylvania." He was born near McVeytown in Mifflin County, and grew up in the forested mountains near the present-day Rothrock State Forest.

Last Monday in April

Arbor Day (WY) — On this date in Wyoming a tree is required to be planted on state grounds with a simple ceremony. Also, planting of seedling trees or some other similar acts may be performed in appropriate ceremonies in the schools of the state.

Last Thursday in April

Take Our Daughters to Work Day (NJ) — This day was born from the Ms. Foundation for Women's desire to bring to the attention of the American public the systematic inequalities that research indicates are affecting negatively the way young girls view themselves and their self-worth. It is hoped that this observance will allow young girls to experience the realities of the workplace, discover their true abilities and think realistically about the future.

Last Friday in April

Arbor and Bird Day (IL, MA) — This is a day for planting trees, shrubs and vines about homes and along the highways and public grounds. It is also a day for showing the value of trees and birds and the necessity of their protection, thus contributing to the comforts and attractions of the state.

Arbor Day (AZ, CT, DE, ID, IN, IA, MN, MT, NE, NV, OH, PA, RI, SD, UT) — In 1854 Nebraska was largely a treeless plain greeting settlers, including J. Sterling Morton of Detroit. They established homes and planted trees, shrubs and flowers. Morton became the editor of the territory's first newspaper and used it to spread agricultural information to his readers. On January 4, 1872, he proposed to the State Board of Agriculture a tree-planting holiday called "Arbor Day," and it was officially proclaimed by the governor in 1874. Arizona citizens are urged to plant trees, shrubs and vines, and promote forest orchard growth and culture in the adornment of public and private grounds, places and ways. In Connecticut there is also emphasis on the economic benefit to be derived from well-cultivated orchards and forests. In Indiana, in addition to planting shade and forest trees, shrubs and vines, citizens are encouraged to give due honor to the conservators of forestry, founders of conservation of state forestry, and Charles Warren Fairbanks, a leading spirit of Indiana forestry conservation.

DeSoto Day (FL) — In Manatee County, this is a legal holiday to commemorate the early Spanish explorer. In late May of 1539 he landed near Shaw's Point in Bradenton in this county, beginning a futile 4,000-mile search for El Dorado, the "city of gold." Once a part of DeSoto Week, celebrated since the 1930s, the celebration has now expanded to a month known as the Florida Heritage Festival, presented by the Hernando DeSoto Historical Society of Manatee County. The Society is charged with keeping alive the memory of Hernando DeSoto and the landing of the conquistadors in Manatee County.

School Janitor Day (PR) — This is a day to celebrate the janitorial staffs serving the public and private schools of Puerto Rico.

Last Saturday in April

Green Up Day (CT) — Connecticut citizens are encouraged to clean up their communities, plant trees and flowers, and otherwise enhance the physical beauty of the state's communities and countryside. It is a day when volunteers traditionally collect thousands of bags of litter and trash, and participate in other projects designed to beautify the state.

Day Corresponding to the 27th day of the month of Nisan on the Hebrew calendar

Holocaust Remembrance Day (NJ) — This day (also known as Yom Hashoah) remembers approximately six million Jews who perished in Nazi concentration and slave labor camps. It honors the memory of those who perished in the Holocaust itself or otherwise as a result of Nazi persecution, and honors and consoles those who survived. Attention is focused on the evils of racism and tyranny. Coordinated efforts at Holocaust education began in New Jersey in 1974. The date of this observance was chosen to correspond with events during the Warsaw Uprising in 1943.

First Sunday Following the Fourth Sunday in April

Family Sunday (GU) — On this day, the people of Guam are to consider the value and importance of the family.

Week Including May 1

Law Week (FL) — This week is an opportunity to expand awareness of our laws and justice system, and its effects on our lives.

Week of May 2

History of Oregon Statehood Week (OR) — This commemorates May 2, 1843, as the date that settlers met at Champoeg to form a provisional government. Later, Oregon became the 33rd state.

OBSERVANCES WITH FIXED DATES

April 1

Cancer Control Month (Fed) — This observance is intended to make all Americans aware of the need for a cancer eradication program.

Cancer Prevention and Control Month (PR) — During this period, the Secretary of Health is to carry out a cancer prevention and control campaign throughout the island of Puerto Rico.

Child Abuse Awareness Month (NJ)—
The New Jersey legislature recognized that the
incidence of child abuse continues to increase in
the state, with over 54,000 cases of suspected
child abuse reported in 1990; as a result, it established this day of observance. This month focuses attention on a serious concern affecting not
only children, but their families and their communities as well.

Equal Pay Day (ME)—The emphasis on
this day is the proposition that all workers who
do the same job should be paid the same amount,
regardless of gender.

Guam Youth Month (GU)—This month,
and one week in it designated as Guam Youth
Week, is planned by the Central Planning Committee, which includes youth from private and
public junior and senior high schools. The time
is set aside to celebrate the achievements of the
island's youth.

Parkinson's Disease Awareness Month
(NJ)—This focuses attention on a disease of
presently unknown origin, which causes diverse
symptoms, including rigidity, slowness of movement, poor balance and tremors. It is debilitating, painful and incurable, impairing the ability
to walk, speak, swallow and breathe. The result
can be a clear mind trapped inside a body that
is losing its ability to function. This is a time to
promote the state's involvement in research efforts,
and to remind the public that even more research
is necessary to combat this disease which affects
approximately one million Americans.

Parliamentary Law Month (MA)—This
month celebrates the certainty and order brought
to organizations through the use of parliamentary procedure, known to most through the most
popular printed version, *Robert's Rules of Order*.

Public Health Month (MA)—During this
month, recognition is given to the achievements
and future successes in identifying and address-
ing patterns of disease, illness and injury. Also
focused upon are the benefits achieved by a modern approach to public health to ensure healthy
living and working environments.

School Library Media Month (MA)—The
Massachusetts School Library Media Association
supports this month's efforts to maintain and improve the libraries which serve the students of the
state. It is recognized that better libraries provide
educational benefits, with the size of a library
media center's staff and collection being the best
school predictor of academic achievement.

Women's Wellness Month (NJ)—Activities this month urge and empower women to take
routine and crucial steps necessary to maintain
and improve their health. It also focuses on their
need to access information and education about
their health and bodies; to schedule routine health
checkups, including pap smears, mammograms,
breast examinations and blood cholesterol and
bone density screenings; to participate in routine
exercise; to maintain a diet based on recommended nutritional guidelines; and to utilize information about available health and social services in their communities.

April 2

Pascua Florida Day (Florida State Day)
(FL)—In 1953 the Florida Legislature established April 2 as State Day to commemorate the
first sighting of Florida by Juan Ponce de Leon
in 1513. The holiday was suggested by Mary
A. Harrell, a social studies teacher in Jackson-
ville.

April 6

Tartan Day (NV)—This day commemorates the contributions that Scots and Scots-
Americans have made to the history and development of the U.S. Nearly half the signers of the
U.S. Declaration of Independence, and the governors of nine of the original 13 states, were of
Scottish ancestry. The day was chosen because it
is the anniversary of the 1320 signing of the Declaration of Arbroath, which was the Scottish declaration of independence from England. This
day of observance was also recognized by the
U.S. Senate in 1998 with a Resolution, but the
observance has not yet been memorialized in the
U.S. Code.

World War I Day (OH)—This is the
anniversary of the U.S. declaration of war against
Germany in 1917. It followed a speech to Congress by Pres. Woodrow Wilson in which he
reaffirmed U.S. friendship with the German people, but that military action had to be taken
against a government which sank not only troop
ships, but also passenger and hospital ships of
the U.S. and other nations. It is also the day
that George M. Cohan composed *Over There*,
which was copyrighted on June 1 of the same
year.

April 7

Cyril Emmanuel King Day (VI)—Cyril Emmanuel King was the second elected governor of the U.S. Virgin Islands, taking over the office in 1975 and remaining until January 2, 1978, when he died in office. The last year of his term was completed by Juan Francisco Luis.

World Health Day (U.N.)—This is the anniversary of the formation of the World Health Organization, sponsored by the United Nations, in 1948. Each year a theme is selected to highlight public health issues of world-wide concern. Global advocacy and awareness-raising activities are a major goal of the World Health Organization, with each U.N. member nation adapting its activities to one or more related issues which are of particular importance to its citizens.

April 8

Buddha Day (HI)—This commemorates the birth of Siddhartha Gautama in 563 B.C. An Indian religious leader later known as Buddha (Sanskrit for "the enlightened one"), he founded Buddhism. He died in about 483 B.C. For his birthday, followers construct temporary platforms at his temples, the roof of each being covered with flowers, based on the legend that at Buddha's birth it rained flowers. On the platform is placed an image of the infant Siddhartha in a tub filled with licorice tea. Believers pour the tea over the figure with bamboo ladles, signifying the act of bathing him, and then drink some of the tea. This is supposed to purify their souls and cause them to become Buddha-like.

Day of Recognition for Bone Marrow Donor Programs (VA)—On this day, Virginians acknowledge the critical value of these initiatives in facilitating bone marrow transplant therapy. Singled out for recognition are those who donate bone marrow to help patients suffering from blood disorders, including Hodgkin's lymphoma, acute leukemia, and diseases of plasma cells and immune systems.

Ramon Emeterio Betances Commemorative Day (PR)—Betances was born to a wealthy landowner on April 8, 1827, in Cabo Rojo, Puerto Rico, and received his medical degree at the University of Paris. He returned to Puerto Rico, founded a hospital, and fought a cholera epidemic. He also formed a clandestine society to liberate slaves, which resulted in his being exiled by the Spanish colonial government. From abroad, and known as "The Father of the Motherland," he organized the armed expedition known as the "Grito de Lares," then moved back to Nevilly, France, where he worked toward Puerto Rican independence until he died on September 16, 1898. He was also awarded the French Legion of Honor medal for his contributions to literature.

April 9

Bataan Day (NM)—This day is in honor of the brave and patriotic New Mexicans composing the 200th and 515th Coast Artillery Regiments (anti-aircraft) who served in the Philippine Islands during World War II. They fought insuperable odds and endured every deprivation, and, following surrender, entered upon a tragic "death march." The day marks the anniversary of the day in 1942 when the island fell to the Japanese after more than three months of siege.

Bataan-Corregidor Day (MA)—This day commemorates the battles of Bataan and Corregidor, in the Pacific Theater during World War II. Corregidor is located 26 miles west of Manila, Philippines, just off the southern tip of the Bataan Peninsula. The island was fortified with big guns to support the Filipino and American defenders of Bataan. Corregidor itself was invaded and taken over by the Japanese in May of 1942. They held it until March 1945, when it was retaken by American paratroopers and landing parties.

Former Prisoners of War Recognition Day (AK, GA, ME, TX, WA) [**Former Prisoner of War Recognition Day** (MA), **POW Recognition Day** (NY), **Prisoner of War Day** (NC), **Prisoners of War Remembrance Day** (AZ, AR, MO, OK)]—This commemorates the sacrifices of men and women who suffered captivity in foreign lands while in the service of our country. Citizens are requested to devote some portion of the day to solemn contemplation on the plight of the men and women of this country who have been prisoners of war. The date of April 9 was set because it was the date during World War II when the greatest number of Americans were captured.

April 12

Anniversary of Signing of Halifax Resolves (NC)—On April 12, 1776, the Halifax

Resolutions of Independence were signed, which in part led to the Declaration of Independence less than three months later. This was the first action of a colony authorizing its delegates to call for independence. The 83 men who comprised the Fourth Provincial Congress unanimously adopted the Resolves, which also recommended to the other colonies that they also take steps toward declaring independence from England.

April 13

Antonio R. Barcelo Day (PR) — This day celebrates the life of Antonio R. Barcelo, who founded the Partido Liberal (Liberal Party). During the 1930s, the party was challenged by youth led by Luis Munoz Marin, but the "old guard," led by Barcelo, held its ground and Munoz left to form the Popular Democratic Party.

Jefferson Day (MO, OK) — This day was established to perpetuate the memory of the public service and the humanitarian principles of Thomas Jefferson.

John Hanson's Birthday (MD) — This celebrates the life of John Hanson (4/3/1715–11/22/1783), who became a member of the Provincial Legislature of Maryland in 1775, and member of Congress in 1777. When the U.S. was formed by the adoption of the Articles of Confederation on March 1, 1781, the Congress unanimously chose John Hanson as its first president. During his tenure, all foreign troops and flags were ordered off American soil, the Great Seal of the U.S. was established, and the Treasury Department, Secretary of State and Foreign Affairs Department were established. His term lasted one year, as did the subsequent terms of Elias Boudinot, Thomas Mifflin, Richard Henry Lee, Nathan Gorman, Arthur St. Clair and Cyrus Griffin. When the Articles of Confederation were superseded by the Constitution, the numbering of U.S. presidents began again with "one" when George Washington was elected.

Thomas Jefferson's Birthday (Fed) — Thomas Jefferson was born on April 13, 1743. He was a politician, architect, educator, and the 3rd President of the U.S. He is considered to have been the prime intellectual force behind the founding of the republic. He died on July 4, 1826. His memorial in Washington, DC, was dedicated by Pres. Franklin Roosevelt on the 200th anniversary of Jefferson's birth.

April 14

Pan-American Day (FL) [**Pan American Day** (CT)] — This is to be observed in the public schools as a day honoring Latin American republics. Citizens are encouraged to recognize and perpetuate mutually friendly relationships with them. It is the anniversary of the first International Conference of American States, in 1889–90. During the lengthy conference, a resolution established the International Bureau of American Republics, which was later renamed the Pan American Union. This became an official day of observance in 1931, when it was proclaimed so by Pres. Herbert Hoover.

April 15

Father Damien DeVeuster Day (HI) — Known as the "Apostle of Molokai," Joseph De-Veuster was born on January 3, 1840, in Tremeloo, Belgium. He decided to become a lay brother with the Sacred Hearts Congregation, and assumed the name of Damien, after the physician-saint who died a martyr's death in the 4th century. He was then persuaded to become a priest, and sailed for Hawaii in 1863 to work at the Sacred Hearts Mission. That same year, leprosy (Hansen's Disease) was growing to epidemic proportions. He worked on the big island, and many of his parishioners were sent to the leper settlement on Molokai to protect the remainder of the population. In 1873 Father Damien volunteered to go to Molokai and live with the outcasts, and devote his life to their care. He ministered to their physical and spiritual needs, and in 1884 it was confirmed that he, too, had contracted the disease. Other Sacred Heart personnel were sent to the island to replace him and carry on his work, but he kept working to care for the natives until a month before his death on April 15, 1889. He was buried there next to the church he built, but in 1936 he was exhumed and re-interred in a shrine at Louvain, Belgium. His right hand was returned to Hawaii in 1995 for use in a ceremony marking his beatification, the penultimate step in becoming a saint, and then was reburied in his original grave at Kalaupapa, Molokai.

Local Government Day (PA) — The government of Pennsylvania calls upon its citizens to recognize the vital role of local government, including municipalities and school districts, in the preservation of the heritage of freedom, justice, equality and self-government. It is a reminder that unless every individual citizen takes an active interest and assumes responsibility in his local government, there can be real danger he will be losing control to the state and federal government over problems which he knows best, such as public education, health and safety.

April 16

Mother Joseph Day (WA) — Mother Joseph was born in April of 1823 in St. Martin, Quebec, to Joseph Pariseau, a carriage maker. She attended St. Martin College, entered the novitiate as a Sister of Charity in Montreal in 1843, and moved to Vancouver, British Columbia, in December of 1856. She and four other Sisters traveled to mining towns, typically raising from $2,000 to $5,000, begging for funds to construct hospitals, schools and missions. They began with a school, the St. Joseph Hospital, and the conversion of an old Vancouver house into an asylum for the mentally ill. She met her goal for Vancouver of the construction of a permanent structure for education, known as the Providence Academy, which still stands. The last of the 29 facilities she raised funds for, and often supervised the construction of, is St. Ignatius in Colfax, British Columbia, which was completed in 1893. In 1892 she was made Mother Superior of a convent, where she served until her death in 1902. Her efforts are continued by the Mother Joseph Foundation, which considers her to be the greatest fund-raiser of all time.

April 17

American Samoa Flag Day (AS) — This is a commemoration of the signing of the Instrument of Cession, making the group of six islands an unorganized U.S. territory in 1900, and also the establishment of the Samoan constitutional government in 1960. Its flag features a bald eagle in a white triangle with a red border, on a field of blue.

New Jersey Day (NJ) — This commemorates and observes the anniversary of the beginning of unified government in New Jersey. It was one of the earliest states to institute its own constitution, in 1776, and was one of the most affected by the ineffectiveness of the Articles of Confederation. Representatives from New Jersey played key roles at the Constitutional Convention, bringing about a government stronger than that which had existed under the Articles.

April 18

Arbor Day (CO) — The people of Colorado are urged to plant forest trees for the benefit and adornment of public and private grounds, places and ways. The founder of Arbor Day, J. Sterling Morton, noted that, "Other holidays repose upon the past. Arbor day proposes the future."

Exemplary Adult Care Provider Day (OH) — This is in recognition of the service and dedication of adult care providers in Ohio, including adult foster homes, adult family homes, adult group homes and residential care facilities.

Renowned Puerto Rican Statesmen's Day (PR) — This is a day to recognize, as a group, the many individuals who have served in governing the island, working for its independence, and fighting for other causes. Included are Pedro Albizu Campos (who championed independence and served as the president of the National Party in the 1930s), Ruben Berrios Martinez (who led the Puerto Rican Independence Party from 1970 to 1993), Nemesio Canales (a member of the Puerto Rican House of Representatives), Luis Alberto Ferre (governor from 1969 to 1973), Rafael Hernandez Colon (governor, senator, and president of the Popular Democratic Party, who opposed statehood), and Felisa Rincon de Gautier (first female mayor of San Juan, from 1946 to 1969).

April 19

Oklahoma City Bombing Remembrance Day (OK) — This day is a commemoration of the sacrifices of those persons who lost their lives or were injured in the bombing, and their loved ones. All in Oklahoma are encouraged to observe a moment of silence at 9:02 A.M., the time the bomb went off at the nine-story Murrah Federal Building on April 19, 1995. Five years later, the Oklahoma City National Memorial was dedicated in a ceremony presided over by Pres. Bill Clinton.

Patriots' Day (AR, FL, MA) — This commemorates the opening events of the American Revolution and the struggle through which the nation passed in its early days. This includes the ride of Paul Revere and Charles Dawes on the night of April 18, 1775, to warn the residents of Boston about the approach of the British army, so the colonists' militia could prepare to meet them at the Lexington meeting house green. The ride is symbolically reenacted through the annual running of the Boston Marathon.

April 20

Bob Bartlett Day (AK) — Edward Louis "Bob" Bartlett, known as the "architect of Alaska statehood," is honored for a lifetime of public service to Alaska and the U.S. He was born on this date in 1904, and spent time as a politician, newspaperman and gold miner. He died on December 11, 1968.

April 21

Confederate Flag Day (AR) — When the term "Confederate flag" is used, most people think of the battle flag with a diagonal blue cross bearing thirteen white stars, all on a red field, but there were several other "Confederate flags" used by the South during the Civil War. These include the Citadel Battle Flag (used by Citadel men in the attack on the ship *Star of the West*), the Bonnie Blue Flag (considered the "first" in the hearts of the people), the Palmetto Guard Flag (flew over Fort Sumter), the South Carolina Secession Flag (which symbolized secession), the C.S.A. Navy Jack (used on ships beginning in 1863), the First National C.S.A. Flag (stars and bars, official from March 1861 to May 1863), the Second National C.S.A. Flag (the "Stainless Banner"), the Third National C.S.A. Flag (officially adopted, but hardly used), and Robert E. Lee's Headquarters Flag (used to identify his command center). State law prohibits the Confederate flag from being used in any advertisement for any commercial enterprise, or in any manner or for any purpose except to honor the Confederate States of America.

Dauphine Day (RI) — This day commemorates the arrival of the ship *Dauphine* in Rhode Island in 1524. It was captained by Italian navigator Giovanni Verrazzano, who had been commissioned to make the voyage by the king of France, making this the first verifiable visit to the state by a European adventurer. He was searching for an all-water route through the North American continent to get to China. As he explored the coast and headed east from the present site of New York, he came upon a triangle-shaped island which reminded him of the size of Rhodes in Greece. He named it Luisa after the Queen Mother of France, and today it is known as Block Island. Roger Williams thought Verrazzano had referred to what the Indians called Aquidneck Island, and changed its name to Rhode Island, which eventually became the name of the entire colony.

John Muir Day (CA) — This day celebrates the life and work of John Muir, who was born in Dunbar, Scotland, in 1838 and emigrated to the U.S. when he was 11. He began pursuing his interest in naturalism with a 1,000 mile walk from Indianapolis to the Gulf of Mexico. After traveling to Cuba and Panama, he went to California in 1868 and began to explore the Yosemite Valley and the Sierras. He was an author, and his writings caught the attention of others who strove to preserve wilderness areas. Muir was recruited to help protect the wilderness of Yosemite and the Sierras, and he was a co-founder of the Sierra Club. He served as its president, then in the 1890s returned to Scotland. Muir died in 1914 of pneumonia. His books include *All the World Over: Notes from Alaska, Gentle Wilderness: The Sierra Nevada, Letters from Alaska, Our National Parks* and *Wilderness Essays*.

San Jacinto Day (TX) — This commemorates the 1836 Battle of San Jacinto. During the previous month, Texas declared independence from Mexico, and expected a fight. Sam Houston and the Texas army camped by the San Jacinto River, awaiting their chance to attack the Mexican army led by General Santa Anna. Houston and his 900 men killed 630 Mexicans and took 730 prisoners, while only nine Texans died. Santa Anna was taken prisoner the following day and signed a treaty under duress. The site of the battle is marked with the 570-foot tall San Jacinto Monument, the tallest monument column in the world. This 18-minute battle is one of the most important in the history of the U.S., as it won the freedom of Texas and resulted in almost one-third of the present-day land area of the U.S. being conveyed by Mexico.

April 22

Birthday of Rafael Martinez Nadal (PR) — Poet Federico Garcia Lorca, prior to his death at the hands of Spain's Civil Guard in 1936, gave his manuscript of an unpublished drama, *The Public*, to author Rafael Martinez Nadal. It was eventually published, with an introduction by Nadal, in 1978. Nadal's books include *Love and Death in the Work of Federico Garcia Lorca*, *Federico Garcia Lorca and "The Public,"* and *History of Europe, of Spain and America*. He also served as the president of the Puerto Rican Senate. He was born in about 1903 and died on March 5, 2001. Nadal's wife, Jacinta, was a renowned sculptor and dancer, and served on the Republican National Committee. Named after this author is the Rafael Martinez Nadal Expressway, running north and south near San Juan.

Earth Day (PA, VI) — First celebrated on April 22, 1970, this is a day of observance around the world, demonstrating a collective concern for the environment. It is hoped that all individuals and institutions, having a mutual responsibility to act as trustees of the Earth, will make choices in ecology, economics and ethics to eliminate pollution, poverty and violence, foster peaceful progress, awaken the wonder of life, and realize the best potential for the future of the human adventure.

Oklahoma Day (OK) — This commemorates the opening of the unoccupied and former Indian lands in the Oklahoma Territory for settlement by whites in 1889. Post–Civil War treaties moved many native tribes to Oklahoma, and there was consideration of using the territory for settlement by emancipated slaves. However, a group known as the "Boomers" pushed for the white settlement of the area, and the western portion of Oklahoma was made available during six land runs between 1889 and 1895. They attracted settlers from all over the U.S. and Europe. The official location designated for this celebration is Guthrie, Logan County. This is also known as 89ers' Day.

April 23

World Book and Copyright Day (U.N.) — UNESCO seeks to promote reading, publishing and the protection of intellectual property through copyright. Since 1948, that agency has pursued an ambitious program to translate and publish more than a thousand representative works from a wide range of cultures. It also backs regional co-publication in Africa and the Asia-Pacific region, where emphasis is placed on books for children, women and individuals who have recently learned to read. In the area of copyright, it introduced in 1952 the universal copyright symbol (an encircled "c") to protect published works.

April 24

Armenian Martyrs' Day (MA) — This day commemorates the 1915 Armenian Genocide, the first mass slaughter of the 20th Century. On April 24, 1915, 235 Armenian professionals and intellectuals were arrested and hanged by Turks as common criminals in public parks, beginning the "final solution" of the problem that the Turks felt the million Armenians caused. By 1923, the Turkish regime deprived the remaining Armenians of their land and human rights, killing a million and exiling half that number. The event is also commemorated by a large memorial monument in the North Burial Grounds of Providence, Rhode Island.

Ernesto Ramos Antonini Day (PR) — Ernesto Ramos Antonini was born in Mayaguez, Puerto Rico, on April 24, 1898, and is known as the "Defender of the Working Class." He was an accomplished musician and lawyer, obtaining a favorable sentence for his clients who were accused in the "Massacre of Ponce." He worked with labor unions for the rights of workers, and testified before the U.S. Congress to denounce the terrible conditions that Puerto Rican workers had to contend with, while earning meager wages working for large U.S. corporations which had branches there. He served in the legislature from 1945 until he died in Santurce on January 9, 1963.

National Wildflower Day (TX) — This day brings focus on a valuable natural resource, wildflowers. Located in Austin, Texas, is the National Wildflower Research Center, which includes 42 acres full of flowers, vines, shrubs and grasses. The Center also mans a telephone hotline providing information on the best wildflower viewing sites throughout the U.S.

April 25

Timothy Theodore Duncan Day (VI) — Tim Duncan was born on February 4, 1976, and grew up on St. Croix. His older sister swam for the Virgin Islands in the 1988 Olympics, and Tim was one of the top-ranked U.S. swimmers for his age group, expected to compete in the 1992 Olympics. However, Hurricane Hugo in 1989 ruined the island's swimming pools and he quit the sport rather than practice with his team in the ocean. As a high school freshman, he took up basketball and caught the attention of a touring NBA player, who was an alumnus of Wake Forest University. He notified the Wake Forest coach, who recruited Duncan, and Tim played for that school for four years, graduating with a degree in psychology. He earned awards as the NCAA Player of the Year, the National Defensive Player of the Year (three years), and the Atlantic Coast Conference Player of the Year (two years). Drafted by the San Antonio Spurs in 1997, he won the Rookie of the Year Award, and was only the third rookie in NBA history to be named Rookie of the Month for each of the six months of the season. In 1999 he was the Most Valuable Player of the NBA Finals, helping the Spurs win their first NBA title.

April 26

Arkansas Bird Day (AR)—This is a day to learn about and appreciate the birds which are indigenous to Arkansas, including the mockingbird, which was designated as the state bird in 1929.

Bird Day (ND)—This day promotes and encourages the conservation and enjoyment of one of nature's most attractive features, and to honor the birth and work of naturalist John James Audubon, who made America's birds known to the world through his drawings and vivid prose.

Confederate Memorial Day (FL, GA)—This day was set aside by the Florida legislature to remember the sacrifices made by Southern soldiers during the Civil War. April 26 marks the anniversary of the end of the Civil War in Georgia, as it was on this day in 1865 that Confederate Gen. Joseph E. Johnston's surrender to Gen. William Sherman in North Carolina became official. Johnston had been in charge of Georgia's defense.

April 27

School Principals' Recognition Day (MA)—This day celebrates the men and women who are tackling the important issues that keep our young people on the road to being productive and competitive in this century's new economy—tough curriculum standards, increasingly diverse student populations, and shrinking education budgets. This is a time to recognize the skill, dedication and commitment of school principals, and support their efforts to provide educational excellence.

April 28

Confederate Memorial Day (AL, MS)—On this day, the South's heritage from the War Between the States is remembered. It is observed with the exhibition of the Constitution of the Confederate States of America, decoration of the graves of Confederate veterans and speeches.

Exercise Tiger Day (MA)—This commemorates the 30,000 servicemen who left Truro, England, on an exercise mission for the D-Day invasion. It took place on April 22–30, 1944, on Slapton Sands in Start Bay, and at Tor Bay, resembling the bluffs of Omaha Beach. The troops and equipment left from most of the same ports that they would use to get to Normandy on D-Day. They were protected from the German E-boats which patrolled the English Channel by two destroyers, three motor torpedo boats and two motor gunboats. Despite that, they were attacked by nine E-boats, which escaped after killing or wounding 551 Allied soldiers. The existence of Tiger was not made known to the public until after D-Day.

Workers' Memorial Day (NY) [**Worker's Memorial Day** (CT, TN), **Workers Memorial Day** (NE, OH)]—This day commemorates and honors workers who have died on the job as a result of injuries or disease. It also focuses on the need for strong safety and health protections in the workplace. The date of April 28 was chosen because it is the anniversary of the Occupational Safety and Health Act.

April 30

Day in Honor of the Aged (PR)—On this day, children are encouraged to feel due respect and veneration for the aged.

MAY

OBSERVANCES WITH VARIABLE DATES

Sunday Following Easter (As early as March 29 and as late as May 2)

Gold Star Mother's Day (NH)—This day recognizes and honors all mothers who have lost sons or daughters while on duty in the U.S. Armed Forces. Gold Star Mothers groups exist to assist veterans, especially those who were wounded or incapacitated during hostilities, and perpetuate the memory of those whose lives were sacrificed in war.

First Sunday Following the Fourth Sunday in April

Family Sunday (GU)—On this day, the people of Guam are to consider the value and importance of the family.

Week of May 1

Law Week (FL)—This week is an opportunity to expand awareness of our laws and justice system, and its effects on our lives.

Week of May 2

History of Oregon Statehood Week (OR)—This commemorates May 2, 1843, as the date that settlers met at Champoeg to form a provisional government. Later, Oregon became the 33rd state.

First Sunday in May

Chaplains Day (IL)—This day recognizes religious chaplains who, far from their homes in places scattered throughout the world, give comfort and solace to Americans wherever they may be found. Illinois chaplains are officially recognized for their valuable and inspiring services.

Loyal Heart Award Day (NJ)—This recognizes and honors the loyal efforts of caregivers in helping patients with disabilities achieve their fullest potential. More than two million New Jersey residents with disabilities have civil rights which are protected by the Americans with Disabilities Act of 1990.

Rhode Island Independence Day (RI)—This commemorates May 4, 1776, when members of the general assembly passed an act renouncing allegiance of the colony to England. It was the first American colony to do so.

Senior Citizens Day (CT)—This is in honor of elderly citizens and recognizes their continued contribution to the state, enriching the lives of all of its citizens.

Week Beginning on the First Sunday in May

Senior Citizens Week (OK)—This week honors all senior citizens and their contributions to the state and all of its citizens.

First Week in May

Correctional Officers and Employees Recognition and Appreciation Week (DE)— This is a time for public recognition and appreciation of those who have dedicated their lives to protecting the rights of the public to be safeguarded from criminal activity, and who are responsible for the care, custody and dignity of human beings in their charge.

Rhode Island Speech-Language-Hearing Awareness Week (RI)— During this time, the people of Rhode Island are presented with educational messages designed to help them understand the varied maladies which affect speaking and hearing. Focus is also made on the advances in the areas of diagnosis and treatment, and the advances in technology which are restoring to many the ability to speak and hear.

First Monday in May

Nurses' Day (RI)— A goal of Nurses' Day is the coming together of nurses and schools to break down the stereotypical image of nursing, and educate the next generation about the realities of modern nursing, midwifery and healthcare. Rhode Island has determined that professional nursing is an indispensable component in the safety and quality of care for hospitalized patients, and that the demand for registered nursing services will be greater than ever because of the aging American population, the continuing expansion of life-sustaining technology, and the explosive growth of home health care services. For that reason, the state honors them on this day to celebrate the ways in which they strive to provide safe and high quality patient care.

Week Beginning on the First Monday in May

Teachers Week (PR)— The National PTA has, since 1984, encouraged all citizens to celebrate Teacher Appreciation Week as a re-affirmation of our commitment to parent-teacher partnerships. It also believes that one way to improve the educational system is to exhibit respect for teachers, and let them know how much we value their contributions. This week is a chance to do that with governmental recognition and support.

First Tuesday in May

Teacher Appreciation Day (NH)— This is an opportunity to focus attention on the outstanding contributions that teachers make to us individually and as a community. Teachers are to be accorded the status and recognition they deserve as professionals, as a way of strengthening the educational system.

Wednesday of Senior Citizens Week (Week Beginning with the First Sunday in May)

Senior Citizens' Day (OK)— This is a day to honor the senior citizens of Oklahoma and recognize the value of what they bring to our culture. It is a celebration of their skills and experiences, and the influences they have on us and our children.

First Thursday in May

Massachusetts Whale Awareness Day (MA)— This is a day to focus on the world's largest mammals, which frequent the waters off the coast of Massachusetts. The types of whales seen there include humpbacks, minkes, rights, seis, blues, sperms and pilots. The area around Cape Ann is close to Jefferey's Ledge and Stellwagen Bank, two major feeding areas frequented by whales.

Commonwealth Day of Prayer (VA) [**Commonwealth Day of Prayer and Celebration of Religious Freedom** (PA), **Day of Prayer in Illinois** (IL), **Prayer Day** (NJ)]— In these states, people are encouraged to engage in group and individual prayer to give thanks and ask for guidance for the betterment of themselves and their society.

First Friday in May

Arbor Day (ND, VT)— This day was set by the legislature to promote and encourage the planting of trees in North Dakota and Vermont, a week later than the most popular date for such observance, as the optimal planting season begins later there than in states located further south.

Teachers' Day (VI)— This day honors all persons having licenses as teachers and who are practicing as such, or are on leave, or are retired, plus officials and employees of the Department of Education, deceased teachers, professors in the Virgin Islands on cultural missions, and guests of honor of Virgin Islands educational institutions.

First Saturday in May

Teachers' Appreciation Day (GU) — This day commemorates the services rendered by the teachers of Guam to its children. They are recognized for their lasting contributions made to the lives of our children.

First Saturday after the First Sunday in May, Through and Including the Third Sunday in May

Covered Bridges Week (PA) — This is a time to celebrate the state's many historic covered bridges. They are preserved through the efforts of the Theodore Burr Covered Bridge Society of Pennsylvania, Inc. Pennsylvanians are encouraged to visit some of the bridges during this week.

Mother's Day and the Saturday Preceding It

Take a Mom Fishing Weekend (MN) — Minnesota fishing licenses this weekend are free for moms. Ordinarily, residents aged 16 or over are required to purchase licenses.

Second Sunday in May

Massachusetts Emergency Responders Memorial Day (MA) — This honors paramedics, emergency medical and public safety personnel, national guard personnel on state active duty, disaster assistance volunteers, and emergency management personnel killed in the line of duty.

Mothers's Day (Fed, DE, IA, KS, KY, MA, NV, NJ, OK, SC, VA) [**Mothers' Day** (ND, PR, TN), **Mothers Day** (AZ, IL)] — This day of remembrance was founded by Anna Jarvis of Grafton, West Virginia, as a public expression of love and reverence for mothers. She began her efforts in 1907, after her mother had died three years before. By 1909, every state was celebrating Mother's Day, and Pres. Woodrow Wilson signed

a proclamation on May 9, 1914, making it a national celebration. In later years Jarvis despised the commercialism that grew up around the observance, especially the greeting cards and flowers. Jarvis essentially became a recluse, never leaving her home and keeping others away with "Warning — Stay Away" signs in her front yard.

Week Beginning with Mother's Day

Osteoporosis Prevention and Awareness Week (NV) — This is to bring to the attention of Nevada's residents factual information regarding the early diagnosis and treatment of osteoporosis, and emphasize the potential for the prevention of the disease.

Week Following the Second Sunday in May

Emergency Management Week (MA) — Special attention is paid to preparedness, response, recovery and mitigation to protect lives and property from national and technological hazards. It is also a time to recognize the work of the Emergency Management Agencies working in the various municipalities to deal with severe weather, natural and man-made disasters. There are programs to educate the public about the EMS system and its appropriate use, and how to respond to a medical emergency.

Second Week in May

First Aid Week (NJ) — During this week, the governor of New Jersey presents an award for the First Aid Volunteer of the Year, from nominations made by presidents of county and municipal first aid, rescue and emergency squads.

Human Potential Week (NJ) — This week promotes greater awareness of the needs and concerns of persons with disabilities, and highlights the significant contributions these individuals have made to their families, communities and society as a whole. This time of observance was established in New Jersey in 1998 to provide a forum to discuss issues of interest to people with physical and mental disabilities, expand communication between disabled and non-disabled people, and promote a greater awareness of the needs and concerns of people with disabilities in order to facilitate a oneness of community.

Second Full Week in May

Long-Term Care Week (NJ)—This week of observance is intended to increase the public awareness of the contributions made by persons in the long-term care field who are providing services to some of the most vulnerable members of our community. During this week, the Governor of New Jersey presents the County Long-Term Care Volunteer of the Year Award.

Second Tuesday in May

Amateur Radio Operators Day (PR)—This day celebrates the numerous amateur radio operators in Puerto Rico, and the services they provide to the island's citizens. In times of natural disaster, radio communication is often the only way to obtain reports of conditions and for families to find out about their loved ones.

Second Wednesday in May

Public School Paraprofessional Day (TX)—This day recognizes education professionals, including teacher assistants, educational trainers, instrumental aides, library attendants, special education associates, bilingual assistants, mentors and trainers.

Second Thursday in May

Rhode Island Hero's Day (RI)—This day is in recognition of Rhode Island residents who have saved a human life and/or performed extraordinary acts of heroism which merit such recognition, as determined by the General Assembly. This observance was established in 1999.

Second Friday in May

Friendship Day (RI)—This is a day to celebrate and encourage friendship among individuals, and among peoples of the world.

Week Including May 15

Law Enforcement Memorial Week (NH)—This recognizes the service given by the men and women who, night and day, stand guard in our midst to protect us through enforcement of our laws. Honored are federal, state and municipal officers who have been killed or disabled in the line of duty.

Police Week (Fed, GA, PA) [**National Police Week** (RI), **Virgin Islands Police Week** (VI), **Police Officers Week** (MA)]—This week recognizes the service given by the men and women who stand guard to protect the people of the U.S. through law enforcement. Declared by the U.S. Congress in 1962, it acknowledges that by the enforcement of our laws, peace officers have given our country internal freedom from fear of the violence and civil disorder that affects other nations. The first law enforcement system in the U.S. was established in Boston in April of 1631. Called the "night watch," it used part-time officers who served without pay. The first full-time paid officers were also hired in Boston, in 1712.

Week Including May 16

National Transportation Week (Fed)—This is a tribute to the men and women who, night and day, move goods and people throughout the U.S. It provides an opportunity for the transportation community to join together for greater awareness about the importance of transportation, and making youth aware of transportation-related careers. The observance was begun by the Women's Transportation Club of Houston, led by Charlotte Jones Woods, who offered a $500 scholarship at the University of Houston for a student seeking a degree in transportation subjects. When no one applied, and it was evident that students were not interested in going into the transportation field, a week to promote transportation was held in 1953 in Houston, and it soon spread to other cities and towns in Texas. It was proclaimed a permanent celebration by Pres. John Kennedy in 1962.

Week of Puerto Rican Danza (PR)—This week has been chosen to make known and divulge this form of musical expression. During the week there is the Annual Contest of Composition of Danzas, with prizes of $1,000, $500 and $250. One particular danza, "*La Borinquena*" (named after the original name for the island, Borinquen), is Puerto Rico's national anthem.

Third Sunday in May

Citizenship Day (IL)—The purpose of this day is to prepare as citizens those individuals who during the previous 12 months have reached the age of 18. Emphasis is placed on the responsibilities attached to the rights and privileges of citizenship.

Joshua James Day (MA)—Joshua James was the first keeper of the Point Allerton Life Saving Station, located in the town of Hull. He was the most decorated member of the U.S. Lifesaving Service, a predecessor of the U.S. Coast Guard.

Police, Firemen and First Aid Recognition Day (NJ)—This day recognizes the dedicated service the members of police and fire departments, and various first aid, ambulance and rescue services in the state, have rendered to their fellow citizens. That service is often provided under difficult circumstances and at great personal risk, to protect the lives and property of their fellow citizens.

Senior Citizens Day (IL)—On this day, the senior citizens of Illinois are honored for their contributions to society and the institution of the family.

Third Week in May

Accountant Week (PR)—This is a time to recognize the services provided by those who keep financial records and, through their reports, keep owners, investors and the public informed about the financial condition of businesses.

American Indian Heritage Week (MA)—This commemorates the Indian tribes of Massachusetts and their contributions to the society and culture of the state.

Maine Small Business Week (ME)—During this week, the state promotes small businesses and the free enterprise system.

Medical Records Transcribers Week (PR)—This celebrates those who work in the field of medical records transcription, which throughout the U.S. has grown to be a multi-billion dollar industry. Medical providers, doctors, psychiatrists, and other medical professionals rely on the judgment and reasoning skills of experienced medical transcriptionists. The accuracy and integrity of medical dictation is essential, and can mean life and death to patients.

National Family Week (MA)—Each year, the Alliance for Children and Families creates a new logo and selects a theme dealing with a topic relevant to families. It works with child- and family-serving organizations, health care agen-

cies and other service groups to celebrate this week and emphasize the importance of family loyalties and ties. National Family Week was founded in 1968 and emphasizes that children live better lives when their families are strong, and families are strong when they live in communities that connect them to economic opportunities, social networks and services.

Virgin Islands African Heritage Week (VI)—The Virgin Islands have historical connections with Africa, beginning with the first group of African slaves brought there in 1665. The islands flourished as a center of slave trade throughout the 18th century. Slavery was abolished in 1848, triggering a decline in the production of sugar cane on the plantations. William Henry Hastie became the first black governor of the Virgin Islands in 1946. In 1969 Melvin Evans was appointed as the first native-born black governor, and he was elected to the position in 1971, serving until 1975.

Visiting Nurse Association Week (MA)—Of the more than 2.2 million registered nurses in the U.S., nearly ten percent work in community or public health settings, including visiting nurse services. They provide skilled nursing services and rehabilitation therapy for both long-term needs resulting from disabilities and illnesses, and for short-term care following hospital stays and accidents.

A Week to Remember Persons who are Disabled or Shut-In (CT)—Residents of Connecticut are encouraged to visit the elderly, infirm, and others who are confined to their homes or care facilities.

Third Full Week in May

Arbor Week (ME)—Citizens of Maine are urged to plant trees, shrubs and vines in the promotion of forest growth and culture, and the adornment of public and private grounds, places and ways.

Wednesday of American Indian Heritage Week

Massasoit Day (MA)—This celebration is in memory of the services of Chief Massasoit performed on behalf of the first European settlers in the commonwealth. Massasoit was born in Pokanoket, a village located near present-day

Bristol, Rhode Island, in about 1590. As a chief of the Wampanoags, he signed a peace treaty with Gov. John Carver of the Pilgrims on March 22, 1621. Unusual for treaties with Native Americans, this one was never broken and helped to provide for a long peaceful coexistence. Massasoit and some of his people were invited to celebrate the first Thanksgiving Day with the Pilgrims. Massasoit's relationship with the settlers helped to keep his tribe neutral in the 1636 Pequot War. He remained an ally of the Pilgrims until he died, in 1661, and he was succeeded as chief by his son, Wamsutta. Peace continued until Wamsutta was succeeded by his brother, Philip, who led an uprising in 1675, now known as King Philip's War.

Week Ending with the Third Saturday in May

Massachusetts National Guard Week (MA) — The national guard is currently involved in protecting the residents of Massachusetts from natural disasters and problems, such as flooding and severe winter storms. They transport people to safe areas, staff hospitals, transport police on patrols and provide ambulance service. Recent action abroad includes service in Bosnia. The service performed by the Guard over the years is remembered in the Massachusetts National Guard Museum in Worcester, which includes an extensive Civil War archive.

Third Friday in May

Glaucoma Day (PR) — This is a time to focus the public's attention on glaucoma, a disease involving optic nerve damage, often resulting from increased pressure within the eye, which may result in blindness. Those at high risk include the elderly, those with a family history of glaucoma, those of African descent, those who have diabetes, and users of steroids or cortisone.

Teacher's Day (FL) — Florida has more than 144,000 teachers and instructional personnel, and the state has recognized that their contribution to Florida's well-being and future prosperity is immeasurable. This day celebrates teachers as champions of youth and members of a noble profession engaged in one of the most important rights of freedom, that of education for all citizens.

Third Saturday in May

Armed Forces Day (OR) — Initially, each branch of the U.S. Armed Forces had its own day to celebrate the anniversary of its establishment. In 1949 Secretary of Defense Louis Johnson announced the creation of a single day to celebrate all, as the Armed Forces were unified under the Department of Defense.

7 Days Ending on the Last Friday Before Memorial Day

National Safe Boating Week (Fed) — This is a time to remind the boating public of the need to follow the nautical "Rules of the Road" for their own safety. Each year, between 700 and 800 individuals in the U.S. die in boating-related accidents, about 70 percent of which involve drowning. As most of the accidents are preventable through increased awareness on the part of boaters, emphasis is placed on identifying hazards, assessing risks, making decisions, implementing controls, and evaluations. It is hoped that by better educating those who operate watercraft, the number of casualties can be reduced.

Second Saturday Before the Last Monday in May

New Jersey Shore Celebration Day (NJ) — This serves as an annual kickoff of the summer shore season. It recognizes the importance of the shore as a symbol of New Jersey's identity, and gives citizens the opportunity to pause and celebrate its beauty and contribution to the overall quality of life, promote the importance of seeking and maintaining a clean ocean and clean beaches for all to enjoy, and demonstrate appreciation for the magnificence and plenty of the sea.

Fourth Week in May

Retired Teachers' Week (IL, KY) — The Illinois legislature has determined that the progress of its state, the U.S. and all civilizations is due to the passing on of knowledge from one generation to the next. This week recognizes the teachers who have tirelessly and selflessly taken on the noble and sacred trust of educating and training the children.

Last Week in May

Massachusetts Art Week (MA)—During this time, there are exhibitions and displays of works in museums, public and private schools, libraries and elsewhere.

Purple Heart Week (OK)—This remembers the Purple Heart, an award established as the Badge of Military Merit by Gen. George Washington in 1782, and revived in 1931. The decoration of honor is awarded to members of the U.S. Armed Forces and U.S. citizens who are honorably wounded resulting from a "singularly meritorious act of essential service." Later, the Purple Heart was extended to other branches of the armed forces, civilians serving with the military, and victims of international terrorist attacks.

Last Friday Before Memorial Day

Long Island Sound Day (CT)—Citizens are encouraged to acknowledge and celebrate the economic, recreational and environmental values of the Long Island Sound. This day of observance resulted from a bill proposed by Senator Eileen Daly to encourage schools, communities and organizations to hold events to bring awareness for the need to preserve and protect this 90-mile long arm of the Atlantic Ocean. Federal and state studies in the mid–1990s pointed out serious problems and recommended a massive cleanup of the sound.

Sunday Before Memorial Day

Neighbor Day (RI)—This was first designated as a statewide observance in 1996 to encourage residents of Rhode Island to get to know their neighbors, and unite with them to work toward solutions to their common problems, such as local crime prevention.

Last Monday in May

Decoration Day (CT, ID, MI, TN)—Henry C. Welles, a druggist in Waterloo, New York, mentioned at an 1865 social gathering that the patriotic dead of the Civil War should be honored by the decoration of their graves. The following year, he mentioned this concept to Gen. John B. Murray, clerk of Seneca County. Murray agreed with it and established a committee to plan a day to honor the dead. Townspeople were strongly in favor of it and created wreaths, crosses and bouquets for veterans' graves, which were placed there on May 5, 1866, in three cemeteries. The celebration was repeated a year later. On May 5, 1868, Gen. John A. Logan, the first commander of the Grand Army of the Republic, issued a General Order establishing "Decoration Day." Graves of comrades who died in defense of their country were to be strewn with flowers.

Jefferson Davis' Birthday (MS)—Jefferson Davis was born in Christian County, Kentucky, on June 3, 1808, and graduated from West Point in 1828. He married the daughter of Zachary Taylor in 1835, and she died shortly thereafter. In 1845 he married the daughter of a Mississippi aristocrat and plantation owner, was elected to the U.S. House of Representatives, and then resigned to join Taylor in Texas to prepare for the Mexican-American War. Davis led a Mississippi regiment at Buena Vista during that war, and afterwards returned home to serve as Secretary of War under Franklin Pierce.

Memorial Day (Fed, AL, AK, AZ, AR, CA, CO, CT, DE, DC, FL, GA, GU, HI, IN, IA, KS, KY, ME, MD, MI, MN, MT, NE, NV, NH, NJ, NM, NY, NC, ND, CM, OH, OK, OR, PA, PR, SD, TN, TX, VI, UT, VA, WA, WV, WI, WY) [**National Memorial Day** (LA, MS, SC)]—In 1882 the name of Decoration Day was changed to Memorial Day, and veterans from all wars were added to the original Civil War dead who were to be honored. Celebrated with speeches and patriotic exercises, the day has been a national holiday celebrated on the last Monday in May since 1971. It marks the unofficial beginning of the summer season, and is a time for families to get together for ball games, picnics and other outdoor activities. The day is also still known as Decoration Day in Connecticut, Michigan and Tennessee.

OBSERVANCES WITH FIXED DATES

May 1

American Loyalty Day (PA) — On this day, Pennsylvania's citizens have the opportunity to learn the meaning of loyalty to one's country, and one's country's loyalty to its citizens, to the end that we shall be a citizenry of united loyalty.

Asian-American Heritage Month (OR) — This celebrates the many and varied contributions to the state by Asian-Americans in the arts, sciences, commerce and education. It is also a time to reflect on the many ways immigrants from Asia suffered — hostile interrogations under prison-like conditions and internment in American concentration camps during World War II are just two examples.

Asian/Pacific American Heritage Month (Fed) — This month has been so designated for the purpose of celebrating the rich cultural heritage which the U.S. has received from Asia and the Pacific Islands. People from there have contributed to cuisine, entertainment, literature, science, art and other aspects of our culture.

Bird Day (OK) — This day's celebration is to be as directed by the Societies for the Preservation of Wildlife.

Family Day (AK) — This day of observance encourages family discussion of the role of families, the rights and responsibilities of children and parents, appropriate methods of resolution of violent feelings in family conflict, and the prevention of child abuse.

Family Preservation Month (AK) — This is the month to celebrate the institution of the family, which is the cornerstone for healthy growth and development of children into responsible adults and good citizens. During this month, the state promotes the proposition that by strengthening families, we strengthen the bonds among parents, children and extended family members — the network which teaches children self-worth, self-confidence and beliefs about the world, attributes which will stay with them throughout their lives.

Keep Massachusetts Beautiful Month (MA) — During this period, programs are held which are designed to encourage and promote the civic and natural beautification of the state.

Kindness Awareness Month (NJ) — All citizens of New Jersey are urged to partake in educational programs and activities to foster kindness.

Law Day, U.S.A. (Fed, MD, NV) [**Law Day** (FL, MO, NJ)] — This is a celebration of the appreciation of liberties and the reaffirmation of loyalty to the U.S., rededication to the ideals of equality and justice under law in relations with each other and with other countries, and for the cultivation of the respect for law which is vital to the democratic way of life. All Florida residents, schools, businesses and clubs, and the mass media are invited to commemorate the role of law in our lives, to be celebrated along a theme selected by the Supreme Court of Florida and supported by the lawyers of the Florida Bar. In Missouri emphasis is placed on ours being a government of laws and not of men, furthering the philosophy that, "The Welfare of the People Shall be the Supreme Law."

Law Enforcement Appreciation Month (FL) — Floridians during this month show their thanks for the services performed by police departments, sheriffs' departments, the highway patrol, and others who risk their lives to protect lives and property.

Law Enforcement Memorial Month (MA) — This is a month to show appreciation for law enforcement officers, especially those who have died in the line of duty. Their names are inscribed on a memorial wall located at Judiciary Square in Washington, DC. On May 13, every year since 1989, a candlelight vigil has been held at the wall to remember those who have made the ultimate sacrifice to protect the residents of their communities. Names of deceased officers which are submitted to the National Law Enforcement Officers Memorial Fund, Inc. are added to the Memorial Wall each May.

Loyalty Day (Fed, CT, MA, SC) — Citizens are asked to reaffirm their loyalty to the U.S., and to recognize the heritage of American freedom. This is a time to recognize the manifold blessings of freedom and liberty secured for the people of the U.S. by their constitutional form of government, and preserved and maintained by the unselfish service and sacrifice of her people. Citizens, mindful of the priceless heritage which has been handed down to them, should ever be vigilant against subversive movements calculated to undermine the American form of government, and embrace this occasion to strengthen their sentiments of faith and loyalty to their country.

May Day Is Lei Day in Hawaii (HI)—This is a celebration of Hawaii's flowers and the colorful leis which are created from them, and their use in greeting visitors to the islands.

Month for Children (VA)—This month's focus is on children's special contributions to family, school and community, and is an opportunity to counter the manifold ills that affect children.

Month of the Composer (PR)—Composers of Puerto Rican music, in various forms, are celebrated during this month.

National Day of Prayer (Fed) [**Alaska Day of Prayer** (AK)]—This is an opportunity for the people of the U.S. to turn to God in prayer and meditation at churches, in groups, and as individuals. In 1952 a law was enacted requiring the President to proclaim a day of his choosing each year for national prayer, and in 1988 the law was amended to designate May 1 as such a day. In his 1987 proclamation, Pres. Ronald Reagan stated, "On our National Day of Prayer, then, we join together as people of many faiths to petition God to show us His mercy and His love, to heal our weariness and uphold our hope, that we might live ever mindful of His justice and thankful for His blessing."

Senior Citizens Month (GU, MA)—In 1965 this replaced Senior Citizens Day in Massachusetts. In Guam this time is to be observed with ceremonies and festivities supervised by the Division of Senior Citizens of the Department of Public Health and Social Services.

Steelmark Month (Fed)—This month recognizes the tremendous contribution made by the steel industry in the U.S. to national security and defense.

V.F.W. Loyalty Day (RI)—On this day, the First District (Rhode Island) of the Veterans of Foreign Wars holds its convention in the hometown of its district commander. That includes a parade with the crowning of the district Loyalty Day queen and her attendants. The V.F.W. dates back to 1899, when veterans of the Spanish-American War and the Philippine Insurrection formed local organizations to secure the rights and benefits they were entitled to as a result of their military service. In addition to medical attention for those who came home sick or wounded, the V.F.W.'s efforts have resulted in the establishment of the Veterans Administration, the national cemetery system, compensation for Vietnam vets exposed to Agent Orange,

and the creation of the National World War II Memorial.

Women Veterans Awareness Month (NJ)—This acknowledges and commemorates the largely unnoticed sacrifices endured, and valor displayed, by American women veterans, having participated in every American conflict since 1776. It is estimated that more than 34,000 live in New Jersey.

May 3

Polish-American Day (CT)—This honors Americans of Polish ancestry, their culture and the contribution they have made to this country.

Polish Constitution Day (MA)—This commemorates the promulgation of the constitution of Poland, ratified on May 3, 1794. Tadeusz Kosciuszko (1746–1817), after helping the Americans defeat England in the American Revolution, returned to Poland in 1784 to live on a small family estate. Five years later, reforms were taking place in the country, and on May 3, 1791, the Polish Diet (parliament) passed a new constitution which reduced Russian influence and strengthened and centralized the Polish government. This resulted in attacks by Russian armies, and Kosciuszko was a key figure in defending against them. Nevertheless, in 1794 the nation was defeated and the constitution no longer had effect. Despite its short duration, it is remembered as being the second modern constitution (the U.S. having the first, and France coming several months after Poland's).

World Press Freedom Day (U.N.)—This date commemorates the Windhoek Declaration on Promoting an Independent and Pluralistic African Press, adopted in 1991. It shows a recognition that a free, pluralistic and independent press is an essential component of any democratic society. It seeks to encourage and develop press freedom initiatives and to assess the state of press freedom worldwide. It is a reminder to national governments to respect their commitments to press freedom, and offer support for media workers who fall victim to any number of measures which restrain, or seek to abolish, freedom of the press. It is also a day to remember those journalists who have been killed because of their profession.

May 4

Horace Mann Day (MA) — This is in recognition of the developer of the modern public school system. Mann was born in Franklin, Massachusetts, on this day in 1796, and spent his life as a public official and educator. He established the State Board of Education and served as its secretary, and as such was able to affect public opinion regarding school problems and increasing the pay of teachers. Mann advocated improving teacher training by founding state schools for the training of teachers. He visited Europe in 1843 to study its schools, and brought back many innovations, including the suppression of corporal punishment. Mann also served in the U.S. Congress as an antislavery Whig, and in 1853 became the first president of Antioch College, where he taught theology and philosophy. He died on August 2, 1859.

May 7

Barrier Awareness Day (KY) — This is a time to become more aware of the barriers which persons with disabilities face, such as buildings or curbs that lack ramps for wheelchairs. Despite the strides made through the Americans with Disabilities Act of 1990, which eliminated many such barriers, more work needs to be done to provide reasonable access to all. On this day, the public is reminded of this.

Vietnam Veterans' Remembrance Day (NJ) — This honors the veterans who served in Vietnam with valor, and is a remembrance of the heroic men and women from New Jersey who lost their lives in the service of their country. Over 300,000 residents of New Jersey saw duty during the Vietnam conflict. Of that number, 1,473 died and 62 were still considered missing as of 1991. May 7 marks the date of the official end of the Vietnam conflict.

May 8

Hernando de Soto Day (MS) — This is in recognition, observation and commemoration of Hernando de Soto, who led the first and most imposing expedition ever made by Europeans into the wilds of North America and the State of Mississippi. It also recognizes the Spanish explorer's 187-day journey from the Tombigbee River basin on the state's eastern border, west-ward to the place of discovery of the Mississippi River on May 9, 1541.

International Red Cross Day (PR) — This day highlights the worth and importance of the Red Cross Movement and its impartial humanitarian efforts towards the prevention and relief of human suffering under any circumstance and in any part of the world. This reaffirms the dignity of man and the rights due to all human beings throughout the globe.

Truman Day (MO) — This celebration is in honor of, and out of respect for, Harry S Truman, the 33rd president of the U.S., a distinguished public servant and the only Missourian ever to be elected to this high office. That was his first full term, having succeeded to the office after the death of Franklin Roosevelt in 1945. His tenure as chief executive included the dropping of atomic bombs on Hiroshima and Nagasaki, the end of World War II, the Korean War, and the McCarthyism era. He died on December 26, 1972.

May 10

Confederate Memorial Day (NC, SC) — This day provides an opportunity to move forward in our efforts to respect everyone's heritage, values, and beliefs, regardless of their race, ethnic background or whatever area of our nation they come from. Citizens are encouraged to use the experience of our past to build a better future.

May 12

Nursing Personnel Day (PR) — Nurses Day was set for May 12 to celebrate the anniversary of the birth of Florence Nightingale. Celebrated around the world, some of its past themes have been "Nurses Always There for You: Caring for Families," "Nurses, Always There for You: United Against Violence," "Partnership for Community Health," "Healthy Aging," and "Safe Motherhood."

May 15

Austrian-American Day (CT) — This honors Americans of Austrian ancestry, their culture and the great contribution they have made to this country. These include Joseph Pulitzer (who created the journalism prize), Arnold Schwarzenegger and Fred Astaire (actors), John D. Hertz (founder of a rental car company), Felix Frankfurter and Earl Warren (Supreme Court justices), August Brentano (bookstore founder), Raoul L. Fleischman (co-founder of *The New Yorker Magazine*), Hermann F. Mark (developer of synthetic fibers), George Low (manager of the Apollo spacecraft program), Victor Frank Hess (physicist), Freidrich von Hayek (economist), and Billy Wilder and Otto Preminger (movie directors). The day was established nationally in 1997 on the fiftieth anniversary of the institution of the Marshall Plan, under which the U.S. helped Austria and the rest of Europe recover from the economic devastation of World War II.

International Day of Families (U.N.)— In 1989 the United Nations General Assembly proclaimed 1994 as the International Year of the Family, and in 1993 it took action to make this day a permanent event. Its goal is to increase awareness of family issues and improve the capability of nations to tackle family-related problems with comprehensive policies.

Peace Officers Memorial Day (Fed, MO, NJ, PA, VI) [**National Police Memorial Day** (RI), **Peace Officer Memorial Day** (GA), **Law Enforcement Memorial Day** (FL), **Police Officers' Week** (MA), **Massachusetts Police Memorial Day** (MA)]—This day honors the federal, state and local officers killed or disabled in the line of duty. It gives citizens an opportunity to recognize, applaud and sincerely thank those men and women who, serving night and day as law enforcement officers, protect and safeguard our lives and property. This day was established by the U.S. Congress in 1962.

Senior Citizen's Day (NJ)—This celebration is intended to increase the state's awareness of the accomplishments and experiences of the senior citizen population. Individuals aged 65 and older comprise 12 percent of the population of the U.S. and 13 percent of that of New Jersey.

Viet Nam Veterans' Day (RI)—On this day, Rhode Island recognizes the 8,744,000 Americans who saw active duty during the Vietnam War, especially those who entered service from the state, and those who resided in the state following their discharge.

May 16

Birthday of Juan Morel Campos and the Day of the Puerto Rican Danza Composers (PR)—Juan Morel Campos was born in 1857 in Ponce, Puerto Rico. He composed more than 300 danzas and at least 250 other songs, and is considered to be the most important figure in 19th century Puerto Rican music. Some of his most famous compositions are *Felices Dias, Vano Empeno, Mis Penas, Tormento, Alma Sublime* and *La Lira Poncena*. As a ballroom dance, the danza flourished in the second half of the 19th century in the salons of the elite landowners having cultural ties to Spain. The dance was heavily influenced by classical music and dances enjoyed by Europeans earlier in the century, incorporating a hint of Afro-Caribbean syncopation.

National Defense Transportation Day (Fed)—On this day we recognize the importance to each community and its people of the transportation system of the U.S., and its maintenance to serve the U.S. in times of peace and national defense. It is also a time to promote the taking advantage of scientific and technological innovations to improve the existing U.S. transportation systems and develop new ones.

May 17

Arbor Day (AR)—This is a day for school children and other residents to plant the state tree (the pine) and other trees, shrubs and vines, on public and private lands.

World Telecommunication Day (U.N.)— This is a commemoration of the founding of the International Telecommunication Union in 1865. Through UNESCO, the United Nations endeavors to strengthen the lines of communication throughout the world.

May 19

Municipal Police Day and **Municipal Police Week** (PR)—These are times for the citizens of the 78 municipalities of Puerto Rico to recognize and celebrate the service provided to them by their respective police departments. Municipal Police Week continues through May 26.

May 20

Anniversary of Death of Lafayette (MA) [**Lafayette Day** (NH)]—This is the anniversary of the death of Marie Joseph Paul Yves Roche

Gilbert du Motier, Marquis de Lafayette, hero of the Revolutionary War, in lasting recognition of his gallant and illustrious service. Born on September 6, 1757, he had entered the French Royal Army at the age of 14, and four years later became enthralled with the American cause for freedom, and the glory and excitement of the possibility of war. At the age of 19 he landed at Charleston, South Carolina, and traveled to Philadelphia where Congress commissioned him as a Major General. He participated in the Battle of Brandywine and helped thwart a move to oust George Washington as head of the army. Lafayette returned to France for a time, and in 1780 came back to the U.S. with French soldiers and supplies. After the war he assisted Thomas Jefferson with French political matters, and Jefferson helped Lafayette draft a Declaration of the Rights of Man and the Citizen, presented on behalf of those overthrowing the monarchy during the French Revolution. Lafayette was granted a huge tract of land in Louisiana and was given honorary U.S. citizenship in 1834, and died on May 20, 1834.

Anniversary of Mecklenburg Declaration of Independence (NC)—This commemorates the declaration of independence from England, signed by the residents of Mecklenburg County, North Carolina, on May 20, 1775. That date is shown on the state flag of North Carolina, but many historians regard the document as spurious. The Mecklenburg residents did, however, adopt on May 31 strong anti–British resolutions. They declared all crown officials, both civil and military, suspended from their offices, thereby implying independence. In 1819 an account of these Mecklenburg Resolves was published, embellished with excerpts from the U.S. Declaration of Independence, and from that some have concluded that there was a May 20 declaration.

May 22

International Day for Biological Diversity (U.N.)—Previously observed on December 29, it was moved to this date to coincide with the anniversary of the adoption of the Convention on Biological Diversity. All are encouraged to celebrate and preserve the diversity of species, and work toward preventing the losses which may result from alien species entering ecosystems following habitat destruction.

International Trade Awareness Week (TX)—Texas businesses are encouraged to engage effectively in the promotion and development of international trade. During this week, focus is placed on opportunities for such trade. This "week" continues through May 26.

Jim Thorpe Day (OK)—This day celebrates the accomplishments of Jim Thorpe, the world's greatest athlete and a native Oklahoman, for the purpose of inspiring the school children of the state to greater personal achievements in physical fitness. In 1950 a panel of American sportswriters and broadcasters chose him as the greatest American athlete, and the greatest football player of the first half of the 20th century. He played football for the Carlisle Indian School, Canton Bulldogs, Cleveland Indians, Oorang Indians, Rock Island Independents, New York Giants and the Chicago Cardinals. At the 1912 Olympics he won both the decathlon and pentathlon. He was born on May 28, 1887, and died on March 28, 1953.

Maine Merchant Marine Day (ME)—This day recognizes the courage and heroism of merchant mariners who have served the nation in times of national emergencies. Merchant mariners have valiantly served as combatant crews on Letters of Marque during the Revolutionary War and the War of 1812, and on armed vessels during the Civil War. During the World Wars, they served on ships equipped with naval armament while transporting supplies and troops between the home front and war fronts.

National Maritime Day (Fed) [**Maritime Day** (MA)]—This is a commemoration of the first transatlantic voyage by a steam-driven vessel, named the S.S. *Savannah*, in 1819. That ship was the first to cross from Savannah, Georgia, to Liverpool, England. This is also a day to honor mariners who gave their lives defending the U.S. during periods of war. During World War II alone, losses included more than 700 American merchant ships and 6,000 merchant mariners.

May 23

Deborah Samson Day (MA)—This is the anniversary of the enlistment of Deborah Samson, under the name of Robert Shurtiff. After her father abandoned his family, five-year-old Deborah was taken in by a spinster and later lived with Deacon Jeremiah Thomas, who already had at least ten sons. By age 15 she grew to five feet eight inches tall, taller than the average male of her day. Her muscles were hardened by strenuous farm work, and, despite a lack of formal education, she became a teacher at age 18 in Middleboro. On May 20, 1782, she enlisted to fight in the American Revolution under an assumed, male name. During one battle she suffered a saber slash on her forehead and took a musket ball in the thigh. After a doctor took care of the head wound and moved on to another patient, she limped out of the hospital and dug out the musket ball with her knife, and, after recovering sufficiently, rejoined her company. The first female of the Continental Army, she is remembered for her courage, determination, outstanding service and unique contribution to the cause for American independence. She received an Honorable Discharge on October 23, 1783, married, bore three children, became the first professional female lecturer, and died on April 29, 1827. On May 23, 1983, she was named the Official Heroine of the Commonwealth of Massachusetts.

Special Needs Awareness Day (MA)— This is in recognition of those who suffer from physical, mental or emotional disability.

May 24

Christa Corrigan McAuliffe Day (CT)— This commemorates the valor of one of the individuals who died in the *Challenger* space shuttle, and honors the commitment and dedication of teachers throughout the U.S. She was born on September 2, 1948, in Massachusetts, and taught social studies in Concord, New Hampshire. She was accepted by NASA out of over 11,000 applicants to be the first "teacher in space," to communicate to Americans the excitement of space travel aboard a space shuttle. During the mission she was to teach two lessons from aboard the shuttle. The first was to introduce each flight member, and show how they lived and worked in space. The second was to explain how the shuttle flew, why people explore space, and focus on the technological advances which have resulted from the space program. She died on January 28, 1986, when the *Challenger* blew up over the Atlantic Ocean just 73 seconds after lift-off.

May 25

African Liberation Day (VI)— Also cele-

brated in a large portion of Africa, this is the anniversary of the formation of the Organization of African Unity in 1963, and celebrates productivity and freedom. It also recognizes renewed and concerted efforts by leaders of Africa to ensure sustainable economic development, democracy and a human rights culture.

Children's Memorial Day (NJ)— Since 1996, this has memorialized the children who have died in New Jersey, and recognizes that their lives made a difference to those who knew them. It is hoped that it will bring comfort to the hearts of their bereaved families.

Missing Persons Month (NJ)— All government agencies and appropriate private agencies are urged to cooperate to make available to the public more in-depth information regarding the true statistics and scope of the missing persons issue. Missing adults and older teenagers represent a largely disenfranchised population, and families are largely forgotten by the present system and general public. This month, rather than corresponding to a calendar month, stretches from May 25 to June 25.

Week of Solidarity with the Peoples of Non-Self-Governing Territories (U.N.)— This observance by the Special Committee on Decolonization was established by the General Assembly of the United Nations in 1999. The week begins on May 25, Africa Liberation Day. Previously, it was known as the Week of Solidarity with the Colonial Peoples of Southern Africa and Guinea (Bissau) and Cape Verde Fighting for Freedom, Independence and Equal Rights. This week continues through May 31.

May 27

Hubert H. Humphrey, Jr. Day (PA)— Hubert Horatio Humphrey was born on this date in 1911. He served as mayor of Minneapolis, Minnesota, beginning in 1945, a U.S. Senator from 1949 to 1965, Vice President from 1965 to 1969, and was the Democratic candidate for U.S. President in 1968. He was known as a liberal, fighting for medical care for the aged and civil rights, although his support of the administration policy of waging war in Vietnam alienated many of his former supporters. He died of cancer on January 13, 1978.

Rachel Carson Day (PA)— This celebrates the May 27, 1907, birth of Rachel Carson in

Springdale, Pennsylvania, generally recognized as the "Mother of the Age of Ecology." She was a biologist, and after becoming the first woman to take and pass the civil service test, worked for 15 years for the Bureau of Fisheries. Carson's books included *Under the Sea Wind*, *The Sea Around Us*, and *The Edge of the Sea*. Her last book published during her lifetime, *Silent Spring*, was the stimulus for worldwide controversy regarding the use of chemical pesticides and herbicides, and their potential dangers. It influenced Pres. John Kennedy, who read the book, to call for testing of the chemicals she mentioned in it. Carson died on April 14, 1964.

May 29

John Fitzgerald Kennedy Day (MI)— John Kennedy was born on this date in 1917 in Brookline, Massachusetts. After gaining fame as a war hero in World War II, he went into politics and won his first election to the U.S. Congress in 1946. While recovering from back surgery in 1956, he wrote *Profiles in Courage*, which won him a Pulitzer Prize. The youngest man elected president, he served as the 35th President of the U.S. from 1961 until he was assassinated on November 22, 1963.

Presidents Day (MA)— This day honors John Adams, John Quincy Adams, Calvin Coolidge and John Fitzgerald Kennedy, former presidents of the U.S. from Massachusetts.

May 30

Memorial Day (AS, IL, MO, VT)— The first observance, called "Decoration Day," was held on May 30, 1868, two years after the town of Waterloo, New York, initiated the tradition of decorating the graves of Civil War veterans. The name was changed to "Memorial Day" in 1882. In May of 1966, the U.S. government recognized Waterloo as the "Birthplace of Memorial Day," and a Memorial Day Museum is located there. Although the actual celebration across the country is now held on the last Monday in May, these four states have kept May 30 as their official statutory Memorial Day.

May 31

World No-Tobacco Day (U.N.)— Since the middle of the 20th century, tobacco has killed more than 60 million people just in the developed countries, and this is recognized as a global public health emergency. This day was established to educate the public about the dangers, and encourage individuals, governments and organizations to help the World Health Organization in the fight against tobacco. It is hoped that efforts will succeed not only in lessening the present three million who die annually, but in altering the current trend, which by the 2020s or 2030s is expected to kill 10 million per year, 70 percent of whom are from developing countries.

JUNE

OBSERVANCES WITH VARIABLE DATES

First Week in June

Atbot de Fuego (Flame Tree) and Arbor Day Week (GU)—This week commemorates the natural beauty of the flame trees of Guam. Also known as the "flamboyant" and "poinciana," this rapid-growing tree bears flowers which are brilliant red with streaks of yellow and sometimes white.

Garden Week (KY)—This is a celebration of gardening and an appreciation of nature.

Gastronomical Week (PR)—This week is an acknowledgement of Puerto Rico's chefs and cuisine professionals.

Puerto Rican Solidarity Week (PR)—This is a time for Puerto Rican workers and citizens to focus on working together for the common good.

First Full Week in June

Garden Week (ME, NJ, OR) [**National Garden Week** (AR), **Michigan Garden Week** (MI)]—This week celebrates gardening, which instills in our people, both young and old, a deeper appreciation of nature and our beautiful land. The official nickname of New Jersey is the "Garden State."

Maine Clean Water Week (ME)—This is a time to bring to the attention of Maine's residents the conditions which pollute, or may pollute, the waters of the state. It is also an opportunity to celebrate the outstanding recreational benefits of the rivers, lakes and ocean shoreline that constitute some of Maine's best natural resources.

First Sunday in June

Children's Day (NY)—The children of New York are celebrated on this day for their various accomplishments. Governments and agencies who deal with children and families also focus on problems and issues that children and their parents must deal with, and ways that they may be dealt with.

Ethnic American Day (MN)—This recognizes the diverse population of Minnesota, from the Native Americans who were this land's first inhabitants to other peoples from all parts of the world who also have contributed their cultures, traditions, and values to their fellow citizens.

Shut-In Day (OK)—The people of Oklahoma are called upon to visit at least one shut-in person on this day.

First Monday in June

Samantha Smith Day (ME)—This commemorates Samantha Smith (born on June 29), whose vision and inspiring message for peace and brotherhood opened the door to greater understanding and friendship among nations of the world. In 1982 she wrote a letter to the President of the Soviet Union, Yuri Andropov. She wrote:

> My name is Samantha Smith. I am ten years old. Congratulations on your new job. I have been worrying about Russia and the United States getting into a nuclear war. Are you going to have a war or not? If you aren't please tell me how you are going to not have a war …. god made the world for us to live together in peace and not fight.

That letter was published in the official state newspaper of the Soviet Union. She and Pres. Andropov exchanged further letters, and upon his invitation, Samantha and her family visited him in Moscow. She became a worldwide celebrity, and gave speeches to promote peace. She died in an auto accident in August of 1985, but she is not forgotten. The Soviet government issued a postage stamp in her honor, and also named a diamond, flower, mountain and planet after her. A foundation bearing her name, founded by her mother, is dedicated to encouraging friendship and peace among children of all nations.

First Wednesday in June

Ocean Day (HI) — On this day is recognized the significant role the ocean plays in the lives of Hawaii's people, as well as their culture, history and traditions. The official celebration began in 1995 with a forum to educate the community about ways that Hawaii's reef can be improved and maintained in a healthy environment.

Public Employees Awareness Day (MA) — This recognizes the service and contributions of civil servants in all levels of Massachusetts government.

First Saturday in June

ITAM-Vets Daisy Day (RI) — This celebrates the Italian-American war veterans of the U.S. They are represented by the Italian American War Veterans of the USA, established in 1932 and chartered by the U.S. Congress in 1981, and headquartered in Youngstown, Ohio.

First Weekend in June

Take a Kid Fishing Weekend (MN) — Normally, all Minnesota residents age 16 or older are required to purchase fishing licenses before going fishing. On this weekend, however, adults accompanying children under the age of 16 may fish without a license.

Week Beginning on the First Saturday in June

Garden Week (MA, SC) — This week recognizes the benefits of gardening in preserving our traditional spirit of independence and individual initiative, which instills in people a greater respect for the environment and our natural resources.

Second Sunday in June

Children's Day (MA) — This day has been designated in recognition of our children of today, from whom will come the leaders of tomorrow.

Fire Fighters' Memorial Sunday (MA) — This day honors all departed fire fighters. It is dedicated to those who have dedicated their lives to the protection of life and property, often ending in the ultimate sacrifice of the firefighter's life.

Flag Day (NY) — The first Flag Day exercises were held in a little country schoolhouse located near Fredonia, Wisconsin, in 1916. Thirty-one years previously, Bernard J. Cigrand began his quest to have the national holiday instituted, resulting in the declaration by President Woodrow Wilson of the start of National Flag Day. Wilson proclaimed, "The Flag has vindicated its right to be honored by all nations of the world and feared by none who do righteousness."

Seamen's Memorial Day (ME) — This honors the many adventurous men and women of Maine who have been lost at sea over the centuries of fishing, whaling and other sea-going enterprises based in Maine.

State Walking Sunday (MA) — This is a day to encourage the residents of Massachusetts to experience the joys and benefits of walking — alone, as families, in groups, or in any other manner which gets people out and about on foot.

Week Including June 14

National Flag Week (Fed)— All citizens are encouraged to honor the American flag by flying it in all appropriate locations.

Second Week in June

Oil Industry Week (PR)— This period is dedicated to the holding of official events to honor and recognize those in this industry. Wednesday is especially for workers in the oil industry, and Friday is for gasoline retailers.

Police Officers Appreciation Day (DE)— This day (actually, the entire week) is an opportunity for public expression of appreciation of those of the state who dedicate their lives to law enforcement.

Rabies Prevention Week (MA)— This is a time to educate the public about the dangers of rabies and efforts to prevent it. Rabies is a deadly viral infection of the central nervous system, spread through the saliva of infected warm-blooded animals. Few in the U.S. die from the disease, but as many as 18,000 each year get shots to fight the disease after coming into contact with infected animals. Worldwide, it is estimated that 40,000 die each year from rabies.

Second Saturday in June

Delaware Bay Day (NJ)— This day recognizes and celebrates the importance and beauty of the Delaware Bay ecosystem, a wetland of international significance and home to 130 species of fish, hundreds of thousands of shore birds, waterfowl and raptors. Delaware Bay is an arm of the Atlantic Ocean between New Jersey and Delaware, with a length of about 50 miles and a depth of from 30 to 60 feet.

Second Saturday in June, Plus the Following Sunday

Gaspee Days (RI)— These two days commemorate the 1772 burning of the British schooner H.M.S. *Gaspee* on the night of June 9–10. The *Gaspee* was sent by the British to patrol Narragansett Bay and prevent the residents from smuggling in goods to avoid the new import taxes. After the ship ran aground in pursuit of a suspected smuggler, locals captured and destroyed it, the last of the hated British vessels that harassed the colony since the days of the Stamp Act, off Namquid Point. It was a supreme act of protest against the British, providing a strong impetus to the colonies' movement toward a fight for independence. The burning of the ship led to the formation of the Committee for Correspondence, which led to the Continental Congress and the Declaration of Independence. This has been celebrated as a holiday since 1966.

Third Week in June

Recreational Leaders Week (PR)— This is a time to recognize and thank the Puerto Rican citizens who supervise and lead sports and other recreational activities throughout the island.

Third Full Week in June

Maine Lighthouse Week (ME)— In 2001 this week was established to urge the people of Maine to commemorate the important role of lighthouses in the history of the state. This brings public attention to the lighthouses to help provide the funds necessary to restore and maintain them.

Third Sunday in June

Father's Day (Fed, AZ, DE, IA, MA, NJ) [**Fathers Day** (IL)]— This was established to express love and reverence for fathers. It was first proposed by Sonora Smart Dodd of Spokane, Washington, a housewife whose father, Henry Jackson Smart, raised his six children alone after his wife died in childbirth. June was chosen because he was born during this month. There was reluctance in the U.S. Congress regarding the designation of this day of observance, because the all-male legislators thought their constituents might believe it to be self-serving. The day was observed by Pres. Woodrow Wilson, but he declined to proclaim it officially. Pres. Calvin Coolidge in 1924 encouraged individual states to proclaim their own Fathers Days, but he also declined to make it a federal holiday. It was finally proclaimed as a U.S. day of observance in 1972 by Pres. Richard Nixon. In Delaware the day is intended to inspire closer ties between fathers and the state. It is a tradition to wear a rose on

Father's Day, red for a living father and white for a deceased one.

Third Saturday in June

Destroyer Escort Day (CT, ME, MA, RI) [**Destroyer Escort Day in Ohio** (OH)]—This day is in recognition of the veterans of the destroyer escort ships which participated in World War II, the Korean Conflict, and the war in Vietnam. Destroyer escorts were built as a less expensive ocean escort to protect against submarines. They also could attack surface ships with guns and torpedoes, and serve as scout ships. In 1975 all surviving destroyer escorts were redesignated as frigates.

Juneteenth National Freedom Day (DE, OK) [**Juneteenth Day** (AK)]—Also called "Jun-Jun," "Emancipation Celebration," and "Freedom Day," this celebration erupted rather spontaneously when slaves learned of their newly declared freedom. Citizens are urged to reflect on the suffering endured by early African-Americans and to appreciate the unique freedom and equality enjoyed by all today. Juneteenth is celebrated on different dates in varying states because liberation only occurred when local Confederate forces were defeated.

Week Ending with the Fourth Sunday in June

Youth Organizations Week (PR)—Celebrated this week are youth organizations operating in Puerto Rico, including the Boy Scouts of America, YMCA and YWCA, and the Puerto Rico Community Foundation.

Fourth Sunday in June

John Carver Day (MA)—This is in memory of John Carver, the first governor of Plymouth Colony. He was born in about 1576 and emigrated to the Netherlands in 1609, joining the Pilgrims in Leiden. He secured financial backing from London and hired and stocked the *Mayflower* with provisions for the trip to the New World. In 1620 he was elected for a one-year term as the governor, and likely was the person who chose Plymouth for the site of the first settlement. He was succeeded by William Bradford upon his death in 1621.

Saint Jean de Baptiste Day (MA)—Also called the celebration of John the Baptist, largely in French-speaking cultures, it previously was the pagan celebration of the summer solstice. King Clovis of France changed it to a Christian celebration of St. John, known as the precursor of Christ. As Christ was known as the Light of the World, early celebrations of this feast day included bonfires, often lit by the king himself. John the Baptist was the son of Zachary and Elizabeth, a kinswoman of Mary, the mother of Jesus. He was likely born at Ain-Karim southwest of Jerusalem, and lived as a hermit in the Judea desert until about 27 A.D., when he was 30 years old. He preached along the Jordan River against the evils of the times and promoted baptism, "for the Kingdom of Heaven is close at hand." He was arrested by Herod Antipas, Tetrarch of Perea and Galilee, and was imprisoned in the Machaerus Fortress on the Dead Sea. John denounced Herod's adulterous and incestuous marriage with Herodias, whose daughter, Salome, had John beheaded.

Youth Day (PR)—On this day the youth of Puerto Rico are honored for their accomplishments. It is also a time to be concerned about their education and welfare.

Last Sunday in June

Log Cabin Day (MI)—This is a celebration of the 81 historical log cabins located in Michigan, and is sponsored by the Log Cabin Society of Michigan. Citizens are encouraged to enjoy crafts, music and refreshments in a log cabin setting, or learn how to build one.

Last Friday in June

Young Blood Donors' Day (PR)—This honors those in Puerto Rico aged 18 to 29 who have donated blood for the good of their communities.

Last Saturday in June

Battleship Massachusetts Memorial Day (MA)—This commemorates the establishment of the *Massachusetts* as a museum and memorial in the city of Fall River. It is a memorial to the citizens of Massachusetts who made the supreme sacrifice during World War II. The battleship, built in Quincy, Massachusetts, was launched on September 23, 1941, and participated in the invasion of North Africa, firing the first American 16" projectile of the war in anger. After sinking four ships and damaging a drydock and buildings in Casablanca, it sailed through the Panama Canal to participate in battles at New Guinea–Solomons, the Gilbert Islands, the Marshall Islands, Truk, Ponaope Island, the Palau Islands, Iwo Jima and Okinawa, and then bombarded the Japanese cities of Kamaishi and Hamamatsu. The ship was deactivated after the war and was ordered to be sold for scrap in 1962. Her wartime crew lobbied for its preservation as a memorial and, with the help of Massachusetts school children, raised enough money to bring the *Massachusetts* to Fall River in June of 1965 for visitation by the public.

R.B. Hall Day (ME)—This commemorates an internationally recognized composer of marches, accomplished conductor, and cornet soloist. Born in Bowdoinham, Maine, on June 30, 1858, Robert Hall took cornet lessons from his father, and by age 19 was the director of the Richmond Cornet Band. He played in and directed several bands, including the Waterville Military Band, which changed its name to R.B. Hall's Military Band. He was known for having an incredible range, often playing well above the rest of the band. He reorganized the Tenth Regiment Band in Albany, New York, which was then selected to play at the 1901 Pan-American Exposition in Buffalo. In 1902 Hall suffered a stroke, and died in poverty as a result of nephritis on June 8, 1907. Hall's birthday has been an official day of observance in Maine since 1981. His many marches include *M.H.A.*, *Independentia*, *The New Colonial*, *The Officer of the Day*, and *Tenth Regiment—Death or Glory*.

Last Sunday on or Before July 4

Independence Sunday (IA)—On this day citizens are to participate in religious-patriotic services and the display of American colors. It is an additional day to commemorate the Declaration of Independence.

OBSERVANCES WITH FIXED DATES

June 1

Missing Persons Month (NJ)—All government agencies and appropriate private agencies are urged to cooperate and to make available to the public more in-depth information regarding the true statistics and scope of the missing persons issue. Missing adults and older teenagers represent a largely disenfranchised population, and families are largely forgotten by the present system and general public. This month, rather than corresponding to a calendar month, stretches from May 25 to June 25.

Portuguese-American Heritage Month (MA)—This month recognizes the significant contributions Portuguese-Americans have made to Massachusetts and the U.S.

Prostate Cancer Awareness Month (NJ)—This month focuses on the most common type of cancer among men, and the importance of early detection. It is estimated that over 180,000 new cases are diagnosed each year, and that nearly 32,000 men will die each year. The public is encourage to participate in early cancer screening and learn about the treatment options.

Statehood Day (TN)—On this date in 1796, Tennessee was admitted to the Union as the 16th state, with Knoxville designated as the state capital. Twenty-four years earlier, residents formed the Watauga Association, which exercised a measure of self-government. In 1784 East Tennessee broke away from North Carolina and formed the state of Franklin, with John Sevier as governor. North Carolina regained control and Franklin ceased to exist in 1788. The area became a federal territory, and once it had a sufficient population for statehood, there was uncertainty as to how to proceed. Split strictly along party lines, Congress on June 1, 1796, narrowly approved admission of Tennessee as a state.

Teachers' Day (MA)—The value of education is enhanced by better teachers. On this day the teachers of Massachusetts are honored for their excellence, and encouraged to continue making strides to improve the educational experience of their students.

June 2

First Lady's Day in Virginia (VA)—This date was chosen because it is the anniversary of the birth of Martha Dandridge in 1731. She married Daniel Park Custis in 1749, and he died in 1757. Two years later she married George Washington, and Martha became the country's first First Lady when George became its first president. When they entertained in the temporary capitals of New York and Philadelphia, her warm hospitality made her guests feel welcome and eased the concerns of strangers. She died on May 22, 1802. This is a celebration of her life, and that of each of her successors.

Jefferson Davis' Birthday (AL)—After serving in the Mexican War and serving as Secretary of War, Jefferson Davis was chosen twice to the U.S. Senate, finishing neither term. When the Confederacy seceded from the Union, the first choice for its leader was Alexander "Little Aleck" Stephens from Georgia, but his prior pro–Union stance met with some resistance. Howell Cobb refused the position, so compromise candidate Davis was chosen in secrecy. By popular vote on February 22, 1862, he became the one and only president of the Confederate States of America. Davis is considered by many to have mismanaged the Confederacy and its conduct of the Civil War. After fleeing the capital in Richmond near the end of the war, Davis was jailed for treason, and afterwards led the life of a businessman and author until he died at the age of 81 in 1889.

Retired Members of Armed Forces Day (MA)—Recognized on this day are those men and women who have retired from service in the U.S. Armed Forces.

June 3

Birthday of Jefferson Davis (FL, GA), [**Jefferson Davis' Birthday** (AR, SC), **Jefferson Davis Day** (KY)]—Jefferson Davis was born on this date in 1808. He served as the president of the Confederate States of America from 1861 to 1865. He died on December 6, 1889. Full U.S. citizenship was restored to him posthumously, on October 17, 1978.

Confederate Memorial Day (KY, LA), [**Memorial or Confederate Decoration Day** (TN)]—This day honors the Confederate veterans of the Civil War, or the War Between the States. The date of June 3 was chosen to coincide with the birthday of Jefferson Davis, who served as president of the Confederate States of America.

Dutch Harbor Remembrance Day (AK)—This commemorates the June 3, 1942, attack by the Japanese and honors the individuals who died as a result. Also remembered are the inhabitants of Attu and Kiska who fell into enemy hands three days later and who were held captive in Japan until after the end of World War II. The Navy servicemen who died in 1943 while recapturing Attu and Kiska from the Japanese are also honored.

June 4

International Day of Innocent Children Victims of Aggression (U.N.)—This day was established by the United Nations General Assembly on August 19, 1982, after it was "appalled at the great number of innocent Palestinian and Lebanese children victims of Israel's acts of aggression."

June 5

World Environment Day (U.N.)—Since 1972, this day of observance proclaimed by the United Nations has been intended to deepen public awareness of the need to preserve and enhance the environment. The date was chosen to correspond to the opening of the United Nations Conference on the Human Environment, which resulted in the establishment of the United Nations Environment Programme.

June 7

American Flag Week (NJ)—This period of observance encourages one of the prime evidences of patriotism, the display of the U.S. flag. The youth of the nation are supposed to be impressed by a forthright display of patriotism by their elders. The week ends every year on Flag Day.

June 8

Flag Week (OK)—All Oklahomans are encouraged to fly the Stars and Stripes, especially during this week, which includes Flag Day.

June 10

Lidice Memorial Day (NJ)—This marks the anniversary of one of the most heinous criminal acts in the history of Western civilization, the brutal extermination of the peaceful village of Lidice, Czechoslovakia, by the Nazi security police on June 10, 1942. Every male resident over the age of 16 was murdered, all women were condemned to the Ravensbrueck concentration camp, four pregnant women were taken to a maternity hospital where their newly-born children were murdered, and all surviving children were dispersed outside of Czechoslovakia. The village was then burned, dynamited and leveled. The action was taken by the Nazis in reprisal for the assassination of Reinhard Heydrich.

June 11

King Kamehameha Day (HI)—This celebrates Kamehameha's unification of the Hawaiian Islands and establishment of law and order there. King Kamehameha I was born in 1758, and is often referred to as Kamehameha the Great. Before his time, many men ruled the Hawaiian Islands, with varying loyalties and alliances. He conquered Oahu in 1795 and Hawaii in 1797, and negotiated an agreement with Kauai. By 1810, Kamehameha was the sole ruler of a unified kingdom. The day, which is not the birthday of the celebrated monarch, was decreed a holiday in 1871 by his grandson, Kamehameha V. The day is celebrated with surf board, canoeing and swimming races, plus feasts and a torchlight procession.

June 12

Women Veterans Recognition Day (NY)—On this day in 1948 the U.S. Congress made the Women's Army Corps a permanent part of the army, and created the Women's Air Force. On June 12, 1998, ground was broken on the site of the Women Veterans Memorial on the grounds of the Empire State Plaza in New York. New York state is home to over 61,000 of the more than 1,200,000 women military veterans living in the U.S. That ground-breaking took place on the 50th anniversary of Pres. Harry Truman's signing a bill granting women a permanent place in the armed services.

June 14

Commemoration of Anniversary of

Founding of the U.S. Army (NH)—The U.S. Army was established on June 14, 1775, more than a year prior to the signing of the Declaration of Independence. On July 16, 1775, George Washington was commissioned as "General and Commander-in-Chief of the Army of the United Colonies and of all forces now raised or to be raised by them, and of all others who shall voluntarily offer their services."

Flag Day (Fed, CT, FL, GA, IL, IN, KS, KY, MA, MO, OR, PA) [**United States of America Flag Day in Puerto Rico** (PR)]—Citizens are urged to observe the anniversary of the adoption on June 14, 1777, by the Continental Congress of the "Stars and Stripes" as the official flag of the U.S. According to George Washington, the white stripes represent the purity and serenity of the nation, the red stripes represent the blood spilled by Americans who made the ultimate sacrifice for freedom, the royal blue field stands for freedom and justice, and the white stars symbolize the purity, liberty and freedom within the nation. Special respect is to be shown to the flag, according to the flag code adopted in 1942 and revised by the National Flag Conference. The law in Illinois states that the flag is a symbol of the guarantee of the sanctity of the home, and therefore should be displayed from every home on this day.

Honor America Days (Fed)—This period of three weeks is an opportunity to display flags and carry on patriotic activities, beginning with Flag Day and continuing through Independence Day.

June 17

Anniversary of Battle of Bunker Hill (MA)—This day commemorates the early events of the American Revolution. On this day in 1775 American forces met the British at Breed's Hill in Boston, but the confrontation became known as the Battle of Bunker Hill. The larger Bunker Hill was involved in the battle, as that is where the retreating Americans regrouped. The Americans were technically defeated since they were driven from the area, but the British suffered heavy losses of nearly 40 percent of their ranks, more than double the American losses.

World Day to Combat Desertification and Drought (U.N.)—The United Nations General Assembly invites all member nations to devote this day to promoting awareness of the need for international cooperation to combat desertification and the effects of drought, and on the implementation of the Convention to Combat Desertification.

June 19

Emancipation Day in Texas (TX)—This commemorates the emancipation of Texas slaves in 1865. On that day, Gen. Gordon Granger arrived with federal troops in Galveston, Texas, to enforce the provisions of Pres. Lincoln's Emancipation Proclamation, to force slave owners to release their slaves. Many of the slaves from other states were brought to East Texas, where it was thought they would be protected from being set free by federal troops. After years of a decline of this celebration, it was made an official Texas state holiday on January 1, 1980.

Juneteenth Day (FL)—This is a commemoration of the traditional observance of the day the slaves in Florida were notified of the Emancipation Proclamation. Federal employees arrived to enforce the proclamation on June 19, 1865.

June 20

Destroyer Escort Day (NH)—This commemorates the bravery and valor of those individuals who lost their lives while serving aboard these gallant vessels during World War II, the Korean Conflict, and the Vietnam Conflict. The goal is to preserve the history of the "trim but deadly" warships and their Navy and Coast Guard crews. The last remaining destroyer escort on display in the U.S., the USS *Slater*, was launched at Tampa, Florida, on February 13, 1944, and is berthed in Albany, New York.

West Virginia Day (WV)—West Virginia was admitted into the Union on this date in 1863 after breaking away from Virginia, of which it had been a part. Approval of the new state was granted by Pres. Lincoln on December 10, 1862. During the Civil War it provided to the Union 31,872 regular army troops, 133 sailors and marines, and 196 United States Colored Troops, and between 16,000 and 20,000 men to the Confederate Army.

World Refugee Day (U.N.)—In 1951 the United Nations, recognizing the plight of refugees, adopted the Convention Relating to the Status

of Refugees. In 2000 the Organization of African Unity agreed to have International Refugee Day coincide with Africa Refugee Day on June 20, and beginning in 2001 it is known as World Refugee Day.

June 23

John Sevier Day (TN)—On this day John Sevier is recognized for his important role in Tennessee attaining statehood, and for his meritorious service as the state's first governor. Sevier was born in 1745 near present-day New Market, Virginia, a town which he founded. He moved with his family to western North Carolina and supported independence from England, and was one of the leaders at the Battle of Kings Mountain in 1780. In 1784 North Carolina ceded its western lands to the U.S., and Sevier served as governor of the state of Franklin. As a result of that, North Carolina arrested him for treason, but he escaped and, following his 1789 election to the North Carolina senate, was pardoned by the governor. When Tennessee was organized in 1796, Sevier was elected as its first governor and served for eleven years, and returned to Congress in 1811, where he served until he died in 1815.

June 24

Flag, Anthem and Coat of Arms Day (PR)—The first flag with the presently used designed was completed in Chimney Corner Hall in New York City on December 22, 1895. Made by Manuela "Mima" Besosa, it inverts the colors of the single-starred flag of Cuba. The island's coat of arms was adopted on March 9, 1905, with a design inspired by the coat of arms granted by Spain on November 8, 1511. It includes a white lamb atop the Book of Revelations, holding the seven seals of the Apocalypse of Saint John the Apostle. The lamb holds a red cross and white flag, and is rimmed by four castles, four lions, four crosses of Jerusalem and four flags. The inscription is "Johannes est nomen ejus" or "John is its name." Puerto Rico formerly was known as San Juan (Saint John), but that name is now applied only to its capital city.

Kentucky National Guard Day (KY)—The Kentucky National Guard was established in 1775, when the area was known as Fincastle County, Virginia. Initially known as the Militia, it was commanded by Capt. James Harrod, and all able-bodied men coming into the territorial frontier were expected to serve as needed. Its earliest duties were as a self-protective association, guarding against attacks from Indians and foreign countries.

Saint Jean-Baptiste Day (ME, RI)—This is a commemoration of the feast of Saint John the Baptist as an important observance, and a show of appreciation for the significant cultural, economic and civic contributions made by Franco-Americans which have served to enrich the culture and lifestyle of the states. John was a relative of Jesus Christ and encouraged many of his followers to follow Jesus, whom John designated as "the Lamb of God." In the New Testament he is portrayed as the last of the Old Testament prophets and the precursor of the Messiah.

Scottish, Scots-Irish Heritage Day (TN)—This day honors and recognizes the contributions people of Scottish and Scots-Irish heritage made to the founding and development of Tennessee. On this day in 1497, Scottish forces, led by Robert Bruce, won the Battle of Bannockburn. The English, led by Edward II, were defeated, surrendering the throne of Scotland to Bruce.

June 25

Korean War Veterans Day (MA, NY)—This day honors the heroic achievements of the members of the U.S. armed forces during this difficult period in America's history. Veterans of this war are also honored at the Korean War Veterans National Museum and Library, which opened in Tuscola, Illinois, on June 3, 2000. The day of June 25 commemorates the North Korean army crossing over the 38th parallel at 0400 on Sunday, June 25, 1950. That army launched its effort toward Seoul, which fell three days later.

Little Big Horn Remembrance Day (SD)—On this day in 1876 the U.S. Cavalry, led by Gen. George Armstrong Custer, were soundly defeated by the Sioux, led by Sitting Bull, at the Little Big Horn River in Montana. The U.S. Army approached from three directions an Indian village comprised of about 10,000 members of six tribes camped along the Little Big Horn River. One prong, the 7th Cavalry, led by Custer, attempted to cross the river near the encampment of the Northern Cheyennes, and their bullets were met by thousands of arrows. They were soon surrounded by two other bands of warriors, led by Two Moons and Crazy Horse, and within a half hour all 215 cavalrymen were dead. The battle continued, with the contingents led by Capt. Frederick Benteen and Maj. Marcus Reno being overwhelmed, surviving only because at sunset most of the warriors returned to the village for a victory dance.

June 26

International Day Against Drug Abuse and Illicit Trafficking (U.N.)—This is the United Nations General Assembly's expression of its determination to strengthen action and cooperation to achieve the goal of an international society free of drug abuse.

International Day in Support of Victims of Torture (U.N.)—Upon the recommendation of the Economic and Social Council, the United Nations General Assembly adopted this day to focus on the eradication of torture. It is also an opportunity to publicize the 1984 Convention Against Torture and Other Cruel, Inhuman or Degrading Treatment or Punishment, which went into effect on June 26, 1987. All member nations are urged to ensure that torture is a crime in their domestic law, and to rigorously pursue perpetrators and bring them to justice.

Motherhood and Apple Pie Day (VA)—This day recognizes the need to prevent infant mortality to preserve our heritage and ensure the health and well-being of future generations. It is a time to thank mothers, who dedicate their lives to the immeasurably important duty of rearing children, and help to shape the character of the Commonwealth of Virginia and nation for generations to come.

June 28

Carolina Day (SC)—This celebrates the anniversary of the Battle of Fort Sullivan (Sullivan's Island) on June 28, 1776. It is considered to be the first victory for the American patriots. British pride was wounded as their sizeable fleet was decisively beaten. This holiday was first celebrated in 1777 with a feast, church services and fireworks. It was first known as Palmetto Day, and also as the 28th of June and Sgt. Jasper's Day, until 1875 when it was changed to Carolina Day.

Pennsylvania German Day (PA)— This day recognizes the cultural, educational and historical contributions from the Pennsylvania German, commonly known as Pennsylvania Dutch. Most emigrated from the Rheinland Provinces, chiefly the Palatinate (Pfalz). Although the most well-known sects are the Anabaptists (the Amish and the Mennonites), they comprise only about ten percent of all the Pennsylvania Germans. The history of these early settlers of Pennsylvania is preserved at the Pennsylvania German Cultural Heritage Center at Kutztown University, which consists of a 60-acre 19th century farmstead with a stone farmhouse, barns and other buildings restored to about 1870. The museum on site includes more than 10,000 artifacts representing Pennsylvania German rural life.

JULY

OBSERVANCES WITH VARIABLE DATES

Date to Be Selected in July

Onate Day (NM) — Each year on a date selected in July, a celebration is held in the Espanola Valley to commemorate the presence of Juan de Onate beginning in 1598. That year he led a caravan to the area with 7,000 livestock, Indian and black servants, and Spanish settlers. He headed up the Rio Grande and established a headquarters at a confiscated pueblo, making it the first permanent European settlement in the American West. He was New Mexico's governor, searched in Kansas for the fabled city of Quivira, and explored westward to the Gulf of California. Onate resigned as governor in 1607. He is credited by many as the originator of the first Thanksgiving Day, when on April 30, 1598, they celebrated when they reached the banks of the Rio Grande. They built a large bonfire and feasted on meat and fish, and gave thanks for the success and hoped-for prosperity.

Last Sunday on or Before July 4

Independence Sunday (IA) — On this day citizens are to participate in religious-patriotic services and the display of American colors. It is an additional day to commemorate the Declaration of Independence.

First Sunday in July (or First Monday, if the First Sunday is July 4)

Aibonito Flower Festival Day (PR) — The island's annual flower festival takes place in Aibonito, whose name is derived from a native word meaning "river of the night." It was founded on March 13, 1824, by Manuel Velez, and is located in the highest land in Puerto Rico. The Festival de las Flores was established in 1969, and is considered to be the most important flower event in Puerto Rico; it includes flower shows, handcrafts display, and music and food.

First Saturday in July

International Day of Cooperatives (U.N.) — This observance was established by the United Nations General Assembly in 1992, marking the centenary of the International Cooperative Alliance. That is an umbrella group of organizations comprising 760 million members of cooperatives in 100 countries. Recognizing that cooperatives were becoming an indispensable factor of social and economic development, the U.N. has invited international organizations, national governments, specialized agencies and cooperative organizations to observe the day annually.

First Week in July

Municipal Assemblymen's Week (PR)—During this time, Puerto Rico pays a tribute of admiration to all members of the municipal assemblies of the commonwealth in just recognition of their meritorious work.

Puerto Rico Domino Players Week (PR)—A recent survey of Puerto Ricans age 12 and older showed that board games and dominos were played frequently by 8.6 percent of the population, trailing only reading and visits to beaches and lakes as the most popular leisure-time activities. Dominos are played in nearly every bar on the island, with the pieces being laid down with a grand flourish and loud slap.

First Full Week in July

Literary Awareness Week (NJ)—This week focuses attention on the needs of citizens to read, and to be able to read. Literacy programs are publicized, especially those for youth and the economically disadvantaged.

Week Beginning with the First Sunday in July

Old Home Week (RI)—During this week, cities and towns may conduct appropriate celebrations to honor returning sons and daughters of the state, and other invited guests. It is a time for residents, both past and present, to reunite to keep the towns alive.

Second Week in July

Transportation Week (PR)—During this week the Luis A. Ferre Award is presented to a person who has excelled in the field of transportation for the development of the infrastructure of Puerto Rico. Ferre was born on February 17, 1904, in Ponce, Puerto Rico, and served as governor from 1969 to 1973. He had a master's degree in engineering from the Massachusetts Institute of Technology, and became a wealthy industrialist and philanthropist, and founder of the New Progressive Party. After him is named the Luis A. Ferre Expressway, a north-south toll road between San Juan and Ponce.

Second Monday in July

Official Public Carrier's Day (PR)—This is a day to celebrate the services performed by motor carriers and other common carriers throughout Puerto Rico.

Week Beginning with the Third Sunday in July

Lead Poisoning Prevention Week (MA)—The observance of this week's events include a continuing effort to promote screening for lead poisoning in young children. Blood tests and educational programs to teach prevention methods are supported by several agencies and private organizations which promote safety. The national goal is to eliminate childhood lead poisoning in the U.S. by 2010.

Third Week in July

Nevada All-Indian Stampede Days (NV)—This celebration held in Fallon, Nevada, commemorates the Indian people and their efforts to maintain their culture, customs and traditions. The town is the site of one of the original Pony Express stations, and events celebrating pioneers and Native Americans are held here annually.

Fourth Sunday in July

Parents' Day (Fed)—This was established to recognize, uplift and support the role of parents in the upbringing of their children. Sponsored by Senators Orrin Hatch and Joe Biden, and Representatives Floyd Flake and Dan Burton, it unanimously passed both houses and was signed into law by Pres. Clinton on October 14, 1994.

Week Including July 24

Abelardo Diaz Week (PR)—Abelardo Diaz Alfaro was born in Caguas, Puerto Rico, on July 24, 1919. He studied to be a social worker with a specialty in psychology, but became a writer, being recognized by the Society of University Journalists in 1947. His written works include descriptions of rural life and show a great love for the earth and Puerto Rico, and a desire to help solve their problems.

Week Including July 27

Jose Celso Barbosa Week (PR) — Born in Bayamon, Puerto Rico, in 1857, Jose Celso Barbosa received his medical degree from the University of Michigan. He was a member of the Autonomous Party, and in 1899 founded the Republican Party of Puerto Rico, which advocated statehood for the island.

Week Including July 31

Press Week (PR) — This week is devoted to highlighting the role of the Press in informing the public of the most outstanding local and international journalistic events.

OBSERVANCES WITH FIXED DATES

July 1

Buffalo Soldiers Heritage Month (TX) — This month is in honor of the bravery and dedication of Texas' Buffalo Soldiers, and in recognition of their contribution to the legendary history of the Lone Star State. The Buffalo Soldiers were the first black soldiers during the Civil War, serving mostly to protect isolated settlements in the Southwest. They were stationed along established settlements, mail routes and stage routes, maintaining law and order while guarding mountain passes, water holes and other areas. The Indians gave them their name, both because of their wooly-like hair and their unmatched courage and superior fighting skills. Of the 12,500 black soldiers in that war, 18 were awarded Medals of Honor. At San Juan Hill in Cuba during the Spanish-American War, about 2,000 blacks served, and many historians believed they played the largest role in the American victory, rather than the "Rough Riders" led by Theodore Roosevelt.

Honor America Days (Fed) — This period to honor this country begins on Flag Day, June 14, and continues through and including Independence Day, July 4.

Puerto Rican Artisan's Month (PR) — This is a time to celebrate the artisans who produce traditional Puerto Rican crafts, includes masks, handmade lace (mundillo), animal carvings, musical instruments (guiro, tiple, cuatro, bordonua, maracas), wood-carved saints (santos), handcrafted jewelry, hammocks and baskets.

Reflex Sympathetic Dystrophy Awareness Month (MA) — This month focuses on a disorder, also known as Complex Regional Pain Syndrome. Nerves become hypersensitive, and strong pain is felt in situations that are normally pain-free. Symptoms include swelling in the painful area, changes in blood flow and sweating, and sometimes changes in the bones, skin and other tissues, making it difficult to move the afflicted parts. This disorder usually follows an injury, especially to major nerves, perhaps seemingly so minor that it is not recalled by the patient. Several therapies are available, and persons afflicted with CRPS should visit pain specialists. Treatment might include a variety of drugs, nerve blocks or surgery to kill nerves, acupuncture or electrical nerve stimulation. Programs this month encourage citizens to support research into the cause, treatment and cure of the syndrome, and to seek care if they exhibit its symptoms.

July 2

Day of the Sports Reporter (PR) — On this day, focus is brought on the importance of the endeavors of sports journalists. Major spectator sports for Puerto Ricans are baseball, basketball, golf, and horse racing.

Ferry Boat Transportation Day (VI) — The three islands comprising the Virgin Islands are tied together with ferries running from Red Hook and Charlotte Amalie (St. Thomas), Cruz Bay (St. John), and St. Croix, as well as nearby West End (Tortola), Great Harbor (Jost Van Dyke), and Fajardo (Puerto Rico). This is a day to recognize the services performed by ferry operators.

Rhode Island Cape Verdian Recognition Week (RI) — During this week (continuing through and including July 9) are recognized individuals who are of Cape Verdian ancestry. Cape Verde is a group of islands in the North Atlantic Ocean, west of Senegal. Most of the inhabitants of Cape Verde descend from both Portuguese colonists and African slaves. In size, it is slightly larger than Rhode Island.

July 3

Drunk Driving Victims Remembrance Day (AK)—This is a day to remember those who have died or been injured as the result of a drunk driver, a time to comfort their families and friends, and an opportunity to educate the public about the dangers of drinking and driving.

Emancipation Day (VI)—This is also known as Danish West Indies Emancipation Day, and commemorates the freeing of the slaves in the Virgin Islands in 1848. In the capital city of Charlotte Amalie is Emancipation Garden, used to hold official ceremonies celebrating the end of slavery. In the garden is a bust of Danish King Christian and a small replica of the U.S. Liberty Bell.

July 4

Independence Day (Fed, AK, AS, AZ, AR, CA, CO, CT, DE, DC, FL, GA, GU, HI, ID, IL, IN, IA, KS, KY, LA, MD, MA, MN, MS, MT, NE, NV, NH, NJ, NM, NY, NC, CM, OH, OK, OR, PA, PR, RI, SC, SD, TX, VI, UT, VT, VA, WV, WI, WY) [**Fourth of July** (AL, ME), **Anniversary of the Declaration of Independence** (ND, WA)]—This is a celebration of the signing of the Declaration of Independence in 1776 by the delegates to the Continental Congress in Philadelphia. The first anniversary was celebrated in 1777 in that same city with a parade, fireworks, shooting of cannon, and the drinking of toasts. In 1779 the 4th fell on a Sunday, initiating the tradition of celebrating a holiday on the following Monday. The first official state celebration pursuant to a legislative resolution occurred in 1781 in Massachusetts.

Indian Rights Day (WI)—This commemorates the U.S. Congress granting home rule and a bill of rights to the American Indians. The tribes native to Wisconsin are the Ojibwe, Stockbridge-Munsee, Oneida, Menominee, Ho-Chunk and Potawatomi. This is a time not only to celebrate their contributions to society, but also to focus on important issues such as sovereignty and treaty rights. The Indian Civil Rights Act, which is celebrated, was important to grant certain rights to Indians, since Constitutional limitations do not apply to tribal governments. Established by the Act are the right to free exercise of religion, freedom of speech, freedom from unreasonable search and seizure, freedom from double jeopardy, freedom from testifying against oneself, and other rights modeled after the U.S. Bill of Rights.

July 8

French Heritage Week (VI)—This ends with Bastille Day, a celebration of the seizure of the Bastille, a state fortress in Paris, in 1789. In the Bastille were political prisoners, such as Voltaire and the "Man in the Iron Mask," and the structure was despised by French revolutionists. The building was destroyed on the first anniversary of its capture as a revolutionary gesture, and the event has been celebrated by the French and descendants of French Canadians in New England and Louisiana.

July 9

Alaska Flag Day (AK)—This celebration honors the creation of the design of the official flag of the State of Alaska by Benny Benson, and its importance as a symbol of the state. Adopted in 1959, it has a blue field representing the sky, sea, mountain lakes and wildflowers, plus eight gold stars representing the Big Dipper constellation and the North Star. It was designed by Benson when he was thirteen years old. A Native American from the village of Chignik, he was awarded a $1,000 scholarship and a watch for his entry in the design contest.

Gilberto Concepcion de Gracia Memorial Day (PR)—Born on July 9, 1909, Dr. Gilberto Concepcion de Gracia is known, among other things, for founding the Independentista Party. As a journalist, lawyer and politician, he fought for the rights of Puerto Rican workers in New York and led a Hispanic newspaper, advocating the recognition of Puerto Rico's independence from the U.S. After teaching in Vermont in the 1940s, he returned to Puerto Rico to found a political party to work for independence. He served in the island's legislature and spoke before the U.S. Congress and the United Nations regarding the rights of Puerto Ricans. He died in San Juan on March 15, 1968.

July 11

World Population Day (U.N.)—This is an outgrowth of the Day of Five Billion, celebrated on July 11, 1987, when the Earth's population hit that number. Now this day seeks to focus attention on the urgency and importance of population issues, especially dealing with overall development plans and programs. As of 2000, world population stood at 6.06 billion, increasing by 78 million per year. The United Nations estimates that in 2050, the total population will be 8.9 billion.

July 13

Nathan Bedford Forrest Day (TN) — Born on this day in 1821, Forrest enlisted in the Confederate army as a private in 1861 and worked his way up to general by July of 1862. His reputation as a tactician earned him the praise of his enemies as well as his allies. He evacuated Fort Donelson without casualty when others were ready to surrender. He himself routed a line of Union skirmishers at Shiloh to protect the retreating Confederate army, and freed a garrison jail of locals in Murfreesboro, Tennessee. He won accolades at Chickamauga, and his engagement of Federal troops at Brice's Crossroads on June 10, 1864, is considered by some experts to be the perfect battle. After the war he served as the first Grand Wizard of the original Ku Klux Klan, and then ordered it to disband in 1869. When it did not, he abandoned it. He died on October 29, 1877.

Northwest Ordinance Day (IN) — This is the anniversary of the adoption of the Northwest Ordinance, which resulted in the creation of the states of Ohio, Indiana, Illinois, Michigan, Wisconsin and part of Minnesota. It is considered to be a great document with strong contributions to freedom and democracy. The Continental Congress passed the Ordinance in 1787, putting the world on notice that this area, previously forbidden to development, would now be settled and made a part of the U.S. It outlawed slavery in the area and accelerated the westward expansion of the country.

July 16

Manu'a Islands Cession Day (AS) — The islands which comprise the Manua Archipelago are Ofu, Olosega and Tau, and are located about 60 miles east of Tutuila. They are marked by high mountains and white, wide sand beaches, and two have small airports. American anthropologist Margaret Mead lived on Tau during the 1920s while researching her first book, *Coming of Age in Samoa*. Samoa was discovered by Dutch explorer Jacob Roggeveen in 1722, and was visited by English missionaries in 1831. The Treaty of Berlin, signed on December 2, 1899, recognized the U.S. to have rights over the eastern portion of the islands, with the western portion being ceded to Germany. This day celebrates the 1904 actions of the king and chiefs of the Manua Islands, ceding them to the U.S.

July 21

Liberation Day (GU) — This holiday celebrates the anniversary of the liberation of Guam from two and a half years of Japanese Occupation on July 21, 1944, and the inauguration of civil government in that country on July 21, 1950. The day is marked with a parade and fireworks. On Nimitz Hill on Asan Beach, one of the landing sites during the 1944 liberation action, is the Asan Memorial, administered by the U.S. National Parks Service. On it are inscribed the names of the American servicemen and local residents who died in the fighting.

Luis Munoz-Rivera Day (PR) — Luis Munoz-Rivera was born in Barranquitas, Puerto Rico, on July 17, 1859. After entering politics in 1887, he became a key figure in the Autonomist Party and founded its newspaper, *La Democracia*. He proposed autonomy for Puerto Rico and attempted to bring about free trade between the island and the U.S. In 1904 he founded the Unionist Party, was elected to the House of Delegates, and in 1910 became the Resident Commissioner to the U.S. House of Representatives. He was largely responsible for the passage of the Jones Act, granting U.S. citizenship to Puerto Ricans and creating a bicameral legislature modeled on that of the U.S. He died on November 15, 1916, before the Jones Act became law on March 4, 1917. He is also known as the best of the Puerto Rican lyricists and political poets, with his most important book of poems entitled *Tropicales*, and for being the father of Luis Munoz Marin, Puerto Rico's most famous statesman.

July 22

Rose Fitzgerald Kennedy Day (MA) —

This honors the matriarch of the Kennedy family, who inspired generations of Kennedys to serve their country with honor, integrity and dedication to justice for all. She was born on this date in 1890, and was the mother of a U.S. President and two Senators. She was married to Joseph Patrick Kennedy, financier and diplomat, who was the first chairman of the Securities and Exchange Commission and ambassador to Great Britain (1937–40). Rose Kennedy died at the age of 104 on January 22, 1995.

July 23

Puerto Rican Recognition Week (RI)— This is a time to recognize the accomplishments and contributions to American society of Puerto Ricans and those of Puerto Rican ancestry. It lasts through July 29.

July 24

Abelardo Diaz Day (PR)—The earliest writings of Diaz include scripts for radio station WIPR, including Teyo Garcia and Retablo del Solar, vignettes of Puerto Rico rural life. He also authored articles of religious character, some dealing with political issues and others focusing on social problems.

Pioneer Day (UT)—The Mormons left their settlement in Nauvoo, Illinois, after the murder of their founder, Joseph Smith. They were led west by Brigham Young, and established Salt Lake City in Utah as their new headquarters. According to tradition, the site for the new settlement was chosen by Young on July 24, 1847, after arising from his sickbed as the party of pioneers emerged from Immigrant Canyon. Over the next year, about 4,000 Mormon settlers arrived over the Oregon Trail to Fort Bridger, then traveled south into Utah, which was then part of Mexico. The first Pioneer Day was celebrated in 1849 with a parade, band music and speeches. That same year, the pioneers began petitioning for statehood, but were denied because of the Mormons' polygamy. An antipolygamy law was passed in 1862, and Mormons were persecuted, fined and imprisoned. The U.S. Supreme Court upheld the laws in 1890, and the Mormons officially banned polygamy under threat of excommunication, clearing the way for statehood, which was granted on January 4, 1896.

July 25

Day of the Constitution (PR)—This day celebrates the moment when political relations between the U.S. and Puerto Rico began on July 25, 1898, and the effective date of the proclamation of the Constitution of the Commonwealth on July 25, 1952. Previously, July 25 was considered to be a holiday for the commemoration of the first landing of American troops on July 25, 1898.

Major-General Henry Knox Day (ME)— This honors a Revolutionary War general from Thomaston, Maine, who served as Secretary of War under Pres. George Washington. He was born in 1750 and became a member of the Boston Grenadier Corps in 1772. He served under Gen. Ward as a volunteer at the Battle of Bunker Hill in June of 1775. When Gen. George Washington arrived in Boston, he recognized Knox as an expert in the field of artillery. Knox was placed in charge of artillery, and on ox sleds brought cannon from captured Fort Ticonderoga to Boston. He placed them on Dorchester Heights in March of 1776, causing the British commander to take his troops out of Boston. After arranging for the defense of Connecticut and Rhode Island, Knox joined Washington's army in New York, later directing the Christmas night crossing of the Delaware River to surprise the Hessian forces, and take captives and supplies. He led troops at Monmouth, Germantown, Brandywine and Jamestown, and after the Revolution ended served as the Secretary of War. He died in 1806 from complications of an accidentally swallowed chicken bone.

Ohio National Guard Day (OH)—This day honors those individuals who have served and contributed to the distinguished service of the Ohio National Guard, and to the state and people of Ohio. The national guard has approximately 15,000 members who maintain a presence in 47 of the state's 88 counties. Their goal is to support the U.S. federal military objectives, to support the governor of the state in protecting its residents, and to actively participate in domestic concerns on the local level.

July 26

Disability Awareness Day (CT)—This day has been designated as such to heighten public awareness of the needs of persons with disabilities.

July 27

Birthday of Dr. Jose Celso Barbosa (PR)—Barbosa, a medical doctor, founded the Republican Party of Puerto Rico, which advocated statehood for the island. Barbosa was black, and his party included poor whites, as he had always stressed equality. Barbosa founded the newspaper *El Tiempo* and established the first Puerto Rican "cooperativa," named "El Ahorro Colectivo." He served as a member of the Executive Cabinet and, later, the Senate. He died in 1921.

Firefighters' Memorial Sunday (PA)—This is a day to recognize and honor those firefighters who have lost their lives in the line of duty protecting lives and property.

National Korean War Armistice Day (Fed) [**Korean War Armistice Day** (IL), **Korean Armistice Day** (CT), **Korean War Veterans' Memorial Day** (RI), **Korean War Veterans' Day** (AZ, NJ), **Korean War Veterans Day** (MO)]—Established in 1998, this day of remembrance is scheduled to expire in 2003. It celebrates the 1953 signing of an armistice by U.S. and Communist delegates, ending the Korean War. It recognizes the courage and unwavering patriotism of those valiant men and women of the U.S. Armed Forces who served during the Korean War, often referred to as the "forgotten war." In that war, 33,665 Americans died and 131 received the Medal of Honor, more than 90 of them posthumously.

July 31

Disabled American Veterans ("D.A.V.") Day (RI)—Reacting to the lack of governmental support for about 300,000 disabled and ill World War I veterans, the Disabled American Veterans of the World War was created in 1920. It was accomplished by leaders of 250 self-help groups formed by the disabled veterans themselves. The prime organizer was Judge Robert S. Marx, who had suffered a disabling injury while fighting in France. Later, the reference to the World War was dropped, and served veterans of all wars.

National Journalist Day (PR)—This date was chosen to coincide with the anniversary of the birth of Cesar Andrew Iglesias. He authored *Memoirs of Bernardo Vega—A Contribution to the History of the Puerto Rican Community in New York*. It described the New York Puerto Rican community from 1916 until after World War II, demonstrating that Puerto Ricans should not be considered "newcomers" to the U.S. This day is an opportunity to further employment and career development for Puerto Rican journalists, and to foster greater understanding of the culture, interests and concerns they are involved with.

AUGUST

Observances with Variable Dates

Date Varies

Virgin Islands Citizenship Day (VI)—The President of the legislature designates a day each year in August or September. It is celebrated in New York City by Virgin Islanders living in or visiting the U.S., and by all friends of the Virgin Islands.

First Week in August

Fire Fighter and Emergency Medical Services Personnel Week (CT)—This recognizes the service, sacrifice and contributions of such personnel to the public health and safety. It is an opportunity to recognize those who have died in the line of duty, and those who continue to risk their own lives to protect the safety and property of us all.

Public Employees' Week (MA)—This recognizes and honors the achievements of public employees who work in professional, scientific, technical, and all other phases of governmental employment.

First Sunday in August

American Family Day (AZ, MI, MN, NC)—This is a day to recognize the accomplishments of families, the value of family life to the members of society, and the important issues facing families in modern society.

First Monday in August

Colorado Day (CO)—This commemorates the admission of Colorado into the Union on August 1, 1876. Much of the land was purchased by the U.S. in 1803 as part of the Louisiana Purchase, but its settlement began in earnest after the remainder was acquired from Mexico in 1848 through the Treaty of Guadalupe Hidalgo. Gold was discovered in 1858 near present-day Denver, then part of the Kansas Territory. Miners petitioned for separate territory status, which was granted in 1861. Statehood proposals were turned down in Washington in 1864, 1866 and 1867, and finally approved by Congress in 1876.

Jamaican Independence Day (MA)—Jamaica formerly was a colony of England, and its major holiday was Emancipation Day, celebrated on August 1. On that date in 1834, Parliament gave the slaves limited freedom, requiring an "apprenticeship" of four additional years. On August 1, 1838, they were considered to be "full free." On August 6, 1962, the island received its independence from Great Britain and now observes that date (or the nearest Monday) as its main holiday celebrating freedom.

First Friday in August

Youth in Government Day (MA)—This day is to call attention to the youth of Massachusetts who intern and volunteer in state government.

First Saturday in August

Volunteer Fire Fighter and Volunteer Emergency Medical Services Personnel Day (CT) — This recognizes the service, sacrifices and contributions of such volunteers to the public health and safety.

Sunday Closest to August 10

Herbert Hoover Day (IA) — This day commemorates the life and principles of Herbert Clark Hoover. He was born on this date in 1874 in West Branch, Iowa, and grew up in Newberg, Oregon, living with his uncle after his parents died. He worked as an engineer in China, and was in London when World War I broke out. He assisted the American Consul General in helping 120,000 Americans to return home. Hoover served as the head of the Food Administration under Pres. Wilson, and organized shipments of food to Europe after the war ended. He was the Secretary of Commerce during the terms of Pres. Harding and Coolidge, and became the 31st U.S. President in 1928. During his term came the stock market crash and repercussions from Europe, and his opponents blamed him for the country's economic woes. He was defeated in his bid for reelection by Franklin Roosevelt. Hoover died on October 20, 1964.

Last Saturday Before the Second Sunday in August

Rhode Island Indian Day of the Narragansett Tribe of Indians (RI) — This is a day to celebrate the Algonquin Native American tribe which was present in Rhode Island when Italian navigator Giovanni Verrazzano visited the future colony and state in 1524. From 1620, settlers from Massachusetts Bay Colony traveled to Rhode Island to trade with the tribe. The Narragansetts and Niantics at that time totaled about 7,000 individuals. After the Narragansetts allied themselves with King Philip during his war in 1675, many of the defeated natives retreated to the forest and swamp lands in the southern part of the state, where there is today a reservation. During the last part of the 19th century the U.S. declared them no longer to be a tribe, and took away most of the reservation lands. Recognition and restoration of some of the land were granted during the 1980s. The present Narragansett population stands at about 2,400, most of whom live in Rhode Island.

Second Sunday in August

Gold Star Mothers Day (GU, IL) — This commemorates the mothers of men and women who gave their lives while serving with the U.S. Armed Forces in time of war or during a period of hostilities. Gold Star organizations also maintain ties of fellowship born of military service, assist and further all patriotic work, and inculcate a sense of individual obligation to the community, state and nation.

Texas Parents Day (TX) — This celebrates the Texas family and emphasizes the importance of parents taking an active role in the raising and future of their children. This observance was created in 1999 to provide educators with an excellent opportunity to coordinate with local community organizations to increase parents' awareness of resources that are available to them.

Second Monday in August

Victory Day (RI) — This is the anniversary of V-J (Victory Over Japan) Day, marking the end of World War II. Rhode Island has celebrated this day since 1948. It followed the dropping of the devastating atomic bombs on Hiroshima and Nagasaki, Japan, on August 6 and 9, 1945. On August 14, Japan surrendered.

Third Week in August

Small and Medium-Sized Retail Merchants Week (PR) — This week focuses on contributions of the small business owners and their employees to the welfare and economics of Puerto Rico.

Third Friday in August

Statehood Day (HI) — This commemorates Hawaii's admission as a state on August 21, 1959. Hawaii had been annexed by the U.S. on July 7, 1898, declaring it to be necessary as a navy base for the conduct of the Spanish-American War, particularly the actions in the Philippines. U.S. interests had coveted the islands for quite some time, and the war gave them an excuse for taking them over. During World War II, Oahu served as the command post for the U.S. operations in the Pacific. Large portions of Hawaii were turned over for U.S. military bases. After the war, two-thirds of the residents favored statehood. However, because of the many ethnicities present, there was resistance to Hawaii's statehood from segregated Southern states. Congress finally passed appropriate legislation to make it the 50th state in March, 1959, and over 90 percent of the Hawaiian voters approved. This was known as "Admission Day" until 2001.

Fourth Thursday in August

Television Non-Violence Day (PR) — This is a time to focus on the effects of violence shown on television, and efforts to remove inappropriate violent content, especially from programming which may be viewed by children.

Fourth Friday of August and the Next 10 Days

Caribbean Friendship Week (VI) — This period is to further friendly relations among the Virgin Islands and its Caribbean neighbors. It lasts for a total of 11 days.

Last Week in August

Caribbean Week (MA) — This week has been designated for observance to celebrate the cultures of the Caribbean nations, and to promote good relations with them and their citizens.

Family Week (SC) — The South Carolina legislature urges the promotion of local festivals, pageants, field days, picnics, reunions and similar activities which would encourage participation by families as units. During this week, the "South Carolina Family of the Year Award" is presented by the Governor.

Last Sunday in August

Family Day (TN) — Tennessee families are celebrated on this day, which focuses on the important issues facing parents in today's society.

OBSERVANCES WITH FIXED DATES

August 2

Disability Day (KY) — This is a time to focus on the contributions to society made by disabled persons, and the needs that they have in order that they may have opportunities that non-disabled citizens have.

August 3

Ernie Pyle Day (NM) — Born on this date in 1900, Ernest Pyle was the managing editor of the *Washington Daily News* from 1932 to 1935. During World War II he was renowned for his reporting of events from the battles, which won him the Pulitzer Prize in 1944. He was killed by enemy machine gun fire on Ie Shima on April 18, 1945.

August 4

Commemoration of Anniversary of Founding of the U.S. Coast Guard (NH) — The Coast Guard was formed as a combination of the Revenue Cutter Service, the Lighthouse Service, the Steamboat Inspection Service, the Bureau of Navigation and the Lifesaving Service. To eliminate overlapping duties, they were combined under the umbrella of the Coast Guard. It traces its origin to the federalization of existing lighthouses on August 7, 1789.

Nicole Robin Day (VI) — This commemorates the return of the *Nicole Robin* and her crew on August 4, 1973, after a harrowing 23-day experience. Most of that time was spent in the hands of Communist Cuban authorities.

August 7

Melvin H. Evans Day (VI) — On January 4, 1971, Dr. Melvin H. Evans became the first elected governor of the U.S. Virgin Islands. He was elected in 1970, 16 years after the U.S. Congress revised the Organic Act to allow such an election. He succeeded himself, having served since 1968 under the auspices of the U.S. Department of Interior.

Purple Heart Day (MA) [**Purple Heart**

Recipient Recognition Day (WA), **Combat Wounded Veterans Purple Heart Day** (MN)]— Established by George Washington as the Badge of Military Merit in 1782, the Purple Heart was largely forgotten until 1927. Then the army chief of staff unsuccessfully petitioned Congress to reinstate the award. Four years later, Douglas MacArthur succeeded, and a new badge was designed by Elizabeth Will. The requirements were redefined, so that it would take more than a "meritorious action" to be awarded the honor.

August 9

International Day of the World's Indigenous People (U.N.)—This day was set on August 9 by the United Nations General Assembly, chosen to commemorate the anniversary of the first meeting (in 1992) of the Working Group on Indigenous Populations of the Subcommission on the Promotion and Protection of Human Rights.

August 12

International Youth Day (U.N.)—This day was established by the United Nations General Assembly in 1999, accepting the recommendation of the World Conference of Ministers Responsible for Youth. Public activities are urged as a way to promote better awareness of the 1995 World Programme of Action for Youth to the Year 2000 and Beyond.

August 14

End of World War II Day (CT)—On this day in 1945, President Truman announced to Americans that Japan had accepted the terms of surrender. This touched off a celebration known as V-J Day. The formal surrender did not occur until September 2, 1945, when Gen. Douglas MacArthur accepted the signed surrender document aboard the battleship *Missouri* in Tokyo Bay.

Liberty Tree Day (MA)—This commemorates the first public shade tree planting in the New World in 1646. One of the trees so planted was known from 1765 as the "Liberty Tree," the first public statement of resistance and a symbol of freedom. When it was removed by British soldiers in 1775, it yielded 14 cords of firewood.

The British also destroyed the liberty tree in Charleston, South Carolina, and then burned its stump. The last remaining liberty tree stood on the campus of St. John's College in Annapolis, Maryland, until it died in October of 1999.

Social Security Day (MA)—This is in recognition of the contribution of the Social Security system to the dignity and well-being of Americans of all ages.

August 16

Bennington Battle Day (VT)—In 1777 the British were heading toward Albany, New York, and then on to New York City. Running low on supplies and having little regard for the American military abilities, General John Burgoyne had Lt. Col. Friedrich Baum lead an expedition into Vermont to capture supplies at American storehouses near the border of Vermont. About five miles from Bennington, Vermont, at a village now called Walloomsac, New York, the British entrenched themselves on a hill, awaiting actions by the Americans. On August 16 John Stark and 1,500 troops from New Hampshire attacked and, in a two-hour battle, defeated the British, killing Baum and over 200 of his men. The American losses were only 40 dead and 30 wounded. Later in the day, another British contingent arrived, and they were pushed back by Stark and the Vermont militia, led by Seth Warner. Burgoyne's army was weakened, and after two more unsuccessful battles, he surrendered on October 17.

Elvis Aaron Presley Day (MS)—This day was named in his honor in recognition of his many contributions, his international recognition and the rich legacy left to us by him. On this date in 1977 he died of a heart attack in Memphis, Tennessee. Presley was born in Tupelo, Mississippi, on January 8, 1935, and was locally successful as a country singer by his late teens. By the mid–1950s he had a recording contract and made appearances on TV shows, building a massive following for his mixture of black and white styles. He had numerous hit records, and some believe that he is still alive.

National Airborne Day (LA, NJ)—This day commemorates the first official U.S. Army parachute jump on August 16, 1940. On that day, 48 volunteers of the U.S. Army Parachute Test Platoon made the first test jump. The first combat jump occurred in November of 1942, when members of the 2nd Battalion, 503rd Parachute Infantry Regiment, participated in the invasion of North Africa.

August 18

Roberto Clemente Day of Remembrance (PR) — Clemente was born in Carolina, Puerto Rico, on August 18, 1934. With the Pittsburgh Pirates from 1955 to 1972, he had a lifetime batting average of .317 and was considered major league baseball's premier defensive outfielder. He won four National League batting titles, one Most Valuable Player award, twelve Gold Glove awards, and twelve All-Star Game selections. In the last game of the season in 1972 he reached the plateau of 3,000 hits. After that season he was in an airplane loaded with supplies for earthquake victims of Managua, Nicaragua, and was killed when it crashed off the Puerto Rican Coast. He was enshrined in the Baseball Hall of Fame in 1973.

August 19

National Aviation Day (Fed) — This is a celebration of the leading role the U.S. played in the development of aeronautics. Initially, in 1937, the contributions of the Wright Brothers were not mentioned in the establishing resolution. Within a couple of years, the National Aviation Day was looked to for help in building excitement for the new science of aeronautics. When the second Congressional resolution in 1939 was signed into law by Pres. Roosevelt, the date for observance was set on August 19, the birthday of Orville Wright.

August 23

International Day for the Remembrance of the Slave Trade and its Abolition (U.N.) — This celebrates the uprising on the night of August 22 to 23, 1791, on the island of Hispanola. It was the beginning of a crucial phase in the fight for abolition of the transatlantic slave trade, and this day inscribes the tragedy of the slave trade in the memory of all peoples. This observance offers an opportunity for the collective consideration of the historic causes, the methods and the consequences of this tragedy, and an analysis of the interactions between Africa, Europe, the Americas and the Caribbean.

August 24

Ukranian-American Day (CT) — This honors Americans of Ukranian ancestry, their culture and the contribution they have made to the country. Before 1999, this was celebrated on January 22.

Wickersham Day (AK) — This holiday was established in 1945 to honor Judge James Wickersham, born in Illinois on August 24, 1857. Beginning in 1898, he served in the Washington Territorial House of Representatives, as well as serving as county probate judge and Tacoma city attorney. When judicial districts were created for the northern portion of Alaska, Wickersham was appointed district judge, the first to sit in the interior of Alaska. His circuit covered 300,000 square miles, and was traveled by boat and dogsled since there were no roads. He presided over trials, and in his spare time enjoyed the outdoors, including in 1903 leading the first attempt to climb Mt. McKinley. In 1908 he was elected as Alaska's delegate to Congress, served until 1920, and was reelected in 1930. His efforts resulted in Alaska gaining territorial status in 1912, the creation of the Alaska Railroad and McKinley Park, and the establishment of what is now known as the University of Alaska. He introduced the first Alaska Statehood Bill in 1916. He died in Juneau on October 23, 1939.

August 26

Susan B. Anthony Day (MA) [**Women's Independence Day** (CT)] — This day honors the woman who was the organizer, lecturer, campaigner and ardent advocate of the fight for American woman suffrage, and whose unfailing efforts culminated in the prohibition of the denial of the right to vote on account of sex. The date was chosen to be the anniversary of the 1920 ratification of the 19th amendment to the U.S. Constitution, extending the right to vote to include women. That amendment was passed by the U.S. House of Representatives and Senate in 1919; and by August 18, 1920, Tennessee's ratification of it made it law. Anti-suffrage legislators left the state to attempt to defeat the existence of a quorum, and there was a strong fight to convince others to vote against the amendment. However, the deciding vote was cast by 24-year-old legislator Harry Burn, who changed his mind after receiving a letter from his mother saying, "Don't forget to be a good boy" and "vote for suffrage."

Women's Equality Day (NJ) — On this day the Governor of New Jersey presents an award to the Woman Police Officer of the Year, recognizing her devotion to duty and heroism. The award is named the Abigail Powlett Award, named after the Plainfield, New Jersey, woman who was the first female New Jersey police officer killed in the line of duty.

August 27

Lyndon Baines Johnson Day (TX) — Johnson was born in a small farmhouse in Stonewall, Texas, on August 27, 1908. He was a teacher and school principal who went into politics after working as an assistant to Congressman Richard Kleberg in the early 1930s. Johnson won his first election to a House seat in 1937, and remained there until 1948 when he was elected to the Senate. He was elected as U.S. Vice President in 1960 and became the 36th President of the U.S. upon the assassination of John Kennedy. Johnson's administration included racial unrest, civil strife and the Vietnam War. He died on January 22, 1973.

August 29

Toms River East Little League World

Champions Day (NJ) — This day is in recognition of the extraordinary accomplishments of the team informally known as the "Toms River East Twelve," the "Windsor Avenue Wonders," and the "Beasts from the East." In their final game on August 29, 1998, the team from Toms River beat Kashima, Japan, by a score of 12 to 9. The Japanese team included Sayaka Tsushima, the first female to play in a final game of the championship series. Toms River two days before beat Greenville, North Carolina, for the U.S. championship.

August 30

Huey P. Long Day (LA) — Long was born on August 30, 1893, in Winnfield, Louisiana. After attending the University of Oklahoma and Tulane University, he practiced law and served as the Chairman of the Louisiana Railroad Commission. In 1928 he became the Governor of Louisiana and was a controversial leader whose regime resulted in almost 13,000 miles of new roads, increased political participation of blacks and poor whites, a new state capitol, an expanded charity hospital system, a medical school, and free textbooks for all school children. He was elected to the U.S. Senate in 1930 and remained as governor until 1932. He appeared to be a real threat to challenge Franklin Roosevelt in the 1936 presidential election, but on September 8, 1935, he was shot by an assassin in a capitol corridor and died two days later.

SEPTEMBER

OBSERVANCES WITH VARIABLE DATES

Date to Be Set Annually by the Governor

National Guard Week (PR) — This is to be set in September by the Governor of Puerto Rico.

Date Varies

Virgin Islands Citizenship Day (VI) — The President of the legislature designates a day each year in August or September. It is celebrated in New York City by Virgin Islanders living in or visiting the U.S., and by all friends of the Virgin Islands.

Vary in September and October

Rosh Hashanah (FL) — This day begins the Jewish New Year, according to the Bible to be proclaimed by "a blast of horns." The earliest Jewish calendar had four "new" years, corresponding to the seasons, and the one in autumn likely gained prominence because of its proximity to Succoth, the harvest festival, and to Yom Kippur, the solemn Day of Atonement. This is a holiday in a judicial circuit only if its chief judge so designates it.

Yom Kippur (FL, NC) — This is the most important Jewish holiday, marked by 24 hours of fasting and prayer. It is the time for the asking of forgiveness for all of mankind's sins, with a focus on jealousy, greed, pride, vanity and lust. It is a solemn day, but is dedicated to joyfulness and the belief that God will forgive old sins and allow all a fresh start. This is a holiday in a judicial circuit in Florida only if its chief judge so designates it.

Day of Opening of the Annual Regular Session of the United Nations General Assembly

International Day of Peace (U.N.) — This observance was established in 1981 to be devoted to commemorating and strengthening the ideals of peace both within and among all nations and peoples. This is a reminder of our permanent commitment to peace, and gives positive evidence of that commitment through actions of cooperative goodwill. At the United Nations headquarters, the day is marked with a special ceremony near the Peace Bell, cast from coins donated from people from about 60 countries, which was donated to the U.N. by Japan. After a special message from the Secretary-General, the bell is rung and then all present observe a moment of silence to reflect on the universal goal of peace.

First Week in September

Grandparents Week (OK) — The first official statewide Grandparents Day proclamation, predating the national observance, took place in West Virginia in 1973. It was the result of a campaign spearheaded by Marian Lucille Herndon McQuade, who lobbied church, civic, business and political leaders, and through Senator Jennings Randolph was able to get the attention of the state and national legislators. The result is a day or week to honor grandparents, who often fill some of the gaps in our mobile society, caring for their grandchildren when parents are unable.

First Full Week in September

Virginia World War II Veterans Appreciation Week (VA) — This week was selected to commemorate the first official week of peace in 1945. Virginia veterans whose service in World War II prevented their finishing high school may be presented this week with Commonwealth of Virginia World War II Veteran Honorary High School Diplomas.

First Monday in September

Grandparents' Day (MA) — This is a day to honor the grandmothers and grandfathers of this country, and the contributions they make to the betterment of the younger generations. September is chosen for the observance, to represent the "autumn years" of life.

Labor Day (Fed, AL, AK, AS, AZ, AR, CA, CO, CT, DE, DC, FL, GA, GU, HI, ID, IL, IN, IA, KS, KY, LA, ME, MD, MI, MN, MS, MT, NE, NV, NH, NJ, NM, NY, NC, ND, CM, OH, OK, OR, PA, PR, RI, SC, SD, TN, TX, VI, UT, VT, VA, WA, WV, WI, WY) — This day was originated by labor union leader Peter J. McGuire. It was his suggestion to the Central Labor Union of New York that the American working man be celebrated, which led to 10,000 workers parading in Union Square. They were supervised by the Knights of Labor, and celebrations included picnics, political speeches and fireworks. The date was chosen as approximately halfway between Independence Day and Thanksgiving, to give workers another day off from work. It is now less tied to trade unions, and marks the unofficial end of the summer vacation season. Major parades and mass displays are now less common than are speeches by leading union officials, educators, industrialists, clerics and government officials, which are covered by print and broadcast media.

Labor Week (MA) — The first Labor Day was observed on Tuesday, September 5, 1882, in New York City. The second was held exactly a year later, but in 1884 it was moved to the first Monday of the month. The Central Labor Union urged other labor organizations to follow their example and celebrate a "workingmen's holiday." In 1885 and 1886, municipal ordinances recognized the day, and the first official state recognition was passed on February 21, 1887, in New York. By the time the U.S. Congress adopted the holiday in 1894, it was already an official observance in 27 states. In 1909 the American Federation of Labor designated the Sunday before Labor Day to be known as Labor Sunday, dedicated to the spiritual and educational aspects of the labor movement.

Santiago Iglesias Pantin Day (PR) — Pantin (February 22, 1870 or 1872–December 5, 1939) served as the Resident Commissioner of Puerto Rico in Washington, DC, from November 8, 1932, until his death. A cabinetmaker born in Spain, he moved to Cuba and served as the Secretary of the Workingmen Trades Circle in Havana from 1889 to 1896, then moved to Puerto Rico where he founded and edited three labor newspapers — *Porvenir Social* (1898–1900), *Union Obrera* (1903–1906), and *Justicia* (1914–1925). After serving as the General Organizer of the Pan American Federation of Labor for the Puerto Rico and Cuba districts, he was a member of the Puerto Rican Senate.

West Indies Solidarity Day (VI) — This celebration recognizes the contributions made by the people of the West Indies to the economic and social life of the Virgin Islands.

First Saturday in September

Colonel Freeman McGilvery Day (ME) — Born in 1824, McGilvery entered the Civil War in 1862 as a captain and commander of the 6th Battery of the Maine Light Artillery. He led that unit at the Battles of Second Bull Run, Antietam and Fredericksburg. After his promotion to Lt. Colonel, he commanded the 1st Volunteer Artillery Brigade in the Army of the Potomac's Artillery Reserve, which he led in the Battles of Chancellorsville, Gettysburg and Mine Run. He is remembered mostly for the second day at Gettysburg, when he and his men bravely made a stand which held off the Confederates until infantry reinforcements arrived. He is credited with saving the Union army on that day, and the next day he helped destroy the Confederate Pickett's Charge. On August 16, 1864, at the Battle of Deep Bottom, he sustained a slight finger wound which he ignored. It became infected, and during surgery for its amputation on September 2 he died from the effects of chloroform.

First Saturday Following Labor Day

Carl Garner Federal Lands Cleanup Day (Fed) — All citizens are encouraged to participate in the cleanup of federally-owned parks, forests and other lands. In 1970 Greers Ferry Lake, an area administered by the U.S. Army Corps of Engineers, was becoming unsightly. It was a popular place to camp, play, boat, swim, fish and sightsee, but visitors left tons of litter along the river and lakeshore. Corps funds were too short to pay for cleaning, so Resident Engineer William Carl Garner contacted local community leaders to organize a volunteer effort to solve the problem. On a Saturday in May of 1970, volunteers began the task of cleaning up 300 miles of shoreline. Over the years, the cleanup campaign has developed into a year-round project involving private industry, civic groups, governments, schools and individuals. The program started by Garner became a model for other lands operated by the Corps of Engineers and other governmental agencies. Garner served as an engineer for Greers Ferry Lake from 1959 until he stepped down in 1996. The Corps of Engineers further honored Garner by naming the visitor center at Greers Ferry Lake as the William Carl Garner Visitor Center.

Native American Day (DE) — This is a time to celebrate the contributions to the state and nation by Native Americans. At the time of the settlement of the state by Europeans, Delaware was the home of the Delaware Indians, also known as the Lenai Lenape. The colonists drove them westward, where they were conquered by the Iroquois. Many of the survivors settled in Ohio. They were allies of the Americans during the Revolutionary War.

First Sunday Following Labor Day

National Grandparents Day (Fed) [**Grand-** **parents' Day** (NJ)] — This day has more than one origin. Some consider it to have been first proposed by Michael Goldgar after he visited his aunt in an Atlanta nursing home. Spending $11,000 of his own money in lobbying efforts to have the day officially recognized, he made 17 trips to Washington, DC, over a seven-year span to meet with legislators. Others consider Marian Lucille Herndon McQuade, a West Virginia housewife, to have been the impetus for the day of observance. In any event, it was finally signed into law by Pres. Jimmy Carter in 1978. Approximately 4,000,000 Grandparents Day greeting cards are sent in the U.S. each year.

Week Following the Sunday Which Follows the First Monday in September

Alzheimer's Awareness Week (MA) — This time is set aside to educate the public about the need for early diagnosis of this debilitating disease, and the opportunities for treatment.

Grandparent Week (NJ) — This is a continuation of the celebration of grandparents in New Jersey.

Second Sunday in September

Family Day (CT, NM) — On this day, residents of Connecticut and New Mexico celebrate the benefits of a strong united family, and focus on important issues that families face.

Second Monday in September

Florida Missing Children's Day (FL) — This day of observance was established in 2000 to remember Florida's past and present missing children through prevention, education and community involvement.

School Safety Patrol Day (CT) — This is to be observed in the public schools with programs on highway safety to call attention to the fine work of school safety patrols.

Week Including September 12

Week Celebrating Manuel Corchado y Juarbe (PR) — Manuel Corchado y Juarbe was born on September 12, 1840, in Isabela, Puerto Rico. He was educated in Madrid, Spain, and became a lawyer. In 1863 he was awarded a prize for his poem, *Oda a Campeche*, giving him a reputation as a poet. Three years later he founded the political magazine *Las Antillas*, dealing with all of Latin America but with a focus on Cuba and Puerto Rico. A memorable speech made in 1871 against the death penalty gave him a reputation for expressive eloquence. He was an advocate for political reform, and fought for the abolition of slavery.

Second Saturday in September

Endangered Species Day (MA) — On this day the work of the Natural Heritage & Endangered Species Program and other organizations is celebrated, especially their efforts to protect the approximately 175 species of animals and 250 species of plants which are endangered, threatened or of special concern in Massachusetts. Their overall goal is to protect the state's wide range of native biological diversity.

First Saturday Following the Full Moon in September

Indian Day (OK) — Oklahoma has the largest Native American population of any state, with over a quarter million individuals descended from the original 67 tribes who resided there. Thirty-nine tribes are presently headquartered there, and the name of the state comes from Choctaw words meaning "red people."

Eighth Tuesday Before the First Tuesday Following the First Monday in November

Election Day (AZ) — This is the date for primary elections, to be held in even-numbered calendar years.

Third Week in September

Constitution Week (NV) — This week includes September 17, which was the date in 1787 that the delegates to the Constitutional Convention in Philadelphia signed the monumental document. It is a time in Nevada to celebrate the freedoms afforded all citizens by the first modern democratic constitution.

Native American Heritage Week (AR) — This honors the integral role that Native Americans have played in the history of the state and the rich contributions they have made to its history, including the state's role as home to many of the roads and trails along the Trail of Tears.

Virginia Championship Applebutter Making Contest (VA) — This week-long contest recognized by the state legislature is held in conjunction with the Rotary Club's Apple Harvest Festival.

Third Full Week in September

Cystic Fibrosis Week (MA) — Special attention is paid to the importance of continued research in, and effective therapy for, this tragic disease. It causes the body to produce an abnormally thick mucus which sticks to and clogs the lungs. As a result, the patient is susceptible to life-threatening infections. It further obstructs the pancreas, which thereby prevents enzymes from reaching the intestines to aid in digestion. Cystic Fibrosis affects about one in every 30,000 children in the U.S.

Prairie Week (IL) — During this week, programs and displays demonstrate the value of preserving and reestablishing native Illinois prairie. The word "prairie" was used by the earliest French trappers and explorers to describe the extensive grasslands which formed a natural meadow. Ecologically, a prairie is a vegetative community dominated by native grasses and colorful flowers. The Illinois Plant Information Network lists 851 species of plants native to prairies of the state. The largest remaining prairie remnant in the state is in the Goose Lake Prairie State Preserve near Morris in Grundy County.

Week Beginning with the Third Monday in September

Hunting Heritage Week (MN) — This commemorates Minnesota's valued heritage of hunting game animals. Residents are urged to reflect upon hunting as an expression of our culture and heritage, and to acknowledge that it is our community of sportsmen, sportswomen and hunters who have made the greatest contributions to the establishment of current game animal populations.

Official Observance of Montana's Hunt-

ing Heritage (MT)—Citizens of Montana are urged to reflect on hunting as an expression of their culture and heritage. They should acknowledge that it is their community of sportsmen, sportswomen and hunters who have made the greatest contributions to the establishment of current game animal populations, and celebrate this culture and heritage in all lawful ways.

Third Friday in September

Native American Day (MA, WY)—In Wyoming, this day of observance was established in 1987 to encourage its citizens to appreciate the special heritage and contributions of Native Americans. All are called upon to recognize the importance of tribal values that have become ingrained in the American spirit, such as respect for our natural resources.

POW/MIA Recognition Day (AR, IL, OK) [POW-MIA Recognition Day (VT), POW-MIA's Day (RI), Prisoners of War and Missing in Action Recognition Day (AK), POW/MIA Day (MA), Pennsylvania POW/MIA Recognition Day (PA), New Jersey P.O.W.-M.I.A. Recognition Day (NJ), Prisoners of War — Missing in Action Recognition Day (ME)]—This day honors those who were prisoners or were still unaccounted for as of the creation of this observance. The missing total 2,282 for actions in Southeast Asia; 8,100 from the Korean War; 78,000 from World War II; and nine from the Persian Gulf War. Prisoners of war surviving today total nearly 50,000. It is a tribute to their bravery, patriotism and courage, which will never be forgotten by their loved ones, nation and community. It is also a day to remember the families of the prisoners and those missing, often not knowing for years whether their loved ones will be returned home. This day of observance was established in 1979.

Tennessee P.O.W.-M.I.A. Recognition Week (TN)—This is a continuation of the recognition of the prisoners of war and those missing in action as a result of service in the U.S. Armed Forces. Where officially recognized in other states, the observance lasts there for one day.

Third Saturday in September

Landowner Recognition Day (ME)—This is a day to recognize those who hold title to lands in the State of Maine.

Third Weekend in September

Take a Kid Hunting Weekend (MN)—To encourage introducing youth to the hunting opportunities in Minnesota, adults are encouraged to take them out this weekend, and fees for licenses this week are waived.

Fourth Sunday in September

Puerto Rico Day (CT)—This day recognizes the contribution to the welfare of Connecticut made by persons of Puerto Rican ancestry.

Fourth Monday in September

American Indian Day (NE, TN)—This honors the first residents of the U.S., who made advances to the growth and development of the state, the U.S. and local communities, first through history and now with human and natural resources. Ceremonies and fellowship are designed to promote greater understanding and brotherhood between American Indians and the non–Indian people of this country.

Fourth Friday in September

Native American Day (CA, NJ) [Michigan Indian Day (MI)]—Established in California in 1984, this was known as California American Indian Day until 1998. In New Jersey it celebrates the state's original inhabitants, who were a great influence on the cultural and agricultural development of the state. The natives are remembered for their forming clearings and trails prior to the arrival of the colonists, making possible the formation of the very earliest colonial towns, supplying colonists with food and guiding them to profitable hunting grounds, and developing corn, squash, beans and tobacco. In Michigan the Chippewa, Ottawa and Potawatomi work to maintain their cultural traditions while serving as citizens of the modern U.S. society.

Fourth Saturday in September

American Indian Day (KS) [Native American Indian Day (OH), Native-American Day

(NY)] — This is a time to recognize the contributions to American society by Native Americans, and to focus on problems of education, employment and other areas which today's Native Americans are facing.

National Hunting and Fishing Day (MA) — A goal of this observance is to create a better public awareness of the important role that outdoorsmen and outdoorswomen have played in conservation and improving our natural resources. It also focuses on the good which has been done, such as the acquisition of thousands of acres of wildlife habitat, as a result of the funds raised from the payment of hunting and fishing license fees. Events include fishing, archery, firearms and muzzleloader shooting, cooking, duck calling, wildlife art, taxidermy, hunter educations, dog training, camping, bird watching, hiking and photography. They are organized by sportsmen's clubs, state wildlife agencies and conservation groups. It has been celebrated nationally since 1972.

Last Full Week in September

Deaf Culture Week (ME) — This is a week which provides an opportunity to recognize the contributions the deaf have made to our communities of the state and nation. It also has a goal of ensuring that people with hearing impairments are afforded the opportunity to fully participate in our society. Many deaf organizations conduct activities to educate the public about deafness.

During the Last Week in September

World Maritime Day (U.N.) — This is held each year on dates selected by each nation's government, but most choose a day in the last week of September. It is used to focus attention on the importance of shipping safety and the marine environment. Each year, a particular aspect of maritime activity is highlighted, such as "IMO: Building Maritime Partnerships," "IMO and the New Millennium," "IMO's 50th Anniversary: Shipping and the Oceans," and "Optimum Maritime Safety Demands a Focus on People."

Last Full Week in September

Indian Solidarity Week (NC) — North Carolina is the ancestral home of Cherokees and other Native American tribes. This week is a time for events which recognize and promote the brotherhood among Native Americans, and encourage cooperation in working on issues of common concern.

Last Sunday in September

Gold Star Mother's Day (Fed, ND, OH) — In 1918 President Wilson approved the wearing of black arm bands bearing a gilt star by those in families whose members had died in the military service to the U.S. This distinguished them from the blue stars, representing a family member presently serving in the Armed Forces. American Gold Star Mothers was incorporated in 1929, obtaining a federal charter from the U.S. Congress. It began with 25 mothers living in the Washington, DC, area, and soon expanded to include affiliated groups throughout the nation. The organization exists to keep alive and develop the spirit that promoted world services.

Parents of Fallen Military Sons and Daughters Day (NJ) — This day is a tribute to all parents whose sons and daughters died as a result of their service with the U.S. Armed Forces, and in acknowledgement of the contributions, commitment and sacrifice made by those parents individually and through American Gold Star Mothers, Incorporated.

Last Friday in September

Children's Day (ME) — This is a day to celebrate the children of Maine, and for parents, teachers and everyone else to dedicate themselves toward providing children with a quality education and opportunities to develop into good citizens.

Indian Day (CT) — This is a celebration of the history and culture of the original natives of Connecticut.

Last Saturday in September

War of 1812 Day (NY) — The War of 1812 began in June of 1812 and lasted until the spring of 1815, despite the peace treaty ending hostilities having been signed in Europe in December 1814. Most of the fighting occurred along the Canadian border, around Chesapeake Bay, and along the Gulf of Mexico. Much of the action was at sea. Initially, American efforts to invade Canada were unsuccessful, and the British tightened a blockade around U.S. coasts, ruining American trade. After the British burned Washington in the fall of 1814, things looked bleak for the Americans until they were successful at the Battle of Lake Champlain on September 11. The focus of the war shifted to New Orleans, where action took place in January of 1815, weeks after the signing of the Treaty of Ghent, unknown to commanders Maj. Gen. Andrew Jackson and Maj. Gen. Sir Edward Pakenham and their armies because of slow communications. The fighting was ended by the treaty, but the issues which brought the war about were not resolved by it.

OBSERVANCES WITH FIXED DATES

September 1

Bible Day (PR) — The early Spanish settlers brought Roman Catholicism to Puerto Rico, with heavy reliance on the Bible. As recently as the beginning of the 20th century, more than 90 percent of the island's population was Catholic. In more recent years, especially with influx from the mainland U.S., membership in Protestant denominations has grown considerably.

Caribbean Friendship Week (VI) — This period, eleven days beginning on the fourth Friday in August, exists to further friendly relations among the Virgin Islands and its Caribbean neighbors.

Literary Awareness Month (MA) — This period encourages the establishment of programs designed to increase the public's awareness of illiteracy.

New Jersey Care About Children with Cancer Month (NJ) — This month is dedicated to promoting the progress made in combating the disease in children, and highlighting the fact that more has to be done in New Jersey to help cancer treatment specialists, health care providers and researchers provide children with the services necessary to prevent these cancers in the future.

Sight-Saving Month (MA) — This is a period of special attention to the importance of the conservation of the gift of sight, one of mankind's greatest treasures.

Support Our Public Schools Month (VI) — This is the time for citizens of the Virgin Islands to become aware of the needs of the islands' public schools, and to become involved in efforts to help support them.

September 2

Queen Lili'uokalani Day (HI) — This day has been named in memory of the birth of Lydia Kamekeha Liluokalani in Honolulu on September 2, 1838. Upon the death of her brother, King Kalakauam, she assumed the throne, and shortly thereafter her husband, John Owen Dominis, died. She never remarried. Although she recommended a new constitution limiting the powers of the monarchy, U.S. businessmen, led by Sanford B. Dole, pushed for the establishment of a republic. In 1894 the American minister called for troops, which took over the Iolani Palace. The Queen was deposed, the monarchy terminated, and a provisional republic government was set up. She was arrested in 1895 after weapons were found in the gardens of her home. Denying any knowledge of them or plans to restore the monarchy, she was released in 1896. She died of complications from a stroke on November 11, 1917. Liliuokalani is also remembered for composing many Hawaiian songs, including *Aloha Oe* and *Farewell to Thee*.

September 3

Prudence Crandall Day (CT) — This celebrates the anniversary of the 1803 birth of Quaker Prudence Crandall in Hopkinton, Rhode Island. In 1831 she established in Canterbury, Connecticut, a private school for girls. Her admittance of a black girl outraged the community and resulted in the withdrawal of many of her white students. In 1833 she opened another school, this one for "young ladies and little misses of color," and 15 to 20 black pupils enrolled. This resulted in the state passing the "Black Law," prohibiting schools for nonresident black students or teaching in one. Crandall was arrested, convicted and imprisoned until an appellate court reversed the decision on a technicality. Her home was then attacked and damaged, and she abandoned her school project and moved to Illinois. She continued to teach and was an outspoken advocate for equality of education and the rights of women. Crandall died on January 28, 1890.

September 4

Marcus Whitman Day (WA)— Whitman was born on this date in 1802. A Congregational missionary as well as a physician and pioneer, he was responsible for settling a large part of the Pacific Northwest, in which he settled in 1843. He was killed by Cayuse Indians on November 29, 1847, after the natives were enraged that their children died while the white children lived. They didn't understand that the survivors had better natural resistance to disease. About 40 natives participated in the Wailatpu Massacre, which began when the Whitmans' home was visited by Chief Tilokaikt. While he distracted Marcus, Tomahas tomahawked him from behind. Wife Narcissa was shot in the house, taken outside and shot several more times, dumped in the mud, and beaten. About a dozen other white settlers died in the attack.

September 8

International Literacy Day (U.N.)— Since 1971, International Literacy Day has been celebrated to focus on the goal of education for all, and the gateway to such end is literacy training. Illiteracy is still a major problem, with one billion illiterates, two-thirds of which are women and one-half of which are speakers of lesser-known languages. On this day, attention is called to the situation that, despite tremendous gains in literacy in recent years, much remains to be done to ensure that people around the world, especially the poor, have access to basic education and lifelong learning opportunities.

September 9

Admission Day (CA)— This commemorates the admission of California as the 31st state on April 9, 1850. After the admission of Wisconsin in 1848, the country consisted of an equal number of slave and free states. California was developing and growing, and was ready for statehood, but its entry would upset the balance. The area was not suited for slave-based agriculture, and the discovery of gold in 1849 and the sudden

massive influx of new residents made slavery even less likely, greatly worrying the South. Proposed by Henry Clay, the Compromise of 1850 solved the dilemma by increasing the strength of the Fugitive Slave Law; while California entered as a free state, the District of Columbia slave trade ended, and Utah and New Mexico became territories.

September 11

911 Day (CT)— This observance was established in 1989 to increase the public's awareness of the emergency telephone number. It is also a time for municipalities to honor emergency operators, public safety dispatchers, telecommunicators and call takers who have performed in an outstanding manner.

Battle of Plattsburgh Day (NY)— Also known as the Battle of Plattsburgh Bay and the Battle of Lake Champlain, it was an American victory over the British navy during the War of 1812. It took place on September 11, 1814. A weak American force faced 10,000 British troops marching from Montreal and New York City. Led by Capt. Thomas MacDonough, the Americans won the battle on Lake Champlain, and the British retreated to Canada, fearing the possibility of a severed line of communications.

Patriot Day (Fed)— In response to the hijacking of four aircraft by terrorists and their being crashed into the World Trade Center in New York, the Pentagon, and into a field in Pennsylvania, the U.S. Congress designated September 11 of each year as Patriot Day. Each year, the President is requested to issue a proclamation calling on all to display the flag at half-staff to honor the individuals who lost their lives as a result of the attacks. To further honor them, the people of the U.S. are to observe a moment of silence on this day.

September 12

Day of Birth of Manuel Corchado y Juarbe (PR)— Corchado y Juarbe returned to Puerto Rico from Madrid in 1879 and became the principal editor of the San Juan newspaper *El Agente*. He served as one of the directors of the Liberal Reformist Party. His writings include *Historia de Ultratumba* (narrative composition), *Dios* (literary-philosophical work), *Al Trabajo* (lyric song), *Maria Antonieta, Biografia de Lincoln, Las Barricadas* (political brochure), *El Capitan Correa* (drama), *Paginas Sangrientas*, and the poems *Confianza en Dios, La Resurrecion del Mundo, A Luisa* and *Amor a Los Padres*. Corchado y Juarbe died in Madrid on November 30, 1884.

Defenders' Day (MD) — This day commemorates an action during the War of 1812, three weeks after the burning of Washington, DC. Approximately 4,000 British troops landed near the present location of Fort Howard, and were met by 3,000 American militia. The British commander, General Ross, was killed, and the British advance was delayed long enough to allow the defensive fortifications around Baltimore to be reinforced. At the end of the day, the Americans, led by Brig. Gen. Sticker, pulled back to join 10,000 troops already assembled at Hampstead Hill. The following day the British attacked Fort McHenry, and after it failed to fall, the British withdrew on September 14. That same day they fought at North Point, but, demoralized after the loss of their commander and their failure to take Fort McHenry, they opted to retreat despite being within sight of Baltimore.

September 13

Commodore John Barry Day (MA, PA) [**John Barry Day** (NY)] — This day is in memory of the service rendered by John Barry during the struggle for American independence. Barry was born in 1745 in Ireland and settled in Philadelphia in about 1760. He was financially successful as the master of a merchant vessel, and in 1776 was appointed to command the brig *Lexington*. He captured the British tender *Edward*, the first capture of a ship by a U.S. commissioned naval officer. In 1778, as commander of the *Raleigh*, he was pursued and run aground by a British man-of-war. While in command of the *Alliance* in 1781, he captured the British ships *Trepassy* and *Atlanta*. He was named senior captain, the highest post in the navy at the time, and had the courtesy title of commodore. In 1794 he helped supervise the reorganization of the U.S. Navy, and directed American naval operations in the West Indies from 1798 to 1801. Barry died on September 13, 1803.

Uncle Sam Day in the State of New York (NY) — In New York, Uncle Sam Day is celebrated with parades, pageants and festivities.

The name of Uncle Sam likely comes from the "U.S." which was stamped on supply containers during the War of 1812, and the image of a man wearing stars and stripes appeared in political cartoons beginning in 1832. He appeared as a shrewd slim Yankee, but after the annexation of Hawaii during the Spanish-American War and the acquisition of Guam, Puerto Rico and the Philippines, was depicted in political cartoons as straddling the world, or with the world in his huge stomach. He was shown as a world power, and later as a protector wielding his army and navy as a "big stick" in Panama, Mexico, Cuba and Haiti. During most of the 20th century he was shown with a short beard, high hat and tailed coat, the image which Congress adopted as a national symbol in 1961.

September 14

Lola Rodriguez de Tio's Birthday (PR) — This Puerto Rican writer penned patriotic lyrics to *La Borinquen*, a revolutionary song and anthem of the rebels who participated in the Grito de Lares revolt for independence in 1868. As a result of this and other separatist activities, she and her husband were deported. She was born in San German on September 14, 1843, and was the first Puerto Rico–born poet to have a reputation known throughout the West Indies. She is known for her patriotic poetry, her most famous work being *Cuba y Puerto Rico Son*, which was part of her collection entitled *Mi Libro de Cuba*, published in 1893. She died while in Cuba on November 10, 1924.

National Anthem Day (PA) — This is the anniversary of the composition of *The Star-Spangled Banner* by Maryland lawyer Francis Scott Key during the Battle of Fort McHenry in the War of 1812. Key, born in 1780, lived in Georgetown near Washington. After the British attacked the city, they captured Upper Marlboro doctor William Barnes, and held him on the British flagship *Tonnant*. Key was asked to help in his release, and offered to exchange himself as prisoner for the doctor. Eventually, the British agreed, but they delayed in letting the doctor and others leave because they had heard too much of the attack plans. On the morning of September 13, 1814, the British began bombarding Fort McHenry, which had a flag purposely oversized (each star was two feet across, and it took 400 yards of material to make) so the British would see it. After

25 hours, the fort had not fallen, and the fleet was about to retreat. When daylight arrived, Key was inspired by the sight of the flag and wrote his famous poem on the back of a letter. After he and the other prisoners were released, he wrote additional lines and called it *Defense of Fort M'Henry*. It was then put to music with the existing tune, *Anacreon in Heaven*, and thereafter was called *The Star-Spangled Banner*. It was made the official U.S. national anthem in 1931.

September 15

Hispanic Heritage Month (Fed) — This month runs from September 15 through October 15. It is a time to focus on the contributions to our society of people of Hispanic ancestry, who make up approximately ten percent of the U.S. population. This includes indigenous peoples of the Americas, such as the Arawaks in Puerto Rico, the Aztecs of Mexico, the Incas of South America, the Mayas of Central America, and the Tainos of Cuba, as well as the early explorers from Spain. This time of celebration began as a single week, approved by Congress in 1968, and was expanded to an entire month in 1988.

September 16

Cherokee Strip Day (OK) — The Cherokee Strip is a parcel of land 226 miles from east to west and 58 miles from north to south, located in Oklahoma. In the last great race for land on September 16, 1893, men, women and children on foot, horses, buggies, bicycles and trains took off at high noon. Over 110,000 individuals with certificates of authority raced for 42,000 claims, and after about two hours those rushing from the south met those coming from the north, effectively filling the Strip with homesteaders entitled to own the parcels which they occupied. The settlement of the area resulted in the death of many Cherokees, making the celebration of this day somewhat controversial.

International Day for the Preservation of the Ozone Layer (U.N.) — The United Nations General Assembly in 1994 began inviting member nations to devote the day to promote activities in accordance with the Montreal Protocol on Substances that Deplete the Ozone Layer. It recognized that the ozone layer, a fragile shield of gas, protects the Earth from the harmful portion of the sun's rays, thus helping preserve life on the planet.

September 17

Constitution Day (MA, NV, UT) [**Federal Constitution Day** (NH), **Citizenship Day** (Fed, VA), **Constitution Commemoration Day** (AZ), **Constitution Week** (Fed, VA), **Constitutional Commemorative Day** (ID)] — This remembers the day in 1787 that the U.S. Constitution was signed by 39 of the 55 delegates to the Constitutional Convention. On this day citizens are to be reminded of the blessings of liberty which they enjoy by the adoption of the Constitution, Bill of Rights, and other amendments. By June 21, 1788, the Constitution was effective, having been approved by nine of the thirteen states.

Friedrich Wilhelm von Steuben Memorial Day (NY) — Baron Friedrich Wilhelm Augustus von Steuben was born on this date in 1730 in Magdeburg, Prussia. At age 17 he became an officer in the Prussian army, and was discharged as a captain at age 33. Heavily in debt in the 1770s, he sought employment in several armies, and with a letter of recommendation from Benjamin Franklin, was accepted into George Washington's army at Valley Forge in February of 1778. Steuben, Alexander Hamilton and Nathaniel Greene drafted a progressive training program for the colonial soldiers, departing from the prior practice of placing untrained recruits into existing units. He also improved the soldiers' speed of reloading their firearms, giving them an advantage over the Redcoats. After the victory at Yorktown, he assisted Washington in demobilizing the army, and was made an American citizen by the Pennsylvania legislature in 1784, the same year he was discharged from the military with honor. He thereafter resided in New York, with the support of a government pension. He died on November 18, 1794.

September 18

Commemoration of Anniversary of Founding of the U.S. Air Force (NH) — The National Security Act established the Department of the Air Force as of September 18, 1947. Personnel serving in the Army Air Force were transferred to the new department eight days later. Aerial activities in the military were first handled by the Army Signal Corps, and balloons were used for reconnaissance during the Civil War. An Aeronautical Division was established in 1907, and the Air Service handled the flying during World War I. Seeing the use of airplanes chiefly as support for infantry, the army's air forces were commanded by local officers, none of them aviators. The Air Service became the Air Corps in 1926, which grew in stature during World War II, when it became the world's most powerful air force, with almost 2.4 million personnel and 80,000 aircraft. After the war, it became a separate branch of the U.S. Armed Forces, to serve on an equal level with the Army and Navy.

September 22

Nathan Hale Day (CT)—Nathan Hale is remembered for his selfless patriotism. On this date in 1776 he was executed by the British. Before the hanging, he stated, "I only regret that I have one life to lose for my country." Hale was born in 1755 in Coventry, Connecticut, and was educated at Yale College. He participated in debates, plays, speeches and parties, and helped form a secular library. After graduating with honors in 1773, he became a teacher, and during the following year enlisted in the local militia. After the Revolutionary War broke out, he resigned as a teacher and served as a soldier in Boston, Manhattan and Long Island, but after a year had still not seen actual combat. When Gen. George Washington needed to find out where Manhattan would be attacked, Hale was sent behind enemy lines to gather information while disguised as an unemployed schoolmaster. On September 21, 1776, he was captured and brought in for questioning by British soldiers. On his person was found intelligence information, and he may have been given up by his cousin, who worked for the Tories. The following morning he was hung in public as a spy near the intersection of present New York City streets East Broadway and Market, and may or may not first have uttered the famous words which have been ascribed to him. His body was left hanging there for several days, and was later buried in an unmarked grave. At the time, he was 21 years old.

September 23

Grito de Lares Day (PR)—This is a tribute to the memory of those brave Puerto Ricans who gave up their lives and who participated in the abortive insurrection of September 23, 1868, known as Grito de Lares. This first and most significant attempt to end colonial dependence on Spain was organized by Ramon Emeterio Betances, who was living in exile in the Dominican Republic. The revolutionary army of several hundred men and women proclaimed independence of the island from Spain, but the army was soon defeated by the Spanish, who retained control over Puerto Rico until autonomy was granted in 1897. The revolution failed largely because the general population was apathetic, the troops were poorly trained and equipped, and the Spanish authorities were aware of their plans in advance.

September 24

American Indian Heritage Day (RI)—On this day the people of Rhode Island celebrate the contributions of Native Americans to their society and culture, and that of the U.S.

September 26

Nevada Indian Day (NV)—The original natives of the state and their descendants are recognized for their culture and contributions to the state and their communities. Focus is placed on the maintenance of the cultural traditions of members of the Paiute, Shoshone and Washoe tribes, while serving as citizens of the modern U.S. society.

September 28

Cabrillo Day (CA)—The people of California on this day celebrate Juan Rodriguez Cabrillo, who is believed to have been born in Portugal. He was with Narvaez on his exploration of Mexico, then allied with Cortes, helped with the founding of Oaxaca, and assisted Alvarado in his conquests in Mesoamerica. Gold mining in Guatemala resulted in his becoming rich by 1542, when he was asked to explore the northern portions of New Spain. He left from Navidad (now known as Acapulco) and sailed to Baja California. He discovered and named San Diego Bay and Santa Barbara, and found the Russian River. He and his men wintered on San Miguel Island in the Santa Barbara Channel, but complications from a broken leg incurred in a fall during an argument with natives resulted in his death on January 3, 1543. Although Cabrillo's explorations did not cause Spain to do anything with its claims on California, he is remembered for his discoveries along the coast.

OCTOBER

OBSERVANCES WITH VARIABLE DATES

Vary in September and October

Rosh Hashanah (FL) — This day begins the Jewish New Year, according to the Bible to be proclaimed by "a blast of horns." The earliest Jewish calendar had four "new" years, corresponding to the seasons, and the one in autumn likely gained prominence because of its proximity to Succoth, the harvest festival, and to Yom Kippur, the solemn Day of Atonement. This is a holiday in a judicial circuit only if its chief judge so designates it.

Yom Kippur (FL, NC) — This is the most important Jewish holiday, marked by 24 hours of fasting and prayer. It is the time for the asking of forgiveness for all of mankind's sins, with a focus on jealousy, greed, pride, vanity and lust. It is a solemn day, but is dedicated to joyfulness and the belief that God will forgive old sins and allow all a fresh start. This is a holiday in a judicial circuit in Florida only if its chief judge so designates it.

First Week in October

Eddie Eagle Gun Safety Week (MA) — Eddie the Eagle is the mascot of the National Rifle Association's GunSafe Program, which teaches elementary school children what to do if they find a gun — Stop!; Don't touch; Leave the area; and Tell an adult. Rather than teach whether guns are good or bad, the program promotes the protection and safety of children. The program was established in 1988, and the safety messages have reached more than eight million children throughout the U.S. and Canada.

Employee Involvement and Employee Ownership Week (MA) — This is a time when Massachusetts promotes the proposition that businesses have a better chance of success when their employees participate in their operation and ownership.

First Full Week in October

Employ Handicapped Persons Week (MA) — The name of this period of observance was changed in 1981 from Employ the Handicapped Week. This is a time to promote the importance for all individuals, including those with disabilities, to prepare for the future by investing in ourselves today, and for employers to focus on the abilities of qualified job applicants with disabilities to meet the increasing need for skilled workers.

First Sunday in October

Children's Day (GA) [**Children and Youth Day** (HI)] — On this day young people of the state are recognized for what they bring to families and society.

Independent Living Center Day (MA)—This day celebrates those facilities which help persons with disabilities reclaim personal power. The independent living program offers opportunities for people with disabilities to experience success at managing the ordinary affairs of their daily lives. By fostering a sense of community and developing an independent living plan for each individual, groups offer support, planning and problem solving.

Senior Citizens' Day (MA)—In 1981 this was changed from Grandparents' Day so that all elderly persons with lifetimes of experiences to pass on to younger generations could be honored, not merely those who have become grandparents.

Stepparents Day (CA)—With an increased number of blended families, it has become appropriate to recognize the care and affection provided by persons who have become parents by marrying others who bring their own children to the relationship.

First Monday in October

Child Health Day (Fed)—This day of observance is intended to make people more aware of the necessity of a year-round program to protect the health of the children of the U.S. Each year, the Health Resources and Services Administration's Maternal and Child Health Bureau, a part of the U.S. Department of Health & Human Services, puts together an informational kit for schools, public health agencies, and communities. Each is on a theme related to children's health, such as tobacco, alcohol or substance abuse, and early childhood development. This day of observance was first proclaimed by Pres. Calvin Coolidge in 1928.

Missouri Day (MO)—Citizens are encouraged to consider the products of the mines, fields and forests of Missouri, and the achievements of the sons and daughters of the state in commerce, literature, statesmanship, science and art. This observance was established in 1915, upon the urging of Anna Brosius Korn, a native of Caldwell County, Missouri.

World Habitat Day (U.N.)—As recommended by the Commission on Human Settlements, the United Nations General Assembly proclaimed this day as an observance of the relationship of human settlements to their surroundings. Each year focuses on a particular area, such as "Women in Urban Governance" and "Cities for All," with the goal of identifying and solving problems in our urbanizing world.

Week Beginning with the First Monday in October

Housing Project Week (PR)—This is a time to celebrate the construction of dwelling units for citizens of Puerto Rico, especially for those of low income who might otherwise be forced to live on the streets or in substandard buildings.

Monday of First Week in October

George Scott Day (VI)—This day to commemorate George Scott was established by the Virgin Islands legislature to coincide with the Monday of Fire Prevention Week, generally observed during the first week of October. Scott is honored for his unselfish service and supreme sacrifice in the protection of his community's safety.

First Saturday in October

Firefighter's Recognition Day (ME)—This is a time to honor those men and women of Maine who dedicate their lives to the protection of property and the lives of the members of their community. It includes those who volunteer in such service, and those who are members of paid fire departments, all of whom spend countless hours on our behalf.

Guam National Guard Day (GU)—This day recognizes the services rendered by the members of the National Guard to the people of Guam.

Social Justice for Ireland Day (MA)—As Massachusetts has a large Irish-American population, it is concerned with the welfare of Ireland and its present citizens. This day focuses the public's attention on human rights issues affecting the Irish, and encourages citizens of Massachusetts to become better informed about them.

A Day Within the First Nine Days of October

Leif Erickson Day (CT)—This day, usually celebrated on October 9, commemorates the explorations of Leif Erickson, who visited North America in about 1003.

On or About October 9

Fire Prevention Day (CT)— Fire Prevention Day was established by the Fire Marshals Association of North America and proclaimed by Pres. Woodrow Wilson on October 9, 1911. The date was chosen since it was the anniversary of the "Great Chicago Fire of 1871," which killed 250 and destroyed 17,430 buildings. After that disaster, focus was shifted from firefighting to fire prevention.

Second Week in October

Government of Puerto Rico Pensioner's Week (PR)— On this day the services provided throughout the working lives of government employees, who have now retired and are receiving pensions, are recognized and appreciated.

Home Composting Recognition Week (MA)— This period recognizes the benefits to the environment by the reduction of solid waste, plus the enhancement it provides to home gardening.

Nuclear Medicine Week (PR)— This is a time to increase public awareness of nuclear medicine and its opportunities to image the body and treat diseases. There are nearly a hundred different nuclear medicine imaging procedures available today, covering every major organ system. Throughout the U.S. an estimated 10 to 12 million nuclear medicine imaging and therapeutic procedures are performed each year.

Week Beginning with the Second Sunday in October

National School Lunch Week (Fed)— The National School Lunch Act was signed into law on June 4, 1946, recognizing the importance of safeguarding the health and well-being of the nation's children, and of encouraging the domestic consumption of nutritious agricultural commodities and other food. The National School Lunch Program now serves appetizing and nutritious meals to more then 23 million children in over 91,000 schools. Nearly half also participate in the School Breakfast Program. This week

we recognize the many concerned citizens who devote their time and skill to providing such meals to school children. This week has been an official national observance since October 9, 1962.

Second Sunday in October

Grandmothers's Day (FL, KY, SC) [**Grandmothers Day** (IL)]— This is a day for public expression of the love, esteem and reverence in which grandmothers are held by the citizens of this country.

National Children's Day (CT)— The objective of this day is to increase the recognition that children today are at risk for many things, including drug and alcohol abuse, child abuse, suicide, peer pressure and the economic and educational challenges of a changing world.

Second Monday in October

American Indian Heritage Day (AL) [**Native Americans' Day** (SD)]— This day, and others throughout the U.S., result in large part from the efforts of Red Fox James, a member of the Blackfoot tribe. He traveled from Montana in 1914 a distance of 4,000 miles to Washington, DC, on horseback to solicit state governors to establish a holiday to honor Indians. After 24 states adopted the holiday, it was approved by 1,250 Indians who gathered in Lawrence, Kansas.

Columbus Day (Fed, AL, AZ, CA, CO, CT, DE, DC, FL, GA, ID, IL, IN, IA, KS, KY, ME, MD, MA, MI, MO, MT, NE, NV, NH, NJ, NM, NY, NC, CM, OH, PA, PR, RI, TX, VI, UT, VT, VA, WV, WI) [**Christopher Columbus Day** (LA, MN)]— The celebration of Columbus Day in the U.S. began on October 12, 1792, organized by the Society of St. Tammany (also known as the Columbian Order). The first official Columbus Day, declared by Pres. Benjamin Harrison, was proclaimed to celebrate the 400th anniversary of Columbus' reaching the New World, in 1892. Following that, the Knights of Columbus lobbied state legislatures to declare October 12 as a legal holiday, with New York being the first to do so. The federal holiday has been celebrated on the second Monday in October since 1971, with parades and festivals in many cities across the country. In Connecticut this is also a celebration of the Italian people, their culture and the great contribution they have made to this county.

Discoverers' Day (HI)— This day is in recognition of the Polynesian discoverers of the Hawaiian Islands. They arrived in outrigger canoes likely from the Marquesas Islands north of Tahiti in about 300 to 750 A.D.

Farmers' Day (FL)— This is a day on which the state of Florida salutes the efforts of its farmers in producing a wide variety of crops and other agricultural products.

Fraternal Day (AL)— This was established as a holiday in Alabama in 1915. Its goal was to encourage all religions, creeds and beliefs to unite together in good will.

Puerto Rico Friendship Day (VI)— This is a day to recognize and promote the friendly relationship the Virgin Islands has with Puerto Rico. Both enjoy a limited amount of benefits of being a part of the U.S., while lacking the full status of statehood.

Yorktown Victory Day (VA)— After a three-week siege by troops led by George Washington, Comte de Rochambeau and Marquis de Lafayette, the Franco-American forces captured two major British redoubts. British General Charles Cornwallis became desperate, and even attempted biological warfare by sending blacks infected with smallpox over enemy lines in an attempt to infect the French and Americans. He then tried an unsuccessful counterattack, and then agreed to surrender. In England, the British Prime Minister, Lord North, subsequently resigned. Those who assumed control of the government concluded that it was not in the best interest of England to continue the war, and entered into the Treaty of Paris recognizing the independence of the U.S. and agreeing to remove all British troops from the country.

Second Wednesday in October

International Day for Natural Disaster Reduction (U.N.)— This day has been observed since 1999, after having been a part of the International Decade for Natural Disaster Reduction (1990–99).

Third Week in October

Clean Water Week (GA)— During this week Georgia focuses on the need to protect its sources of clean water for its residents, while celebrating the popular recreational uses of its lakes, rivers and Atlantic shoreline.

Natural Resources Rangers Corps Week (PR)— Puerto Rico recognizes and acknowledges the efforts of its Rangers Corps in conserving and protecting its rich natural resources, including its parks, beaches and underwater areas.

Puerto Rico Business and Professional Women's Week (PR)— During this week Puerto Rico exalts the contributions of its business women to the personal, family and social welfare of the Puerto Rican people.

Third Full Week in October

Maine Business Women's Week (ME)— During this week the Maine Department of Educational and Cultural Services may make appropriate information available to the people and the schools to honor and recognize the accomplishments of women in business.

Third Sunday in October

I Am an American Day (FL)— This is a day for Floridians to celebrate the benefits of citizenship, and to be reminded of the responsibilities that come with them.

Respect for Our Elders Day (HI)— On this day Hawaiians pay homage to the older residents of the islands, and recognize the contributions they make to society and family life as a result of their wisdom and experience.

Shut-In Day (OR, PA)— Citizens are encouraged to pay special tribute and recognition to their citizens who are confined to their homes, and still continue to live useful lives and contribute so much to the progress of their communities. A National Shut-In day was proclaimed by Pres. Nixon in 1972, and its first chairman was Marian McQuade of West Virginia. She was also one of the main proponents of the establishment of National Grandparents Day. Her goal was to have those who are home-bound be visited and remembered not only at Christmas and perhaps birthdays, but instead to have attention paid to them throughout the year.

Third Wednesday in October Through the Following Saturday

Washington Parish Free Fair (LA)—This annual fair started in 1911 in a livery stable, and is now believed to be the largest county/parish free fair in the U.S. Held in Franklinton, this is a family fair with exhibits of cut flowers, homemaking, livestock and agricultural products. Also on site is the Mile Branch Settlement, an authentic historical pioneer village.

Third Thursday in October

Ohio Mammography Day (OH)—The sponsors of the National Breast Cancer Month estimate that 192,000 cases of breast cancer occur among U.S. women each year. To increase the victims' chances of survival, early detection is strongly encouraged through the use of mammograms. On this day the dangers of cancer, the value of early detection, and the options for treatment are publicized through educational programs and messages disseminated through the media.

Friday and Saturday of the Third Weekend in October

International Rice Festival (LA)—This is Louisiana's oldest Agricultural Festival and one of its largest. Held in downtown Crowley, it focuses attention on the importance of rice as food and its place in the world economic picture. Parades are held on Friday (the Children's Parade on Children's Day) and Saturday (the Grande Parade). Special events include a Livestock Show, Arts and Crafts Exhibit, Rice Cooking Contest, Rice Eating Contest, Farmers Banquet and Queens Ball.

Fourth Friday in October

Frances Willard Day (SC)—South Carolina residents are encouraged to use this day as an opportunity to teach the children of the state about the evils of intemperance. Willard was born in 1838 in Churchville, New York, and came to believe that women could obtain political power through the temperance crusade. She supported women's suffrage, and, after serving as

president of Evanston College, became the president of the Women's Christian Temperance Union, which she allied with the Prohibition Party. She authored *Women and Temperance*, which was published in 1883. Willard died in 1898 and is remembered with a statue located in the U.S. Capitol.

Fourth Saturday in October

Robert Frost Day (MA)—This day is in recognition of Robert Frost's years in Massachusetts. Frost (3/26/1874–1/29/1962) was named after Confederate General Robert E. Lee, and had his first poems published in the Lawrence High School *Bulletin*. He attended Dartmouth and Harvard, but although he did not graduate, he later taught at Amherst College. He received a Pulitzer Prize, a gold medal from the U.S. Congress, and was honored by a U.S. Senate resolution on his 75th birthday. Later he served as an Honorary Consultant in the Humanities at the Library of Congress.

Last Week in October

Quality of Life Week (PR)—This promotes an awakening of the conscience of the community regarding the importance and responsibility we all have of uniting our efforts to improve the expectations and quality of life of our fellow citizens individually, and of Puerto Rico as a whole. During this week, the annual Quality of Life Award is presented to the municipalities that are most outstanding in their efforts to improve their quality of life.

Virgin Islands Taxi Week (VI)—Virgin Islands residents and commercial enterprises are encouraged to join together to give special recognition to the commonwealth's taxi industry.

Last Friday in October

Nevada Day (NV)—This is a commemoration of Nevada's entry into the Union as the 36th state, in 1864, and its frontier legacy. Five years earlier it was an empty place that nobody seemed to want. Following Henry Comstock's discovery of gold in 1859, with his Comstock Lode producing over a billion dollars from silver and gold mining, settlers flocked to Nevada. Within two years it became a territory, and just two years later it was a state. No other part of the

U.S. went from emptiness to statehood in a shorter time.

Saturday of the Last Week in October

Virginia Drug-Free Day (VA)— This is a day to recognize and support education about the dangers of drug abuse, the penalties for drug crimes, the availability of substance abuse programs, and the need to eradicate drug abuse in Virginia's communities.

OBSERVANCES WITH FIXED DATES

October 1

Children and Youth Month (HI)— October in Hawaii is a time to focus on the islands' young people, both as to their accomplishments and as to the social issues which they have to deal with.

Head Injury Awareness Month (MA)— This day is promoted by the Massachusetts Brain Injury Association to educate the public about services, programs and treatments available to those who have suffered head injuries, and efforts to prevent such injuries. The goal is to create a better future through prevention, research, education and advocacy. Areas focused on include motor vehicle safety, alcohol, firearm-related injuries, and the benefits of bicycle helmets.

International Day of Older Persons (U.N.)— This day has been observed by United Nations members since 1990, following up on U.N. initiatives such as the Vienna International Plan of Action on Aging, adopted in 1982.

Italian-American Heritage Month (MA)— This month recognizes the significant contributions Italian-Americans have made to Massachusetts and the U.S. Italian-Americans make up the fifth largest ethnic group in the U.S. This month is an opportunity for them to discover, understand and bond with their families' background, heritage and native language. The state has a variety of methods to promote the appreciation for the contributions of Italians and Italian-Americans, including essay contests for school age children, performances, exhibits, and the publication of biographies about notable Italians and Italian-Americans.

Lupus Awareness Month (MA)— This month of observation is intended to increase public awareness of systemic lupus erythematosus, to encourage early recognition of symptoms and diagnosis. It is a chronic, auto-immune disease affecting various parts of the body, including the heart, lungs, brain, kidneys, joint, blood system and skin, and can take up to seven years to diagnose. Nine out of ten victims are women, but it can strike any person of any age. The immune system fails to distinguish between good and bad, so it attacks everything, resulting in inflammation of what would otherwise be healthy tissue. Untreated lupus can kill. Treatment, if accomplished early enough, results in a 97 percent survival rate; but it varies depending on the portion(s) of the body afflicted.

Month of Mental Health (PR)— This month focuses on the various mental and emotional maladies which affect citizens of Puerto Rico, research being conducted to alleviate them, and options and opportunities for treatment.

National Disability Employment Awareness Month (Fed)— Public support is enlisted for the employment of workers with disabilities, who are otherwise qualified employees. The observance was begun in 1997 at the urging of the Department of Labor to expand the opportunities open to the disabled.

New Jersey Seafood Promotion Month (NJ)— This period celebrates New Jersey as a leader in the nation's commercial and recreational seafood industries, and focuses on the renewable seafood resources supporting a commercial fishing industry worth half a billion dollars, and recreational value of twice that much.

Ohio Breast Cancer Awareness Month (OH)— This month is observed nationally, and the Board of Sponsors of the National Breast Cancer Awareness Month is dedicated to increased awareness of issues dealing with the disease, with a focus on the importance of early detection. It estimates that 192,000 new cases of breast cancer occur each year among the women of the U.S.

Ohio Hepatitis C Awareness Month (OH)— This month focuses on increasing the public's awareness of Hepatitis C as an emerging health concern. The institution of this month of observance was urged by the Ohio hemophilia community, as the incidence of hepatitis C is substantially higher among hemophiliacs. Mortality from hepatitis C is high, and further research into treatment is encouraged.

Polish-American Heritage Month (MA)— This month recognizes the significant contributions Polish-Americans have made to Massachusetts and the U.S. This is a celebration of Polish history, culture and pride, in cooperation with the Polish American Congress and Polonia Across America. Nationally, celebrations are coordinated by a committee headquartered at the Polish American Cultural Center Museum in Philadelphia, Pennsylvania.

Pro-Life Month (MA)— The people of Massachusetts are to consider this a period of special attention to the importance of every stage of human life.

Recycling Day (IL)— Residents of Illinois are encouraged to purchase products made from, or sold in packaging manufactured from, recycled materials. This is a time to educate the public on the benefits of recycling and the location of recycling centers.

October 4

World Space Week (U.N.)— This week was proclaimed by the General Assembly to celebrate the contributions of space science and technology to the betterment of the human condition. The October 4 beginning date commemorates the October 4, 1957, launch of Sputnik I, the first artificial satellite. The October 10 ending date corresponds with the date in 1967 that the Treaty on Principles Governing the Activities of States in the Exploration and Use of Outer Space took effect. This week continues through October 10.

October 5

Raoul Wallenberg Day (NY)— By Spring of 1944, plans were being formulated by Nazi Adolf Eichmann to annihilate the 700,000 Jews remaining in Budapest, Hungary, the last remaining significant Jewish community in Europe. The Germans invaded Hungary on March 19, 1944, and began their deportation to the Auschwitz-Birkenau concentration camp. Swedish businessman Raoul Gustav Wallenberg (August 4, 1912–?) was sent to Budapest to speak on their behalf. He remained there six months and, through the use of bribes, extortion threats and other unconventional negotiation techniques, was responsible for the saving of at least 100,000

Jews. The city was liberated by the Soviet asrmy in January of 1945. The Soviets arrested Wallenberg and he was never heard from again. The Soviets claim he died in captivity in 1947, but many believe that he may still be alive. He was made an honorary U.S. citizen in 1981.

Rothschild Francis Day (VI)— After World War I the reason for the U.S. acquisition of the Virgin Islands had passed, in that there was no more German threat to U.S. interests in the Caribbean. Administration of the islands was under the Department of the Navy, which made little change to the preexisting governmental structure. During the "Naval Regime," from 1917 to 1931, hospitals and roads were built, and improvements were made in the areas of education and sanitation. During that time there was a strong movement toward self-government, breaking from Naval administration with carried-over Danish laws. With Rothschild Francis and others as proponents of greater civil liberties and a change in administration, U.S. citizenship was granted in 1927, administration of the islands was shifted to the Department of the Interior in 1931, and self-government was granted by the U.S. Congress in 1936.

World Teachers' Day (U.N.)— On this day teachers around the world resolve to work toward the goal of a quality education for all to promote a culture of peace. The world pays homage to the role of teachers in expanding the learner's horizons in the new knowledge society of the 21st century.

October 6

German-American Day (CT)— This honors Americans of German ancestry, their culture and the great contributions they have made to this country. The date of October 6 is significant because it is on that date in 1683 when 13 Mennonite families from Krefeld, Germany, disembarked from the *Concord* (also known as the "German Mayflower") in Philadelphia. They founded the town of Germantown. They were the first group of German immigrants to the U.S., and over the next 300 years they would be followed by more than seven million more, making German-Americans the largest ethnic group in the nation. As of 1990, the U.S. Census reported that one-fourth of all Americans reported German ancestry.

Italian-American History and Heritage Week (NJ) — This celebrates the heritage of Italy, including the classic civilization of Rome, the fine arts of the Renaissance, the scientific and artistic genius of Leonardo da Vinci, the literary works of Dante and Petrarch, the opera of Verdi and Puccini, and many other contributions that have enriched today's civilization. Over two million New Jerseyans are of Italian descent (as of the 1990 census). The week always ends on October 12, the original designation of Columbus Day.

October 8

Mighty Eighth Air Force Week (MN) — This celebration honors the largest military unit to serve in World War II. Its members showed heroism during the week of October 8–14, 1943, during events which served as a turning point for daytime strategic bombing. The Mighty Eighth had 26,000 troops killed in action, had over 28,000 captured as prisoners of war, had uncounted numbers missing in action, and had over 100 heavy bombers lost in action. The celebration continues through October 14.

Town Meeting Day (MA) — This commemorates the holding of the first town meeting in Massachusetts.

William A. Egan Day (AK) — This day honors William "Bill" Allen Egan, the first governor of the State of Alaska, for his lifetime of service to the territory and state. Born in Valdez, Alaska, on October 8, 1914, he served in the territorial Senate and the House of Representatives (and was its Speaker), served as the mayor of Valdez, and was a delegate to the state constitutional convention. He was the governor from 1959 to 1966 and from 1970 to 1974. Egan died on May 6, 1984. He was honored by having the University of Alaska library in Juneau named after him. In Anchorage the Civic & Convention Center, blending Alaskan hospitality, Native Alaskan art and modern technology, is also named after Egan.

October 9

Leif Erikson Day (Fed) [**Leif Ericson Day** (MA), **Leif Erickson Day** (CO)] — This commemorates the Scandinavian peoples and their culture and the great contribution they have made to this country in the past, and which they continue to make; it is also a tribute to the gallant explorations of the Vikings. Specific attention is shown to Leif Erikson, the Norse explorer who ventured across unchartered waters in about 1003 to North America, and whose stories are recorded in the Icelandic sagas. He was commissioned by King Olaf I to convert the Greenland Vikings to Christianity, and may have been blown off course, arriving on the North American mainland. Another story holds that he purposely set out from Greenland and wintered at Vinland, between Virginia and Nova Scotia. This date was chosen in 1964 because the first organized body of Norwegian settlers arrived in the U.S. on October 9, 1825, and also because it is shortly before Columbus Day.

World Post Day (U.N.) — This day marks the anniversary of the Universal Postal Union, established in 1874 to promote world communication through international mail.

October 10

Oklahoma Historical Day (OK) — This is celebrated to remember the first settlement of whites in the Oklahoma Territory in 1802. The date is chosen because it is the anniversary of the birth of Pierre Chouteau of St. Louis in 1758. He is known as the "Father of Oklahoma," and his 1802 trading post constituted the first permanent white settlement in the territory. The settlement was located on the east bank of the Grand River where the present city of Salina is located, and afforded trading opportunities with the Osage tribe.

Republic of China on Taiwan-American Day (CT) — This honors Americans of Chinese-Taiwanese ancestry, their culture and the great contribution they have made to this country. On Taiwan this day is celebrated as National Day (also called Double Tenth Day) to commemorate the proclamation of the Republic in 1912. The Chinese Revolution began the same date in 1911 with a revolt of military officers in Hankow.

World Mental Health Day (U.N.) — The aim of this day is to promote and raise awareness of the function of mental health. As defined by the World Health Authority, "health" is a state of complete physical, mental and social well-being, and not merely the absence of disease or infirmity. The WHA feels that the enjoyment of the highest attainable standard of health is one of the fundamental rights of every human being, without distinction of race, religion, political belief, or economic or social condition.

October 11

General Pulaski Memorial Day (OH, PR) [**General Pulaski's Day** (KY), **General Pulaski's Memorial Day** (KS, SC), **Anniversary of Death of General Pulaski** (MA), **Casimir Pulaski Day** (MI), **General Casimir Pulaski Day** (RI), **Pulaski's Memorial Day** (NE)]—This is a commemoration of the 1779 death of Gen. Pulaski, hero of the American Revolution. After being placed in command of the cavalry of the American forces, he successfully liberated Charleston, South Carolina, from a British siege. From there he went to Savannah, Georgia, for a joint military operation with French allies. Against Pulaski's advice, the commander of the French forces ordered an assault at the strongest point of the British position on October 9, 1779. Pulaski saw this failing, and charged into the battle to rally the troops. He was struck by cannon fire and died from his wounds two days later, on October 11.

New Netherland Day in the State of New York (NY)—This day commemorates the chartering of the New Netherlands Company to settle what is now New York, on October 11, 1614.

October 12

Columbus Day (AR, OR, WA)—On August 2 or 3, 1492, Christopher Columbus and 90 men left Palos, Spain, in three ships—the *Santa Maria*, the *Nina*, and the *Pinta*. He stopped at the Canary Islands for supplies and repairs on September 6, and sighted land in what is now the Bahamas on October 12. On October 28 he discovered Cuba and claimed it for Spain. He spent about eight more months exploring and returning to Spain. The *Santa Maria* was wrecked in a storm on Christmas Day, and the *Nina* became the new flagship for the remainder of the trip home to report to his benefactors, King Ferdinand and Queen Isabella of Spain.

Washington State Children's Day (WA)—This is a time to focus on education, drug abuse, and other issues affecting the children of Washington and the U.S.

October 13

Commemoration of Anniversary of Founding of the U.S. Navy (NH)—On this date in 1775 the Continental Congress in Philadelphia voted to fit out two sailing vessels with ten carriage guns and swivel guns, and carry crews of 80 each. They were to cruise for three months in an attempt to intercept transports bringing munitions and supplies to the British army in North America. Congress soon established a Naval Committee to equip a fleet, draft naval legislation, and establish rules and regulations to govern the conduct of the Continental Navy. During the Revolutionary War the navy sent out more than fifty armed ships, and took nearly two hundred British vessels as prizes.

Day of the Retired Educator (PR)—This is the time to celebrate the lifetimes of service to youth which have been dedicated by teachers, school principals, and other personnel within the educational system of Puerto Rico.

October 14

Bird Day (GA)—The first bird day was observed on May 4, 1894, upon the suggestion of Charles A. Babcock, the superintendent of schools in Oil City, Pennsylvania. In many parts of the U.S. this observance is combined with Arbor Day.

Dwight D. Eisenhower Day (KS)—This is a special tribute to his life and legacy. He was born in Denison, Texas, on this date in 1890, and a year later the family moved back to Kansas. He graduated from West Point in 1915 and served stateside during World War I. He worked his way up through the ranks, and after serving during World War II in Europe and North Africa, was appointed as the Supreme Commander of the Allied Expeditionary Force on December 24, 1943. After the war he retired from the army and served as president of Columbia University, then in 1950 became the commander of NATO forces in Europe. He served as the 34th President of the U.S. from 1953 to 1961. Eisenhower died on March 28, 1969, and was buried in Abilene, Kansas, near his childhood home.

October 15

Poetry Day (ME, MD)—This is a commemoration of the cultural and human values of poetry and poetic expression. On this day the citizens of Maine give recognition to the poets who have helped or who are helping to make Maine famous in the field of poetry throughout the world. Cultural, educational, patriotic and religious organizations are urged to participate in the commemoration. This day is also observed around the world as World Poetry Day.

White Cane Safety Day (Fed, AR, IA, MA, RI) [**White Cane Day** (PR)] — Especially on this day, citizens are called upon to take precautions necessary for the safety of the visually handicapped, hearing impaired, and other physically handicapped persons.

World Rural Women's Day (PR) — This day has been chosen to recognize rural women both in Puerto Rico and the rest of the world.

October 16

World Food Day (U.N.) — This observance was proclaimed in 1979 by the Conference of the FAO of the United Nations. Its goal is to heighten public awareness of the world food problem and to strengthen solidarity in the struggle against hunger, malnutrition and poverty. October 16 was chosen, as it was the day of the founding of the FAO in 1945.

October 17

International Day for the Eradication of Poverty (U.N.) — Celebrated since 1992, this day has as its focus the promotion of awareness of the need to eradicate poverty and destitution in all countries, particularly in the developing ones.

School Lunchroom Employee Day (PR) — Attention is brought on this day to the role lunchroom employees play in providing nutritious meals to children in public and private schools.

October 18

Alaska Day (AK) — After 68 years of Russian rule in Sitka, Alaska, the Russian flag at the governor's house was lowered on October 18, 1867, and replaced with a U.S. flag. Two years before, the transcontinental telegraph line reached Sitka, and old expansionist dreams were rekindled. The U.S. purchased the territory for 7.2 million dollars, releasing the Russians from the costly maintenance of a foothold in the Western Hemisphere. Little happened to interest the residents of the rest of the U.S. until gold was discovered in the Klondike in 1897.

October 19

National Forest Products Week (Fed) — This is a time to celebrate the many products that come from our forests, including lumber for furniture and housing, paper, wood for pencils and toys, cellulose for plastic and chemicals, clean water and air, and many others. The natural resources which comprise the forests are reusable, recyclable and biodegradable, and require less energy to produce than many other materials. National Forest Products Week was established by Congress in 1960 to recognize these products, and to honor the industry which produces them.

Yorktown Day (VA) — In late September of 1781 the British General pleaded for troop reinforcements and considered ferrying his men to safety away from the battlefield of Yorktown. The reinforcements did not arrive, the troops remained, and the French and Americans began a long, continuous bombardment of the British position. A night attack was led by Lt. Col. Alexander Hamilton, and Gen. Cornwallis came to the realization that there was little hope left. On October 19, 1781, Cornwallis surrendered to Gen. Benjamin Lincoln, second in command to George Washington, after they unsuccessfully tried to surrender to the French. This essentially ended the Revolutionary War, which officially ended with the signing of a peace treaty on September 3, 1783.

October 22

Day of Recognition for Early Childhood and Day-Care Providers and Professionals (VA) — This is the time for the people of Virginia to recognize and appreciate the important services provided to their children by those who take care of them when parents are elsewhere.

October 23

Hungarian Freedom Fighters Day (CT) — This commemorates the bravery of the Hungarian freedom fighters during the Hungarian Revolution of 1956. On October 23 of that year, students held demonstrations in front of a Budapest statue of General Bern, and demanded reforms, democracy and the return of Premier Imre Nagy. Police reacted with tear gas, beatings and arrests. The crowd tried to free those who had been arrested, and the police opened fire. The demonstration turned into a street riot and revolution, and the government called in Soviet soldiers, tanks and jets. Fighting broke out in other parts of the country, with "freedom fighters" taking over weapons depots, factories and some of the Soviet tanks. Radio Free Europe and Voice of America encouraged the Hungarians to fight, which they did, and the troops pulled back. Nagy and one of his generals were invited by the Soviets to negotiate peace, and although they came under a flag of truce, the Soviets arrested and executed them. Fighting ceased on November 4, but freedom fighters never totally gave up. They finally succeeded by having all Soviet troops removed in 1989.

October 24

Birthday of William Penn (PA) — This day celebrates the great founder, proprietor and governor of Pennsylvania. Penn was born on October 24, 1644, in London, and while attending school at Oxford converted to be a Quaker. When his father sent him to Ireland in 1666 to oversee the family estates in County Cork, William was imprisoned because his religious convictions brought him into conflict with local authorities. After he returned to England, he wrote a religious tract, *The Sandy Foundation Shaken*, but since it was published without a license, he was imprisoned in the Tower of London. While there, he wrote *Innocency with Her Open Eyes* in 1669, and during another period of imprisonment in 1671 he wrote *The Great Case of Liberty of Conscience*. In 1681, in payment for a debt owed his father, he obtained a grant of territory in North America and sailed there the following year. He planned and named Philadelphia, and governed the colony for two years. He returned to England to aid persecuted Quakers, and was twice accused of treason and corresponding with the exiled king. He made a second trip to Pennsylvania in 1699 to suppress piracy and issue the Charter of Privileges, guaranteeing religious freedom. He left for England in 1701, leaving an agent who wound up nearly ruining Penn's interests. Penn was crippled by a stroke in 1712 and died on July 30, 1718.

Day of Remembrance of Rafael Hernandez (PR) — Rafael Hernandez Colon was born in Ponce, Puerto Rico, on October 24, 1936, and attended Johns Hopkins University and the University of Puerto Rico Law School. After practicing law, he served as president of the Senate and president of the Popular Democratic Party. In 1972 he was elected as the island's youngest governor. He sponsored programs of housing construction and economic development, and opposed making Puerto Rico the 51st state. He was reelected as governor in 1984 and 1988.

Disarmament Week (U.N.) — Celebrated on the anniversary of the founding of the United Nations, it is a time for member nations to highlight the danger of the arms race, propagate the need for its cessation, and increase public understanding of the urgent tasks of disarmament. When the week of observance was established, the United Nations Secretary-General was invited to continue using the U.N. information entities as widely as possible to promote a better understanding among the public of disarmament problems and the aims of this week.

United Nations Day (MA, U.N.) — This celebrates the effective date of the United Nations Charter on October 24, 1945. Earlier that year, representatives of more than 50 nations began meeting in San Francisco to finalize the Charter, and on October 24 a sufficient number of ratifications had been obtained to officially consider the United Nations to be in existence. Throughout the world in the 189 member nations, this day has been observed since 1947 by meetings, conferences and exhibits on the achievements and goals of the U.N. In the U.S. the President annually issues a proclamation asking citizens to observe United Nations Day, but it is not officially made a day of observance in the U.S. Code. Present observance in this country usually involves focus on world issues on the U.N. agenda which affect every American citizen.

World Development Information Day (U.N.) — This day was established in 1972 to draw the attention of world public opinion to development problems and the need to strengthen international cooperation to solve them. It was felt by the United Nations General Assembly that improving the dissemination of information and the mobilization of public opinion, particularly among young people, would lead to greater awareness of the problems of development, thus promoting efforts in the sphere of international cooperation for development.

October 25

State Constitution Day (MA)—This is the anniversary of the October 25, 1780, adoption of the constitution of Massachusetts. It is to be a constant reminder of the courage and wisdom of our forefathers who, having won their independence, secured their liberty by establishing on a new foundation a government of law and order, and who did their work so well that the constitution is the oldest written constitution in operation.

October 26

Statue of Liberty Awareness Day (MA)—The celebration for this day focuses on elementary school students. The Statue of Liberty was formally presented to the U.S. on July 4, 1884. The cornerstone of the base was laid on August 5 of the same year, and the official dedication was proclaimed on October 28, 1886, by President Grover Cleveland.

October 27

Ramon Power y Giralt Day (PR)—This day honors Don Ramon Power y Giralt, born in San Juan in 1775. In 1809 he was elected as Puerto Rico's first representative to the parliament of Spain. His birthplace in San Juan has been restored as the headquarters of the Puerto Rico Conservation Trust.

Theodore Roosevelt Day (NY)—Roosevelt was born on this date in 1858. During the Spanish-American War he commanded the First U.S. Volunteers Cavalry, known as the "Rough Riders," in Cuba, becoming a national hero. He served as the 26th President of the U.S., pursuing the preservation of wilderness areas and the passage of anti-trust legislation. In 1905 he was awarded the Nobel Peace Prize for his part in the negotiation of the end of the Russo-Japanese War. He died on January 6, 1919.

October 31

Youth Honor Day (IA, MA)—This recognizes and honors the outstanding achievements of youthful citizens, and reminds them to prepare for their responsibilities and obligations as the future leaders of the states and nation.

NOVEMBER

OBSERVANCES WITH VARIABLE DATES

First Sunday in November

Family Sunday (WI)—Wisconsin families are encouraged on this day to spend time together, engage in discussions of issues facing families today, and strengthen their own family bonds.

New Jersey Retired Teachers Day (NJ)—This day has been set aside in grateful recognition of the instruction and guidance teachers have provided, and the example they have set for the youth of New Jersey. The retired teachers of the state chose what should be recognized as the most important profession in the world.

First Tuesday Following the First Monday in November

Election Day (AZ, GU, IN, NH, NJ, NC, OH, OK, PA, RI, WV) [**General Election Day** (DE, FL, IL, MT, WI), **Presidential Election Day** (KY), **General State Election Day** (MO)]—On this day ballots are cast for national, state and/or local public offices. Although this occurs throughout the country, election day is officially designated as a holiday or special day in a minority of the jurisdictions.

First Wednesday in November

Parade Day (FL)—A holiday in Hillsborough County, this opens the annual Hillsborough County Fair in Tampa.

Second Day Following General Election Day

Return Day (DE)—Although modern methods of vote-counting have rendered the determination of winners nearly instantaneous, this day is still observed as the time when voting results are officially announced.

First Friday in November

Arbor Day (HI)—The people of Hawaii are encouraged on this date to plant shrubs and trees, including the state tree, the kukui.

Second Week in November

American Education Week (DE, MA)—Each year there is a national theme to direct the public's attention toward an important aspect of education and opportunities to reach out to communities and neighborhood schools. This week of observance was established during the 1920s to eliminate illiteracy among World War I draftees and to generate public support for education.

Geographic Education Awareness Week (MA)—This celebration focuses attention on the need for citizens of the commonwealth to further their knowledge of geographic matters. It is sponsored by the Massachusetts Geographic Alliance, a grassroots organization of more than 3,000

Massachusetts teachers, and is dedicated to improving geography education.

Massachusetts Hospice Week (MA)—This is a time to recognize and appreciate hospice workers, who are committed to the dignity of human life and compassion, particularly in times of great crises.

Week of the Historian (PR)—This week recognizes and appreciates the work performed by those who chronicle the history of Puerto Rico.

Wednesday During the Week of the Historian

Day of the Historian (PR)—Coming in the middle of the Week of the Historian, further emphasis is placed on the historians of Puerto Rico.

Week Including November 11

Veterans' Week (ME)—This is a time to recognize and thank all military veterans for their service to the cause of freedom.

Last School Day Before Veteran's Day

Korean War Veteran's Day (IL)—Illinois has done more than most states to honor the veterans of the Korean War, known as the "Forgotten War." On June 16, 1996, the Illinois Korean War Memorial was dedicated at Springfield's Oak Ridge Cemetery. It is a four-ton bronze sculpture designed by Prof. Robert Youngman of the University of Illinois. It is bell-shaped, with four niches for figures representing four branches of the U.S. Armed Forces. On it are inscribed the names of the 1,743 Illinois residents who died in the war. Also in Illinois is the Korean War Veterans National Museum and Library, located in Tuscola.

Second Saturday in November

Veterans' Recognition Day and **Vietnam War Memorial Dedication Day** (VA)—On November 9, 1984, the statue *Three Servicemen* was unveiled as the final portion of the Vietnam Veterans Memorial in Washington, DC. This day was proclaimed in Virginia to honor the 2.7 million American soldiers, sailors, airmen and marines who served in Vietnam, especially the 300,000 wounded, 75,000 permanently disabled, and 1,300 who remain missing. Of the veterans who came home, more than 600,000 lived in Virginia when the proclamation was made in 1999.

Week Including November 16

Oklahoma Heritage Week (OK)—The coordinating and planning agency for celebrations this week is the Oklahoma Heritage Association. It is a time to celebrate the accomplishments of its famous citizens, including Olympian Jim Thorpe, "Cherokee Cowboy" Will Rogers, African-American author Ralph Ellison, jazz musician Charlie Christian, astronaut Thomas Stafford, and country music stars Vince Gill, Reba McEntire and Garth Brooks.

Third Week in November

Historical Archives Week (PR)—This celebrates the work of historical archivists and the importance of original historical records of all kinds as keys to Puerto Rico's cultural heritage.

Sunday Commencing the Third Week in November

Retired Teachers' Day (FL)—Events on this day, under the supervision of the Florida Retired Educators Association, which was established in 1954, honor the state's retired teachers. The organization, which also accepts active educators and other school personnel, has approximately 12,000 members and is affiliated with the National Retired Teachers Association.

Third Monday in November

Oklahoma Native American Day (OK)—This is a day to celebrate the Native Americans who lived, and who continue to live, in Oklahoma. When the first white men arrived, already present were Caddo, Wichita, Quapaw, Osage, Comanche and Ute. After it was formally designated as Indian Territory in 1830, tribes from many regions were relocated there, including Cherokee, Creek (Muskogee), Chickasaw and Choctaw.

Third Wednesday in November Through the Following Friday

Silver-Haired Legislature Days (MA)—Silver-haired legislatures are groups of volunteer citizens aged 60 or older who are elected by their peers. They represent the interests of older residents of their state. They are modeled after the respective state legislatures, and communicate their legislative priorities to the governor and state legislature.

Friday of Historical Archives Week

Historical Archivist's Day (PR)—On this day those in Puerto Rico who endeavor to preserve, restore and index historical records are celebrated. It is recognized that our connection to the past is enhanced by accurate and accessible historical records.

Week Beginning with the Last Sunday Before Thanksgiving Day

Native Heritage Week (WV)—This is a time to celebrate the history and culture of Native Americans in West Virginia, and their contributions to the welfare of the state and the U.S.

Wednesday Before Thanksgiving Day

Day of Appreciation for American Indians (VA)—This day commemorates the special place the tribes native to Virginia have in the life and history of the commonwealth. It is a time to celebrate the working relationship between the early settlers and the indigenous people which has, since 1607, provided stability, education and support for the founding of Virginia.

Fourth Thursday in November

Thanksgiving Day (Fed, AK, AZ, AR, CA, DE, DC, FL, GA, GU, HI, ID, IL, IN, IA, KS, LA, MD, MI, MN, MS, MO, MT, NE, NV, NH, NJ, NM, NY, NC, ND, CM, OH, OK, OR, PA, PR, RI, SC, SD, TN, TX, VI, UT, VT, VA, WA, WV, WI, WY) [**Thanksgiving** (AS)]—Pilgrims who had migrated to Massachusetts first celebrated Thanksgiving in 1621 to give thanks for their harvesting a good crop in their first year

there. It was officially celebrated in Massachusetts for the first time in 1631, and was first officially proclaimed by Pres. Lincoln, who set the date as the last Thursday in November. In 1939 it was changed to the fourth Thursday of the month.

Friday Following Thanksgiving Day

Acadian Day (LA)—This commemorates the arrival in Louisiana of the Acadian people from the French colony Acadie following the ceding of that colony to England in 1713. It also recognizes the fact that much of the early economic and political development of Louisiana is directly attributable to the industry of the Acadian people, through cultivation of land, utilization of Louisiana's natural resources, and the interest of the Acadian people in political self-determination and American democracy.

Day After Thanksgiving Day (IA, MD, NE, SC, TX, VA, WA)—In Iowa this is a day for state employees to have a day off, with pay. It is a school holiday in Maryland. This is an opportunity to turn a one-day holiday into a four-day weekend.

Family Day (NV)—This is a day to celebrate the families of Nevada, and the positive influence a family has on its children.

Sunday Following Thanksgiving Day

Family Day (KS)—This is a day for the people of Kansas to celebrate the benefits of raising children in a family situation, and focus on the problems which families must face.

Last Sunday in November

John F. Kennedy Day (MA)—This is in memory of John Fitzgerald Kennedy, the 35th president of the U.S. He is remembered at the Kennedy Library and Museum, located at Columbia Point on the Dorchester waterfront in Boston. Designed by I.M. Pei, the museum includes a multimedia show, campaign posters, personal items (including the family Bible), and exhibits involving important events, such as the Cuban Missile Crisis, the space program, and his assassination. There are also displays concerning his brother, Robert F. Kennedy, who served as John's attorney general.

OBSERVANCES WITH FIXED DATES

November 1

All Saints' Day (LA)— This day is celebrated to honor all saints, known and unknown, and, according to Pope Urban IV, to supply any deficiencies in the celebration of any saints' feast days during the year. The date of November 1 was fixed by Pope Gregory III (731–741), who consecrated a chapel in the Basilica of St. Peter in Rome to all the saints.

Alzheimer's Disease Awareness Month (NJ)— This period calls attention to the fourth leading cause of death in the U.S., affecting between two and four million Americans between the ages of 40 and 80, including about 400,000 residents of New Jersey.

American Indian Month (VA)— This month honors the culture and heritage of the American Indian, and recognizes the historic and continuing contribution of that heritage to American society.

D. Hamilton Jackson Day (VI)— After World War I the reason for the U.S. acquisition had passed, in that there was no more German threat to U.S. interests in the Caribbean. Administration of the islands was under the Department of the Navy, which made little change to the preexisting governmental structure. During the "Naval Regime" from 1917 to 1931, hospitals and roads were built, and improvements were made in the areas of education and sanitation. During that time there was a strong movement toward self-government, breaking from Naval administration with carried-over Danish laws. With D. Hamilton Jackson and others as proponents of greater civil liberties and a change in administration, U.S. citizenship was granted in 1927, administration of the islands was shifted to the Department of the Interior in 1931, and self-government was granted by the U.S. Congress in 1936.

Day of Peace (PR)— This is the time to make evident the importance of peace in achieving the progress and material and spiritual well-being of all people.

Month of Musical Arts (PR)— This is a month-long celebration of composers, conductors and musical performers of Puerto Rico.

Native American Indian Month (KY)— This is a time to recognize the contributions of Native American Indians with suitable ceremony and fellowship designed to promote greater understanding and brotherhood between Native American Indians and the non–Native American people of Kentucky.

Wisconsin Family Month and **Wisconsin Family Week** (WI)— These times focus attention on the principles of family responsibility to spouses, children and parents, as well as on the importance of the stability of marriage and the home for our future well-being.

November 2

All Soul's Day (GU)— This was begun as a Christian adaptation of a pagan festival for the dead. It was a day of intercession for deceased souls which had not yet been sufficiently purified, based on the belief that they could be aided by the prayers of the living. Beginning as a memorial during the 10th century, it was later abolished by the Church of England, although it continues to be celebrated informally by many Protestants.

South Dakota Statehood Day (SD)— This is a celebration of the anniversary of South Dakota's admittance into the Union as the 40th state on November 2, 1889. North Dakota became the 39th state on the same day. Both became part of the U.S. through the Louisiana Purchase in 1803, and were partially explored by Lewis and Clark. The area became the Dakota Territory in 1861, but did not show much growth in population until gold was discovered in the Black Hills in 1874.

November 3

Father of Texas Day (TX)— This day is in memory of Stephen Fuller Austin, a great pioneer and the real and true father of Texas. He was born on November 3, 1793, and moved to Texas shortly after Mexico granted his father a large parcel of land. His father died shortly thereafter, and Stephen remained. Many other pioneers were heading to Texas, having no allegiance to Mexico, and relations between the two countries were straining. In 1833 Austin went to Mexico to plead for reform, and they imprisoned him for nearly two years. After his release, Austin became active in the Texas Revolution against Mexican dictator

Antonio Lopez de Santa Anna. Austin died on December 27, 1836. The capital city of Texas is named for him.

November 4

Citizenship Day (CM) — This day commemorates the granting of U.S. citizenship to qualified residents of the Northern Mariana Islands on November 4, 1986. Earlier that same year the United Nations Trusteeship Council concluded that the U.S. had satisfactorily discharged its obligations to the islands, having been appointed to administer the Northern Marianas as a trust territory in July of 1947.

Will Rogers Day (OK) — William Penn Adair Rogers was born on this date in 1879 near Oologah, Oklahoma, and had an international reputation for his satirical observations and wry wit. Part Cherokee, he was known as the "Indian Cowboy," starred in wild west shows and vaudeville, and then went into movies. He starred in silent films and talkies, and in 1934 was voted the most popular male actor in Hollywood. His political commentary carried a lot of weight with voters and politicians, and he served as the mayor of Beverly Hills and helped get Franklin Roosevelt elected for his first term as president. He was killed, with Wiley Post, in a plane crash near Point Barrow, Alaska, on August 15, 1935. He claimed that he "never met a man he didn't like" and that his "ancestors didn't come over in the *Mayflower*— they met the boat."

November 9

Kristallnacht Memorial Night (NJ) — On this night in 1936, organized gangs of Nazi Gestapo agents instigated a horrible wave of wanton destruction aimed at Jews, Jewish synagogues, homes and shops throughout Germany. "The Night of Broken Glass" resulted in 199 burned synagogues, 76 of which were completely destroyed. Destroyed or looted were 7,500 shops and homes. At least 36 Jews were killed, and the same number were seriously injured. The gangs rounded up 20,000 "for their own protection" and sent them to Dachau, Oranienburg-Sachenhausen and Buchenwald. Every room and office in each state building within the New Jersey Capitol Complex remains lit for the entire night as a remembrance of the terrible events and a symbol of hope that humanity will finally unite and put an end to genocide.

Pedrin Zorilla Memorial Day (PR) — Zorilla was a scout for the Brooklyn Dodgers baseball team and also owned the Santurce Crabbers, a team in a league in Puerto Rico. At the suggestion of his friend, Roberto Marin, Zorilla observed a young man playing for the Juncos, an amateur baseball team at the AA level. That boy was Roberto Clemente, who Zorilla signed for the Crabbers at the age of 18 in 1952 for a $400 bonus and a salary of $40 per week. Within a year Clemente was approached by nine professional teams, and he signed with the Dodgers, who assigned him to a farm team in Montreal. He was later drafted by the Pittsburgh Pirates, and there he became a star, enshrined in the Baseball Hall of Fame in 1973, the year following his death in a plane crash while taking provisions to Nicaragua after a devastating earthquake.

Witness for Tolerance Day (NY) — In 2000 this day of observance was established for the purpose of encouraging communities to join together to stand up to hate and violence against minority groups. The date of November 9 was chosen because it was on that date in 1938 that Nazi Gestapo agents carried out a wave of destruction and violence aimed at German Jews, called "Kristallnacht" and "The Night of Broken Glass." This day is intended to remind society that the hate and violence that resulted in Kristallnacht and the Holocaust must not continue today.

Women Veterans Day (AK) — This commemorates the sacrifices endured and valor displayed by American women veterans, and recognizes their increasing role in the military.

November 10

United States Marine Corps Day (MA) — This is the anniversary of the founding of the United States Marine Corps by the Continental Congress in 1775. The day is in recognition of the distinguished patriotic services rendered by that branch, and by the citizens of Massachusetts who have gallantly served. On this date in 1954 the Marine Memorial, based on a photograph of the raising of a flag on Iwo Jima during World War II, was dedicated in Arlington, Virginia.

Veterans Educate Today's Students (V.E.T.S.) Day (OH) — On this day elementary and secondary schools are encouraged to invite veterans to visit the schools and discuss their military experiences with the students.

November 11

Armistice Day (MA, MS, NJ, NM) — This day is in honor of the service and sacrifice of those sons and daughters of Massachusetts who served in the armed forces of the U.S. during World War I, and in thanksgiving for the termination of hostilities at 11:00 A.M. on Armistice Day, November 11, 1918. Armistice day became a holiday in 1926, and an official national observance in 1938. The name was changed on June 1, 1954, to honor all U.S. veterans.

Oklahoma Week (OK) — This time is so designated to let the world know that "we are proud of Oklahoma, and prouder to be Oklahomans." It extends through November 16.

Veterans' Day (Fed, AL, AK, AZ, AR, CO, CT, DE, DC, FL, GA, HI, KS, LA, ME, MD, MI, MS, MO, MT, NV, NJ, NM, NY, ND, OH, OK, PA, SC, SD, TN, VT, WA, WV, WI) [**Veteran's Day** (DC, GU, CM, RI), **Veterans Day** (AS, CA, ID, IL, IN, IA, KY, MA, MN, NE, NH, NC, OR, PR, TX, VI, UT, VA, WY)] — The date for this holiday was changed to the fourth Monday in October in 1970, but soon it became apparent that the date of November 11 had historic and sentimental significance, so in 1978 Congress changed it back to its previous date. On this date in 1921 the Tomb of the Unknown Soldier was dedicated at Arlington National Cemetery, following a tradition started earlier at Westminster Abbey in London and beneath the Arc de Triomphe in Paris. Initially holding the remains of a World War I veteran, in 1958 two more unidentified American veterans were added, one from each of World War II and the Korean War. As of 1973, it was authorized to have a veteran from the Vietnam War buried there, but it took until 1984 to find one that was unknown. With the development of DNA testing, those remains were identified in 1998, and he was disinterred and reburied by his family in St. Louis, Missouri.

November 13

Coal Miners Day (IL) — This honors and remembers the coal miners of Illinois who have given their lives while laboring in the mines for the welfare of their families and the prosperity of the state.

November 15

Kentucky Harvest Day (KY) — This commemorative day, to spotlight the agricultural industries of Kentucky, was established by the state legislature in 1998.

November 16

International Day for Tolerance (U.N.) — This day was established by the United Nations General Assembly after 1995 had been observed as the United Nations Year for Tolerance.

Oklahoma State Flag Day (OK) — The first Oklahoma state flag, which served the state from 1911 to 1925, had a white star edged in blue in the center of a field of red. Then a contest was held to design a flag which represented the diversity of cultures present in the state, and Mrs. George Fluke, Jr. submitted one which was adopted in 1925 and is essentially the same as the one used today. It bears the image of an Osage warrior's shield made from buffalo hide, decorated with seven eagle feathers, all on a field of sky blue. It honors more than 60 groups of Native Americans present in Oklahoma, and their ancestors. It also has six white crosses representing high ideals, and a peace pipe and olive branch, as symbols of peace and unity. In 1941 the name of the state was added beneath the shield.

Oklahoma Statehood Day (OK) — On this date in 1907 Oklahoma was admitted to the Union as the 46th state. After the discovery of oil, it became known as the place to go to strike it rich, and fortune seekers came from all parts of the world.

November 17

Day to Commemorate the Birth of Don Miguel Angel Garcia (PR) — In 1956 the Partido Estadista Republicano chose Garcia as its leader to serve with Luis Alberto Ferre. While Ferre had the charisma to attract votes, Garcia was chosen to handle the party's organizational, legislative and administrative activities. Garcia was considered to be a brilliant orator and served for a time as Speaker of the Puerto Rican House of Representatives.

November 19

Discovery of Puerto Rico Day (PR)— This commemorates the discovery of the island by Christopher Columbus on his second voyage in 1493. He began his voyage in Cadiz, Spain, on September 25, 1493, and made the crossing in 17 ships, carrying almost 1,500 men. They arrived at the island on November 19 and found a population of Taino Indians, who showed him gold nuggets in the river and invited him to take all he wanted. Columbus named the island San Juan, and the first effort to colonize it began in 1508.

November 20

Africa Industrialization Day (U.N.)— Since 1989, this day has been observed by the members of the United Nations, with the goal of mobilizing the commitment of the international community to the industrialization of Africa. It is an opportunity to recognize the tireless efforts of African governments and societies to create sustainable development and improved living conditions. The celebration calls for further concerted efforts at national, regional and international levels to transform the continent's natural resources into processed goods and to raise the overall growth rate of manufacturing value added.

Bill of Rights Day in New Jersey (NJ)— This day recognizes and heightens awareness of the importance of the Bill of Rights to the people of New Jersey and the U.S.

Time for Survivors of Homicide Victims Awareness (MA)— During this time the families and friends who have been killed are recognized and comforted. It lasts from November 20 through December 20.

Universal Children's Day (U.N.)— This is observed as a day of worldwide fraternity and understanding between children, and of activity promoting the welfare of the world's children. This day is the anniversary of the adoption of the 1959 Declaration of the Rights of the Child and the 1989 Convention on the Rights of the Child. An important goal of the day is to increase awareness of the Convention, recognizing the rights of

children and youth under the age of 18 and their basic human rights, and providing them with additional rights to protect them from harm. The Convention has been signed or ratified by more countries than any other international treaty, and is a valuable tool for promoting children's rights around the world.

November 21

World Television Day (U.N.)— Proclaimed in 1996, this commemorates the date in that year that the World Television Forum was held at the United Nations. Member nations are invited to encourage global exchanges of television programs focusing on issues such as peace, security, economic and social development, and the enhancement of cultural exchanges.

November 23

Virgin Islands Freedom Fighters Day (VI)— This is a commemoration of an African slave revolt which took place on the island of St. John. On the morning of November 23, 1733, a group of slaves killed the guard at the gate of the fort in Coral Bay, then killed six of the seven other soldiers who were sleeping inside the fort. Upon the firing of the fort's cannon as a signal, slaves throughout the island ransacked houses, set fire to cane fields and murdered their white masters and overseers. The one soldier who had escaped from the fort was able to alert other soldiers on St. Thomas, who tried unsuccessfully to put down the revolt. The slaves remained free for six months, until the Danish governor was able to deploy 200 men, including a corps of free blacks skilled in hunting runaways.

November 25

Day of No More Violence Against Women (PR)— This observation is to make the citizenry aware of the need to eradicate the problem of violence against women in Puerto Rico.

International Day for the Elimination of Violence Against Women (U.N.)— Governments are invited by the United Nations General Assembly to organize activities to raise public awareness of violence directed at women. This date has been observed since 1981, the 20th anniversary of the assassination of three Mirabal sisters, political activists in the Dominican Republic, on the order of the Dominican leader, Rafael Trujillo.

November 29

International Day of Solidarity with the Palestinian People (U.N.)—This day has been observed since 1977, based on the finding of the United Nations that it has a permanent responsibility with respect to the question of Palestine. It will continue to feel so responsible until the Palestine question is resolved in a satisfactory manner in accordance with international legitimacy. The General Assembly in 2000 authorized the Committee on the Exercise of the Inalienable Rights of the Palestinian People to continue to promote the exercise of these rights. It works toward mobilization of international support for the achievement by the Palestinian people of its rights, and for a peaceful settlement in Palestine.

Nellie Taylor Ross' Birthday (WY)—This day honors the first woman governor of any state in the U.S. She was born on this date in 1876, and served as the governor of Wyoming from 1925 until 1927. She was also the first female Director of the U.S. Mint, holding that position from 1933 until 1953. She died on December 19, 1977.

November 30

Anthony J. Dimond Day (AK)—Since 1955, this day has honored Anthony Joseph "Tony" Dimond (1881–1953), born in Palatine Bridge, New York. After teaching school in New York, he moved to Alaska to mine and prospect for gold. He studied law and opened a practice in Valdez, Alaska. He served as a member of the Alaska territorial senate, and was a delegate to the U.S. Congress and the Democratic National Convention. After World War II until his death in Anchorage, he served as a district judge. Dimond was a key sponsor of the Anti-Discrimination Act adopted in 1945 to fight discrimination against Native Alaskans.

DECEMBER

OBSERVANCES WITH VARIABLE DATES

First Week in December

Troubadour's Week (PR) — This is a time to commemorate and promote participation of the citizenry in activities recognizing the musical contributions of troubadours.

First Full Week in December

Alcohol Awareness Week (ME) — This is a time to educate the public about the dangers related to overuse of alcohol, and the opportunities available to those who are afflicted with alcoholism.

First Sunday in December

Army and Navy Union Day (MA) — This is a day to celebrate the Army and Navy Union, which has advocated and strongly supported legislation for an adequate national defense. During peacetime, its theme has been "Devotion to Country, Respect for the Flag, and the practice of true Americanism." Founded in 1886, it is the oldest veterans' organization in the U.S. It is open to all who have served, or who serve, honorably in the U.S. Armed Forces.

Disabled American Veterans' Hospital Day (MA) — The Disabled American Veterans were chartered by the U.S. Congress in 1932 as the official voice of the disabled veteran. Three hundred national service centers in 68 cities provide free counseling, employment services, and help in obtaining health care. This day is celebrated at the veterans hospital in West Roxbury, Massachusetts, with speeches, a military color guard, a feast, and recognition of the services rendered to veterans by the hospital staff.

First Friday in December

Arbor Day (SC) — On this day South Carolina citizens are encouraged to plant trees on school property. The only other state which celebrates Arbor Day later than the first Friday in May is Hawaii, which observes it in November.

Second Week in December

Human Relations Day (VI) — This focuses on the need for people to work together in society, and recognizes the achievements in this area which have already been accomplished. Although it is officially named a "day," the observance lasts for an entire week.

Second Monday in December

Candle Safety Day (MA) — This day promotes the safe use of candles within the commonwealth. Because of the deaths and millions of dollars of damage caused each year by candles, a Candle Subcommittee of the Massachusetts Public Fire and Safety Education Task Force promotes candle fire safety messages. They include the burning of candles only within a one-foot circle of safety, extinguishing after use, keeping candles out of the reach of children and pets, using a saucer as a candleholder, and never leaving lit candles unattended.

Week of December 17

Ohio Aviation and Aerospace History Education Week (OH)—This remembers the anniversary of the Wright Brothers' first flight. This is an opportunity to educate and inspire the public in the celebration of the achievements of the Wright Brothers, and as of 2003, a century of powered flight. It is also an opportunity to stimulate a new generation of inventors, innovators and dreamers.

OBSERVANCES WITH FIXED DATES

December 1

Romanian-American Day (CT)—This is in honor of Americans of Romanian ancestry, their culture and the great contribution they have made to this country.

Time for Survivors of Homicide Victims Awareness (MA)—During this time, the families and friends who have been killed are recognized and comforted. It lasts from November 20 through December 20.

World AIDS Day (U.N.)—The World Health Organization proclaimed December 1, 1998, as World AIDS Day. The United Nations General Assembly, wishing to express its deep concern about the pandemic proportions of the acquired immunodeficiency syndrome (AIDS) caused by the human immunodeficiency virus (HIV), established this as a permanent day of observance. It estimates that over 41 million people worldwide are living with HIV/AIDS, with the majority in Sub-Saharan Africa. This day is intended to be a time for all peoples of the United Nations to appreciate, understand and acknowledge the danger that the disease poses, and the extent to which it has spread. It calls attention to the need to show solidarity, sympathy and support for victims, and work to combat AIDS.

December 2

International Day for the Abolition of Slavery (U.N.)—This date was chosen by the United Nations General Assembly on the anniversary of the December 2, 1949, United Nations Convention for the Suppression of the Traffic in Persons and the Exploitation of Others. After more than fifty years, it is still needed, as slavery is present in many areas. New forms of slavery are now recognized, such as child labor, sexual exploitation of children, serfdom, bonded labor, migrant labor, domestic labor, forced labor, and slavery for ritual or religious purposes.

December 3

International Day of Disabled Persons (U.N.)—The United Nations Decade of Disabled Persons concluded in 1992, after ten years of raising awareness and enacting measures to improve the situation of persons with disabilities, so that they would be provided with equal opportunities. This annual day was established to encourage member nations to further integrate people with disabilities into society, and to celebrate and acknowledge the experience and capabilities of people with disabilities. An important concern is the providing to the more than half a billion disabled people an equal access to new technologies, especially those dealing with information and communications.

Organ Donor Awareness Day (ME)—This day of commemoration was instituted in 1999, with a day honoring Kate James, born on December 3, 1980, who died on March 6, 1999, while awaiting a double lung transplant. The Maine Transplant Program endeavors to make the number of organs and tissues available for transplantation, and reduce the average of eleven people who die each day waiting for transplants. Educational programs encourage the public to become donors, and train hospital personnel to recognize potential donors and obtain the necessary consents.

December 5

International Volunteer Day for Economic and Social Development (U.N.) — Governments are invited to observe this day, and the United Nations urges them to heighten awareness of the contribution of volunteer service. The goal is to stimulate more people in all walks of life to offer their services as volunteers, both at home and abroad.

December 7

Delaware Day (DE) — This commemorates Delaware's ratification of the U.S. Constitution at a convention in Dover on December 7, 1787, being the first state to do so.

International Civil Aviation Day (U.N.) — In 1992 this day was observed by the International Civil Aviation Organization, a specialized agency of the United Nations. Four years later the General Assembly proclaimed it an annual observance to highlight and advance the benefits of international civil aviation. It reinforces awareness worldwide of the importance of international civil aviation in the social and economic development of nations. Events on this day recognize that even the essentials of life, such as food, health and education, have depended to a great extent upon air transport.

National Pearl Harbor Remembrance Day (Fed) [**Pearl Harbor Remembrance Day** (AK, IL, KS, MO, NV, NJ, NC, VA, WA), [**Pearl Harbor Recognition Day** (WY), **New Hampshire Pearl Harbor Remembrance Day** (NH), **Oklahoma Pearl Harbor Remembrance Day** (OK), **Pearl Harbor Day** (CA, MA, NY)] — This remembers and commemorates the attack on Pearl Harbor, Hawaii, on December 7, 1941, and honors the individuals who died as a result of the attack. American losses included 188 aircraft and many ships. The following day, President Roosevelt in a speech to Congress stated that the bombing of Pearl Harbor was "a date which will live in infamy." That same day, the U.S. declared war on Japan.

December 8

Bodhi Day (HI) — This commemorates the day that Prince Siddhartha Gautama, after six years of study and rigorous ascetic practices and meditation, attained "enlightenment" or "awakening" to the true nature of existence, which was later conceptualized as the "Four Noble Truths."

Civil Rights Week (MA) — This is a time to remember the need to protect four basic rights which have been the core of our democratic philosophy of government: (1) the right to safety and security of person; (2) the right of citizenship and its privileges; (3) the right to freedom of conscience and expression; and (4) the right to equality of opportunity. This period extends through and includes December 15.

Constitution Day (CM) — The current constitution and government of the Northern Mariana Islands went into effect in 1978. Under the constitution, the islands form a self-governing commonwealth with a political union with the U.S. Most U.S. federal laws apply in the Northern Marianas.

Our Lady of Camarin Day (GU) — In the apse of the Agana Cathedral Basilica stands a small wooden statue, known as Our Lady of Camarin (Santa Marian Kamalen). Tradition holds that over 300 years ago it floated onto the shores of Merizo, escorted by two crabs with lit votive candles on their backs. It is thought by some to be a miracle, since it is made of ironwood which does not float. It is said that it was noticed by a partially clad fisherman who approached it repeatedly, but the statue drew away until he fully clothed himself, and then he could pick it up and present it to the Spanish governor. The statue's hands and face are made of ivory, and the jewel-studded gold crown sits atop a cap of natural hair. It has survived earthquakes, fires, typhoons and fierce fighting during World War II.

December 10

Human Rights Day (MA, U.N.) — This celebration, proclaimed by the U.N. General Assembly, is in recognition of the 1948 adoption of the Universal Declaration of Human Rights by the United Nations. It recognizes that the inherent dignity and the equal and inalienable rights of all members of the human family are the foundation of freedom, justice, and world peace. It encourages the development of friendly relations between nations, and the protection of human rights by the rule of law. This celebration serves as a source of reinvigorated commitment by the international community, to the necessity that much still must be done to ensure the realization and universality of human rights for all people.

Wyoming Day (WY) — This day commemorates the action of Wyoming Territorial Governor A.J. Campbell who, on December 10, 1869, approved the first law found anywhere in legislative history which extends the right of suffrage to women. Wyoming is known as the "Equality State" because women there were the first in the nation to vote, hold public office and serve on juries. On February 17, 1870, Ester Hobart Morris of South Pass City, Wyoming, became the first woman appointed as a justice of the peace.

December 11

Indiana Day (IN) — This is a celebration of the anniversary of Indiana's admission to the Union as the 19th state, on December 11, 1816. It was formed from a portion of the Northwest Territory.

December 12

Foster Children's Day (NJ) — This recognizes the unique needs and experiences of foster children, and provides an opportunity for state and local government, private organizations and the general public to engage in charitable efforts which acknowledge that these foster children are important and loved.

December 13

Day of the Blind (PR) — This week aggrandizes and dignifies the education, culture and welfare of the sightless in Puerto Rico.

December 14

Margaret Chase Smith Day (ME) — Born on December 14, 1897, she became the first woman to be elected to both houses of Congress. She served in the U.S. Senate from 1949 to 1973, after serving in the House of Representatives from 1940 to 1949. Her first victory was on June 3, 1940, in a special election held to fill the House vacancy resulting from the death of her husband, Clyde Harold Smith. She was also the first woman to be placed in nomination for the presidency at a major party convention, in 1964. She died in her hometown of Skowhegan, Maine, on May 29, 1995.

December 15

Bill of Rights Day (GA, OK, SD, UT, VA) — Activities this day are intended to affirm the fundamental freedoms embodied in the Bill of Rights, ratified on December 15, 1791, and commemorate the sacrifices made to preserve these essential rights. These include the freedom of religion, speech, press, assembly and petition for grievances; the right to bear arms; prohibition against quartering soldiers in homes without consent; protection from unreasonable search and seizure; prohibition against double jeopardy, the prohibition of testimony against oneself, and the right to due process; the right to speedy trial and confrontation of witnesses; the right to trial by jury; and protection from cruel and unusual punishment.

December 16

Bastogne Day (NY) — This commemorates the World War II Battle of Bastogne, which took place in Belgium in 1944. The German army unsuccessfully attacked Allied positions in the snow, and suffered heavy casualties before it withdrew. As a result, they were unable to capture the key village of Bastogne, which sat at the entrance to a wide complex of roads leading westward. The German counteroffensive and siege is known as the Battle of the Bulge, of which the Battle of Bastogne was a part. On December 26, Bastogne was relieved by Gen. Patton's Third Army.

Bill of Responsibilities Day (OK) — Citizens are urged to reflect upon and accept the responsibilities of being citizens of this nation in order to secure and expand our freedom as individual members of a free society.

December 17

Pan American Aviation Day (Fed) — This day celebrates and stimulates interest in aviation in the Western Hemisphere as an important stimulus to the development of more rapid communications and cultural development.

Wright Brothers Day (Fed) — This commemorates the first successful flight in a heavier-than-air, mechanically propelled craft, made on December 17, 1903, near Kitty Hawk, NC. Their first aircraft, named *Flyer*, covered just 120 feet on its maiden flight. This has been observed nationally to honor Wilbur and Orville Wright since 1963.

December 18

International Migrants Day (U.N.)— Upon the recommendation of the Economic and Social Council, the United Nations General Assembly established this day to commemorate the 1990 adoption of the International Convention on the Protection of the Rights of All Migrant Workers and Members of Their Families. It focuses on the need to make further efforts to ensure respect for the human rights and fundamental freedoms of all migrants, with approximately 130 million people living outside their countries of origin.

December 19

Senator Hattie W. Caraway Day (AR)— This day commemorates Hattie Ophelia Wyatt Caraway (1878–1950), the first woman elected to the U.S. Senate. A Democrat, she also holds the distinctions of being the first woman to head a Senate committee and the first to preside over a Senate session. She was born and raised on a farm near Bakersville, Tennessee. Later, her husband was elected to the Senate from Arkansas, and after his death Governor Harvey Parnell appointed her to complete the remainder of his term. When that was over, she ran for election on her own and won. After serving in the Senate from 1931 to 1945, she relinquished her seat to another Democrat who defeated her in a primary election.

December 20

Samuel Slater Day (MA)— This day recognizes the beginning of America's Industrial Revolution along the banks of the Blackstone River. There, Samuel Slater established his first mill, later relocating it and establishing the town of Webster. Slater was born in Derbyshire, England, on June 9, 1768. He apprenticed in the textile industry at age 14, and rose to become superintendent of Jedediah Strutt's mill. Slater emigrated to the U.S. in 1789 to make his fortune in the new textile industry, and since he was the first to know how to build as well as operate the necessary machines, his mill built in Pawtucket, Rhode Island, in 1793 was the first successful water-powered textile mill. Slater's mill and his methods (known as the Rhode Island System) became a model for subsequent mills in the Blackstone River Valley. Slater died in 1835. This day also recognizes the contributions of countless working men and women to America's national greatness.

December 21

Chester Greenwood Day (ME)— This day is in honor of Chester Greenwood (1858–1937), whose inventive genius and native ability, which contributed much to the enjoyment of Maine's winter season, marked him as one of the state's outstanding citizens. His most famous invention was a pair of "ear protectors" (now known as earmuffs), for the protection of men's ears while their heads were covered by fashionable beaver fur derby hats. He came up with the idea at age 15, and eleven years later was producing them through his Farmington Manufacturing Company. He had about 100 other inventions, including a mousetrap, fluid shock absorber, self-priming spark plugs, and the spring-tooth steel rake. His hometown of Farmington celebrates this day with a parade of floats, fire trucks, and dogs in earmuffs.

December 24

Christmas Eve (AL, AR, MD, ND, SC, TX)— In North Dakota the holiday begins at noon and continues until midnight. In South Carolina it is a holiday only if the Governor so declares it. This day is declared a holiday in that state to give employees and students an additional day to prepare for and celebrate Christmas. In Alabama the Superintendent of Banks may authorize banks to close at noon on this day.

Unnamed School Holiday (MD)— Students and teachers have this additional day to prepare for and begin to celebrate Christmas.

December 25

Christmas Day (Fed, AK, AZ, AR, CA, CO, DC, FL, GA, HI, ID, IL, IN, IA, KS, KY,

LA, ME, MD, MI, MN, MS, MO, MT, NE, NV, NH, NJ, NM, NY, NC, ND, CM, OH, OK, OR, PA, PR, RI, SC, SD, TN, TX, VI, VT, VA, WA, WV, WI, WY) [**Christmas** (AL, AS, CT, DE, GU, UT)] — December 25 was fixed during the 4th century by the Roman Catholic Church as the date of the feast of Christ's birth, moving it from January 6. This gave rise to the "Twelve Days of Christmas," connecting the two days. The eastern half of the church kept January 6, as that was when Christ was manifested to the world.

Clara Barton Week (MA) — This recognizes Clara Barton's countless humanitarian efforts in the cause of peace and aiding the victims of wartime and natural disasters, and in further recognition of her founding of the American Red Cross. Barton was born on Christmas Day in 1821 in North Oxford, Massachusetts, and taught school there for more than ten years. At age 29 she began attending an advanced school for teachers, working on her writing and studying French. She went back into teaching, and when she was passed over for a promotion in favor of a man, she quit and went to work as a clerk in the U.S. Patent Office. She left that when the Civil War began, becoming a volunteer who delivered supplies to the front for two years, and in 1864 was named as superintendent of Union nurses. While serving as a volunteer in Europe during the Franco-Prussian War, she learned about the Red Cross, and later actively lobbied for the creation of such an organization in the U.S. When it was formed in 1881, she served as its first president, a post she held until 1904. She died on April 12, 1912.

December 26

Christmas Second Day (VI) — The "two turtle doves" in the song *The Twelve Days of Christmas* symbolize the Old and New Testaments, bearing witness to God's self-revelation in history. It also remembers John the Evangelist,

who spoke eloquently of Christ as the "light that shatters the darkness." As a result, it is a custom to light candles on this day.

Day After Christmas Day (OK, SC, TX) — In Oklahoma, to make a long weekend including Christmas, the day afterwards is a holiday in years in which Christmas falls on a Thursday. In years Christmas falls on a Tuesday, the day before Christmas is a holiday.

December 29

Wounded Knee Day (SD) — After being pursued 150 miles by the U.S. Army for their alleged practice of the Ghost Dance religion, 350 Miniconjou Sioux, led by Big Foot, camped on the Pine Ridge Indian Reservation in South Dakota. On December 28 they were promised by Maj. Samuel M. Whiteside that if they surrendered, they would be allowed to live. The Sioux agreed, and spent the night at the soldiers' camp, under the watch of sentinels with rapid-fire guns. On the morning of the 29th, an accidental shot by deaf warrior Black Coyote started a panic, ending 20 minutes later with the death of Big Foot and 150 to 250 others (plus 25 soldiers), with 50 more injured. Most of the rest died in a blizzard three days later. This massacre marked the virtual end of the Indians' hope for freedom in this country.

December 31

New Year's Eve (AL) — The country focuses on Times Square in New York City, where a lighted ball is dropped precisely at midnight. That tradition began with a ball constructed by Russian immigrant metalworker Jacob Starr, who built the first ball for New Year's Eve in 1907 because the city had outlawed the use of fireworks for the celebration. In Alabama the Superintendent of Banks may authorize banks to close at noon on this day.

Unscheduled Observances

Bird Day (DE)—This is a time for residents of Delaware to become more aware of the many species of birds found in their state.

Citizenship Recognition Day (OK)—This is a day to celebrate the benefits of citizenship and the obligations placed on citizens.

Election Day (PR)—When these are scheduled throughout the island, they are official special observances. They are not fixed on any particular dates by statute.

Indian Day (NC)—Public schools and citizens are to place emphasis on Indian lore on this day.

Lithuanian Day (CT)—The statute provides for a holiday on "a date certain" to celebrate the independence of Lithuania, but no such date is stated. It commemorates the February 16, 1918, signing of the Declaration of Independence by the Council of Lithuania, proclaiming to the world the reestablishment of an independent Lithuanian state founded on democratic principles, with Vilnius as its capital.

National POW/MIA Recognition Day (OR)—Although this will likely be celebrated along with most of the country in September, the laws of Oregon give the state discretion in choosing the date each year. On the date chosen, Oregon uses it for recognition of those who have made the ultimate sacrifice while serving their country.

Native Industries Week (PR)—During this week, 15-minute talks are to be given in school classes, with displays of native products. These industries include agriculture, tourism, pharmaceuticals, electronics and clothing.

Natural and Environmental Resources and Environmental Quality and Health Education Term (PR)—The length of observance and dates are not specified by statute, and are to be determined by the Department of Natural and Environmental Resources, the Environmental Quality Board, the Department of Health, and the Department of Education. Its purpose is to emphasize the importance of preserving our natural resources and maintaining the purity of the environment.

Official Day for Each Indian Tribe (OK)—Each tribe in Oklahoma may pick its own day for celebrating its culture, history and contributions to society.

Powered Flight Day (CT)—The statute states that "a date certain" is to be set to commemorate the first heavier-than-air powered flight, but the law itself does not set a particular date. The celebrated flight by Wilbur and Orville Wright took place at Kitty Hawk, North Carolina, at 10:35 a.m. on December 17, 1903. The first flight, with Orville at the controls, lasted 12 seconds and covered a length of 120 feet. The fourth and final flight that morning, with Wilbur flying, went 852 feet in 59 seconds.

Veteran Firefighters' Muster Day (RI)—In New England there is a tradition of firefighters competing with one another. In the days when they battled blazes with hand-pumped fire engines (called "handtubs"), it was a matter of pride for a fire company to be able to perform quickly and efficiently. Competitions were held to see who could douse a fire the fastest, or whose hose shot the longest stream. Today, regional leagues compete with antique equipment which spends most of its time in museums. The day is also marked with parades and other festivities to honor the communities' firefighters.

Women Devoted to the Religious Vocation Commemorative Week (PR) — This celebration may be set at any time by the Puerto Rican Governor, with the first having taken place on November 13–19, 1994. It is an opportunity to honor those women who have dedicated their lives to religious vocations.

Holidays and Observances
Listed by Jurisdiction

FEDERAL (FED)

Variable Dates:

Birthday of Martin Luther King, Jr. — 3rd Mon in Jan

Washington's Birthday — 3rd Mon in Feb

Save Your Vision Week — 1st week of Mar

Mother's Day — 2nd Sun in May

Police Week — Week including May 15

National Transportation Week — Week including May 16

National Safe Boating Week — 7 days ending on the last Fri before Memorial Day

Memorial Day — Last Mon in May

National Flag Week — Week containing Jun 14

Father's Day — 3rd Sun in Jun

Parents' Day — 4th Sun in Jul

Labor Day — 1st Mon in Sep

Carl Garner Federal Lands Cleanup Day — 1st Sat following Labor Day

National Grandparents Day — 1st Sun following Labor Day

Gold Star Mother's Day — Last Sun in Sep

Child Health Day — 1st Mon in Oct

National School Lunch Week — Begins 2nd Sun in Oct

Columbus Day — 2nd Mon in Oct

Thanksgiving Day — 4th Thu in Nov

Fixed Dates:

New Year's Day — Jan 1

Stephen Foster Memorial Day — Jan 13

American Heart Month — February

National Freedom Day — Feb 1

National Poison Prevention Week — Mar 16–22

Cancer Control Month — April

Thomas Jefferson's Birthday — Apr 13

Asian/Pacific American Heritage Month — May

Law Day, U.S.A. — May 1

Loyalty Day — May 1

National Day of Prayer — May 1

Steelmark Month — May

Peace Officers Memorial Day — May 15

National Defense Transportation Day — May 16

National Maritime Day — May 22

Flag Day — Jun 14

Honor America Days — Jun 14–Jul 4

Independence Day — Jul 4

National Korean War Armistice Day — Jul 27

National Aviation Day — Aug 19

Patriot Day — Sep 11

Hispanic Heritage Month — Sep 15–Oct 15

Citizenship Day — Sep 17

Constitution Week — Sep 17–23

National Disability Employment Awareness Month — Oct

Leif Erickson Day — Oct 9

White Cane Safety Day — Oct 15

National Forest Products Week — Oct 19–25

Veterans' Day — Nov 11

National Pearl Harbor Remembrance Day — Dec 7

Pan American Aviation Day — Dec 17

Wright Brothers Day — Dec 17

Christmas Day — Dec 25

ALABAMA (AL)

Variable Dates:

Martin Luther King, Jr.'s Birthday — 3rd Mon in Jan
Robert E. Lee's Birthday — 3rd Mon in Jan
George Washington's Birthday — 3rd Mon in Feb
Thomas Jefferson's Birthday — 3rd Mon in Feb
Mardi Gras — 40 days before Easter
Memorial Day — Last Mon in May
Labor Day — 1st Mon in Sep
American Indian Heritage Day — 2nd Mon in Oct
Columbus Day — 2nd Mon in Oct
Fraternal Day — 2nd Mon in Oct

Fixed Dates:

New Year's Day — Jan 1
Confederate Memorial Day — Apr 29
Jefferson Davis' Birthday — Jun 2
Fourth of July — Jul 4
Veterans' Day — Nov 11
Christmas Eve — Dec 24
Christmas — Dec 25
New Year's Eve — Dec 31

ALASKA (AK)

Variable Dates:

Martin Luther King, Jr.'s Birthday — 3rd Mon in Jan
Presidents' Day — 3rd Mon in Feb
Seward's Day — Last Mon in Mar
Memorial Day — Last Mon in May
Juneteenth Day — 3rd Sat in Jun
Labor Day — 1st Mon in Sep
Prisoners of War and Missing in Action Recognition Day — 3rd Fri in Sep
Thanksgiving Day — 4th Thu in Nov

Fixed Dates:

New Year's Day — Jan 1
Ernest Gruening Day — Feb 6
Elizabeth Peratrovich Day — Feb 16
Former Prisoners of War Recognition Day — Apr 9
Bob Bartlett Day — Apr 20
Alaska Day of Prayer — May 1
Family Day — May 1
Family Preservation Month — May
Dutch Harbor Remembrance Day — Jun 3
Drunk Driving Victims Remembrance Day — Jul 3
Independence Day — Jul 4

Alaska Flag Day — Jul 9
Wickersham Day — Aug 24
William A. Egan Day — Oct 8
Alaska Day — Oct 18
Women Veterans Day — Nov 9
Veterans' Day — Nov 11
Anthony J. Dimond Day — Nov 30
Pearl Harbor Remembrance Day — Dec 7
Christmas Day — Dec 25

AMERICAN SAMOA (AS)

Variable Dates:

Good Friday — Fri before Easter
Labor Day — 1st Mon in Sep
Thanksgiving — 4th Thu in Nov

Fixed Dates:

New Year's Day — Jan 1
Washington's Birthday — Feb 22
American Samoa Flag Day — Apr 17
Memorial Day — May 30
Independence Day — Jul 4
Manu'a Islands Cession Day — Jul 16
Veterans Day — Nov 11
Christmas — Dec 25

ARIZONA (AZ)

Variable Dates:

Sundays
Martin Luther King, Jr./Civil Rights Day — 3rd Mon in Jan
Lincoln/Washington Presidents' Day — 3rd Mon in Feb
Arbor Day — Last Fri in Apr
Mothers Day — 2nd Sun in May
Memorial Day — Last Mon in May
Father's Day — 3rd Sun in Jun
American Family Day — 1st Sun in Aug
Labor Day — 1st Mon in Sep
Election Day — biennial primary election day on the 8th Tue before the general election
Columbus Day — 2nd Mon in Oct
Election Day — biennial in even-numbered years on the 1st Tue after the 1st Mon in Nov
Thanksgiving Day — 4th Thu in Nov

Fixed Dates:

New Year's Day — Jan 1
Dr. Cesar Estrada Chavez Day — Mar 31
Prisoners of War Remembrance Day — Apr 9

Independence Day — Jul 4
Korean War Veterans' Day — Jul 27
Constitution Commemoration Day — Sep 17
Veterans' Day — Nov 11
Christmas Day — Dec 25

ARKANSAS (AR)

Variable Dates:

Dr. Martin Luther King, Jr.'s Birthday — 3rd
  Mon in Jan
Robert E. Lee's Birthday — 3rd Mon in Jan
Daisy Gatson Bates Day — 3rd Mon in Feb
George Washington's Birthday — 3rd Mon in Feb
Arkansas Teachers' Day — 1st Tue in Mar
Arbor Day — 3rd Mon in Mar
Good Friday — Friday before Easter
Memorial Day — Last Mon in May
National Garden Week — First full week in Jun
Labor Day — 1st Mon in Sep
Native American Heritage Week — 3rd week in
  Sep
POW/MIA Recognition Day — 3rd Fri in Sep
Thanksgiving Day — 4th Thu in Nov

Fixed Dates:

New Year's Day — Jan 1
General Douglas MacArthur Day — Jan 26
Abraham Lincoln's Birthday — Feb 12
Arkansas Agriculture Recognition Day — Mar 7
Prisoners of War Remembrance Day — Apr 9
Patriots' Day — Apr 19
Confederate Flag Day — Apr 21
Arkansas Bird Day — Apr 26
Arbor Day — May 17
Jefferson Davis' Birthday — Jun 3
Independence Day — Jul 4
Columbus Day — Oct 12
White Cane Safety Day — Oct 15
Veterans Day — Nov 11
Senator Hattie W. Caraway Day — Dec 19
Christmas Eve — Dec 24
Christmas Day — Dec 25

CALIFORNIA (CA)

Variable Dates:

Saturdays (noon to midnight)
Sundays
Dr. Martin Luther King, Jr. Day — 3rd Mon in
  Jan
Good Friday — Fri before Easter (noon to 3 p.m.)
Memorial Day — Last Mon in May

Labor Day — 1st Mon in Sep
Native American Day — 4th Fri in Sep
Stepparents Day — 1st Sun in Oct
Columbus Day — 2nd Mon in Oct
Thanksgiving Day — 4th Thu in Nov

Fixed Dates:

New Year's Day — Jan 1
Lincoln Day — Feb 12
A Day of Remembrance: Japanese American
  Evacuation — Feb 19
Arbor Day — Mar 7
Cesar Chavez Day — Mar 31
John Muir Day — Apr 21
Independence Day — Jul 4
Admission Day — Sep 9
Cabrillo Day — Sep 28
Veterans Day — Nov 11
Pearl Harbor Day — Dec 7
Christmas Day — Dec 25

COLORADO (CO)

Variable Dates:

Birthday of Dr. Martin Luther King — 3rd Mon
  in Jan
Washington-Lincoln Day — 3rd Mon in Feb
Memorial Day — Last Mon in May
Colorado Day — 1st Mon in Aug
Labor Day — 1st Mon in Sep
Columbus Day — 2nd Mon in Oct

Fixed Dates:

New Year's Day — Jan 1
Susan B. Anthony Day — Feb 15
Arbor Day — Apr 18
Independence Day — Jul 4
Leif Erickson Day — Oct 9
Veterans' Day — Nov 11
Christmas Day — Dec 25

CONNECTICUT (CT)

Variable Dates:

Martin Luther King Day — 1st Mon after Jan 15
Youth to Work Day — 2nd Wed in Feb
Washington's Birthday — 3rd Mon in Feb
Retired Teachers Day — 3rd Wed in Feb
Friends Day — 4th Sun in Apr
Arbor Day — Last Fri in Apr
Green Up Day — Last Sat in Apr
Senior Citizens Day — 1st Sun in May

A Week to Remember Persons Who are Disabled or Shut-In — 3rd week in May

Long Island Sound Day — Last Fri before Memorial Day

Memorial (Decoration) Day — Last Mon in May

Destroyer Escort Day — 3rd Sat in Jun

Fire Fighter and Emergency Medical Services Personnel Week — 1st week in Aug

Volunteer Fire Fighter and Volunteer Emergency Medical Services Personnel Day — 1st Sat in Aug

Labor Day — 1st Mon in Sep

Family Day — 2nd Sun in Sep

School Safety Patrol Day — 2nd Mon in Sep

Puerto Rico Day — 4th Sun in Sep

Indian Day — Last Fri in Sep

Fire Prevention Day — On or about Oct 9

Leif Erickson Day — A day within the 1st nine days of Oct, likely Oct 9

National Children's Day — 2nd Sun in Oct

Columbus Day — 2nd Mon in Oct

Lithuanian Day — Date not set by statute

Powered Flight Day — Date not set by statue

Fixed Dates:

New Year's Day — Jan 1

Lincoln Day — Feb 12

Iwo Jima Day — Feb 23

Gulf War Veterans Day — Feb 28

St. Patrick's Day — Mar 17

Greek-American Day — Mar 25

Pan American Day — Apr 14

Worker's Memorial Day — Apr 28

Loyalty Day — May 1

Polish-American Day — May 3

Austrian-American Day — May 15

Christa Corrigan McAuliffe Day — May 24

Flag Day — Jun 14

Independence Day — Jul 4

Disability Awareness Day — Jul 26

Korean Armistice Day — Jul 27

End of World War II Day — Aug 14

Ukrainian-American Day — Aug 24

Women's Independence Day — Aug 26

Prudence Crandall Day — Sep 3

911 Day — Sep 11

Nathan Hale Day — Sep 22

German-American Day — Oct 6

Republic of China on Taiwan-American Day — Oct 10

Hungarian Freedom Fighters Day — Oct 23

Veterans' Day — Nov 11

Romanian-American Day — Dec 1

Christmas — Dec 25

DELAWARE (DE)

Variable Dates:

Saturdays

Martin Luther King, Jr. Day — 3rd Mon in Jan

Presidents' Day — 3rd Mon in Feb

Delaware Head Start Week — Last week of Mar

Good Friday — Last Fri before Easter

Arbor Day — Last Fri in Apr

Correctional Officers and Employees Recognition and Appreciation Week — 1st week in May

Mother's Day — 2nd Sun in May

Memorial Day — Last Mon in May

Police Officers Appreciation Day — 2nd week in Jun

Father's Day — 3rd Sun in Jun

Juneteenth National Freedom Day — 3rd Sat in Jun

Labor Day — 1st Mon in Sep

Native American Day — 1st Sat after Labor Day

Columbus Day — 2nd Mon in Oct

General Election Day — Biennially on the 1st Tue after the 1st Mon of Nov

Return Day — 2nd day following General Election Day (Sussex County only)

American Education Week — 2nd week in Nov

Thanksgiving Day — 4th Thu in Nov

Bird Day — Date not set by statute

Fixed Dates:

New Years Day — Jan 1

Delaware Swedish Colonial Day — Mar 29

Independence Day — Jul 4

Veterans' Day — Nov 11

Delaware Day — Dec 7

Christmas — Dec 25

DISTRICT OF COLUMBIA (DC)

Variable Dates:

Saturdays (from noon to midnight)

Dr. Martin Luther King, Jr.'s Birthday — 3rd Mon in Jan

Washington's Birthday — 3rd Mon in Feb

Memorial Day — Last Mon in May

Labor Day — 1st Mon in Sep

Columbus Day — 2nd Mon in Oct

Thanksgiving Day — 4th Thu in Nov

Fixed Dates:

New Year's Day — Jan 1

Inauguration Day — Jan 20 quadrennially

Independence Day — Jul 4

Veteran's Day — Nov 11
Christmas Day — Dec 25

FLORIDA (FL)

Variable Dates:

Sundays
Arbor Day — 3rd Fri in Jan
Gasparilla Day — 1st Sat in Feb
Washington's Birthday — 3rd Mon in Feb
Shrove Tuesday — 40 days prior to Easter
Save the Florida Panther Day — 3rd Sat in Mar
Children's Day — 2nd Tue in Apr
Good Friday — Last Fri before Easter
DeSoto Day — Last Fri of Apr (only in Manatee
    County)
Law Week — Week including May 1
Teacher's Day — 3rd Fri in May
Memorial Day — Last Mon in May
Labor Day — 1st Mon in Sep
Florida Missing Children's Day — 2nd Mon in
    Sep
Rosh Hashanah — Varies in Sep-Oct
Yom Kippur — Varies in Sep-Oct
Grandmother's Day — 2nd Sun in Oct
Columbus Day — 2nd Mon in Oct
Farmers' Day — 2nd Mon in Oct
I Am an American Day — 3rd Sun in Oct
General Election Day — 1st Tue after the 1st Mon
    in Nov in even-numbered years
Parade Day — 1st Wed in Nov
Retired Teachers' Day — Sun commencing the
    3rd week in Nov
Thanksgiving Day — 4th Thu in Nov

Fixed Dates:

New Year's Day — Jan 1
Birthday of Martin Luther King, Jr. — Jan 15
Birthday of Robert E. Lee — Jan 19
Alzheimer's Disease Day — Feb 6
Lincoln's Birthday — Feb 12
Susan B. Anthony's Birthday — Feb 15
Parade Day — Feb 28
Pascua Florida Week — Mar 27–Apr 2
Pascua Florida Day (Florida State Day) — Apr 2
Pan-American Day — Apr 14
Patriots' Day — Apr 19
Confederate Memorial Day — Apr 26
Law Day — May 1
Law Enforcement Appreciation Month — May
Law Enforcement Memorial Day — May 15
Birthday of Jefferson Davis — Jun 3
Flag Day — Jun 14

Juneteenth Day — Jun 19
Independence Day — Jul 4
Veterans' Day — Nov 11
Christmas Day — Dec 25

GEORGIA (GA)

Variable Dates:

Sundays
Birthday of Martin Luther King, Jr. — 3rd Mon
    in Jan
Home Education Week — 1st week in Feb
Firefighter Appreciation Day — 1st Tue in Feb
Girls and Women and Sports Day — 1st Thu in
    Feb
Washington's Birthday — 3rd Mon in Feb
Wildflower Week — 4th week in Mar
Police Week — Week including May 15
Memorial Day — Last Mon in May
Labor Day — 1st Mon in Sep
Children's Day — 1st Sun in Oct
Columbus Day — 2nd Mon in Oct
Clean Water Week — 3rd week in Oct
Thanksgiving Day — 4th Thu in Nov

Fixed Dates:

New Year's Day — Jan 1
Birthday of Robert E. Lee — Jan 19
American History Month — Feb
Georgia History Month — Feb
Law Enforcement Officer Appreciation Day —
    Feb 10
Former Prisoners of War Recognition Day —
    Apr 9
Confederate Memorial Day — Apr 26
Peace Officer Memorial Day — May 15
Birthday of Jefferson Davis — Jun 3
Flag Day — Jun 14
Independence Day — Jul 4
Bird Day — Oct 14
Veterans' Day — Nov 11
Bill of Rights Day — Dec 15
Christmas Day — Dec 25

GUAM (GU)

Variable Dates:

Sundays
Gubernatorial Inauguration Day — 1st Mon in Jan
President's Day — 3rd Mon in Feb
Chamorro Week — 1st Mon in Mar through eight
    days later
Guam Discovery Day — 1st Mon in Mar

Farmers' Appreciation Days — Last Sat in Mar
   and the following Sun
White Cane Safety Days — 2nd Sat and Sun of Apr
Good Friday — Fri before Easter
Children and Youth Sunday — 4th Sun in Apr
Earth Week — Last week in Apr
Teachers' Appreciation Day — 1st Sat in May
Family Sunday — 1st Sun following the 4th Sun in
   Apr
Memorial Day — Last Mon in May
Atbot de Fuego (Flame Tree) and Arbor Day
   Week — 1st week in Jun
Gold Star Mothers' Day — 2nd Sun in Aug
Labor Day — 1st Mon in Sep
Guam National Guard Day — 1st Sat in Oct
Election Day — 1st Tue after 1st Mon in Nov
Thanksgiving Day — 4th Thu in Nov

Fixed Dates:

New Year's Day — Jan 1
Guam Youth Month — Apr
Senior Citizens Month — May
Independence Day — Jul 4
Liberation Day — Jul 21
All Soul's Day — Nov 2
Veteran's Day — Nov 11
Our Lady of Camarin Day — Dec 8
Christmas — Dec 25

HAWAII (HI)

Variable Dates:

Dr. Martin Luther King, Jr. Day — 3rd Mon in Jan
Presidents' Day — 3rd Mon in Feb
Good Friday — Last Fri before Easter
Memorial Day — Last Mon in May
Ocean Day — 1st Wed in Jun
Statehood Day — 3rd Fri in Aug
Labor Day — 1st Mon in Sep
Children and Youth Day — 1st Sun in Oct
Discoverers' Day — 2nd Mon in Oct
Respect for Our Elders Day — 3rd Sun in Oct
Arbor Day — 1st Fri in Nov
Thanksgiving Day — 4th Thu in Nov

Fixed Dates:

New Year's Day — Jan 1
Bahai New Year's Day — Mar 21
Prince Jonah Kuhio Kalanianaole Day — Mar 26
Buddha Day — Apr 8
Father Damien DeVeuster Day — Apr 15
May Day Is Lei Day in Hawaii — May 1
King Kamehameha Day — Jun 11
Independence Day — Jul 4

Queen Lili'uokalani Day — Sep 2
Children and Youth Month — Oct
Veterans' Day — Nov 11
Bodhi Day — Dec 8
Christmas Day — Dec 25

IDAHO (ID)

Variable Dates:

Sundays
Martin Luther King, Jr.–Idaho Human Rights
   Day — 3rd Mon in Jan
Washington's Birthday — 3rd Mon in Feb
Arbor Day — Last Fri in Apr
Decoration Day — Last Mon in May
Labor Day — 1st Mon in Sep
Columbus Day — 2nd Mon in Oct
Thanksgiving Day — 4th Thu in Nov

Fixed Dates:

New Years Day — Jan 1
Independence Day — Jul 4
Constitutional Commemorative Day — Sep 17
Veterans Day — Nov 11
Christmas Day — Dec 25

ILLINOIS (IL)

Variable Dates:

Saturdays (noon to midnight)
Martin Luther King, Jr.'s Birthday — 3rd Mon in Jan
Presidents Day — 3rd Mon in Feb
Casimir Pulaski's Birthday — 1st Mon in Mar
Good Friday — Last Fri before Easter
Arbor and Bird Day — Last Fri in Apr
Chaplains Day — 1st Sun in May
Day of Prayer in Illinois — 1st Thu in May
Mothers Day — 2nd Sun in May
Citizenship Day — 3rd Sun in May
Senior Citizens Day — 3rd Sun in May
Retired Teachers' Week — 4th week in May
Fathers Day — 3rd Sun in Jun
Gold Star Mothers Day — 2nd Sun in Aug
Labor Day — 1st Mon in Sep
Prairie Week — 3rd full week in Sep
POW/MIA Recognition Day — 3rd Fri in Sep
Grandmothers Day — 2nd Sun in Oct
Columbus Day — 2nd Mon in Oct
General Election Day — 1st Tue after 1st Mon in
   Nov biennially
Korean War Veteran's Day — Last school day be-
   fore Veterans Day
Thanksgiving Day — 4th Thu in Nov

Fixed Dates:

New Year's Day — Jan 1
Christa McAuliffe Day — Jan 28
American History Month — Feb
Lincoln's Birthday — Feb 12
Susan B. Anthony's Birthday — Feb 15
Mayor's Day — Mar 4
Viet Nam War Veterans Day — Mar 29
Memorial Day — May 30
Flag Day — Jun 14
Independence Day — Jul 4
Korean War Armistice Day — Jul 27
Recycling Day — Oct 1
Veterans Day — Nov 11
Coal Miners Day — Nov 13
Pearl Harbor Remembrance Day — Dec 7
Christmas Day — Dec 25

INDIANA (IN)

Variable Dates:

Sundays
Martin Luther King, Jr.'s Birthday — 3rd Mon in Jan
George Washington's Birthday — 3rd Mon in Feb
Casimir Pulaski Day — 1st Mon in Mar
Good Friday — Last Fri before Easter
Arbor Day — Last Fri in Apr
Memorial Day — Last Mon in May
Labor Day — 1st Mon in Sep
Columbus Day — 2nd Mon in Oct
Election Day — General elections on the 1st Tue after the 1st Mon in Nov, plus days of municipal and primary elections
Thanksgiving Day — 4th Thu in Nov

Fixed Dates:

New Year's Day — Jan 1
Abraham Lincoln's Birthday — Feb 12
George Rogers Clark Day — Feb 25
Flag Day — Jun 14
Independence Day — Jul 4
Northwest Ordinance Day — Jul 13
Veterans Day — Nov 11
Indiana Day — Dec 11
Christmas Day — Dec 25

IOWA (IA)

Variable Dates:

Dr. Martin Luther King, Jr.'s Birthday — 3rd Mon in Jan
Washington's Birthday — 3rd Mon in Feb

Arbor Week — Week including Apr 25
Arbor Day — Last Fri in Apr
Mother's Day — 2nd Sun in May
Memorial Day — Last Mon in May
Father's Day — 3rd Sun in Jun
Independence Sunday — Sun on or before Jul 4
Herbert Hoover Day — Sun closest to Aug 10
Labor Day — 1st Mon in Sep
Columbus Day — 2nd Mon in Oct
Thanksgiving Day — 4th Thu in Nov
Day After Thanksgiving Day — Fri after Thanksgiving Day

Fixed Dates:

New Year's Day — Jan 1
Lincoln's Birthday — Feb 12
Iowa State Flag Day — Mar 29
Independence Day — Jul 4
White Cane Safety Day — Oct 15
Youth Honor Day — Oct 31
Veterans Day — Nov 11
Christmas Day — Dec 25

KANSAS (KS)

Variable Dates:

Martin Luther King, Jr. Day — 3rd Mon in Jan
Washington's Birthday — 3rd Mon in Feb
Arbor Day — Last Fri in Mar
Mother's Day — 2nd Sun in May
Memorial Day — Last Mon in May
Labor Day — 1st Mon in Sep
American Indian Day — 4th Sat in Sep
Columbus Day — 2nd Mon in Oct
Thanksgiving Day — 4th Thu in Nov
Family Day — Sun following Thanksgiving Day

Fixed Dates:

New Year's Day — Jan 1
Lincoln's Birthday — Feb 12
Flag Day — Jun 14
Independence Day — Jul 4
General Pulaski's Memorial Day — Oct 11
Dwight D. Eisenhower Day — Oct 14
Veterans' Day — Nov 11
Pearl Harbor Remembrance Day — Dec 7
Christmas Day — Dec 25

KENTUCKY (KY)

Variable Dates:

Martin Luther King, Jr.'s Birthday — 3rd Mon in Jan

Washington's Birthday — 3rd Mon in Feb
Mother's Day — 2nd Sun in May
Retired Teachers' Week — 4th week in May
Memorial Day — Last Mon in May
Garden Week — 1st week in Jun
Labor Day — 1st Mon in Sep
Grandmother's Day — 2nd Sun in Oct
Columbus Day — 2nd Mon in Oct
Presidential Election Day — 1st Tue after 1st Mon
   in presidential election years

Fixed Dates:

New Year's Day — Jan 1
Robert E. Lee Day — Jan 19
Franklin D. Roosevelt Day — Jan 30
Lincoln's Birthday — Feb 12
Environmental Education Month — Mar
Commonwealth Cleanup Week — Mar 23–29
Statewide Cleanup Day — Mar 29
Barrier Awareness Day — May 7
Confederate Memorial Day — Jun 3
Jefferson Davis Day — Jun 3
Flag Day — Jun 14
Kentucky National Guard Day — Jun 24
Independence Day — Jul 4
Disability Day — Aug 2
General Pulaski's Day — Oct 11
Native American Indian Month — Nov
Veterans Day — Nov 11
Kentucky Harvest Day — Nov 15
Christmas Day — Dec 25

LOUISIANA (LA)

Variable Dates:

Wednesdays and Saturdays (noon to midnight)
   (Sabine and Vernon Parishes)
Saturdays (in some parishes)
Sundays
Dr. Martin Luther King, Jr.'s Birthday — 3rd
   Mon in Jan
Washington's Birthday — 3rd Mon in Feb
Mardi Gras — 40 days before Easter (some
   parishes and all municipalities)
Good Friday — Last Fri before Easter
National Memorial Day — Last Mon in May
Labor Day — 1st Mon in Sep
Christopher Columbus Day — 2nd Mon in Oct
Washington Parish Free Fair — 3rd Wed-Sat in
   Oct (Washington Parish only)
International Rice Festival — Fri and Sat of 3rd
   weekend in Oct (Acadia and Lafayette
   Parishes only)

Thanksgiving Day — 4th Thu in Nov
Acadian Day — Fri after Thanksgiving Day

Fixed Dates:

New Year's Day — Jan 1
Battle of New Orleans — Jan 8
Robert E. Lee Day — Jan 19
Inauguration Day — Jan 20 in presidential inau-
   guration years (only in city of Baton Rouge)
Confederate Memorial Day — Jun 3
Independence Day — Jul 4
National Airborne Day — Aug 16
Huey P. Long Day — Aug 30
All Saints' Day — Nov 1
Veterans' Day — Nov 11
Christmas Day — Dec 25

MAINE (ME)

Variable Dates:

Saturdays
Sundays (The Lord's Day)
Martin Luther King, Jr. Day — 3rd Mon in Jan
Washington's Birthday — 3rd Mon in Feb
Maine Cultural Heritage Week — Week including
   Mar 15
Arbor Week — 3rd full week in May
Patriot's Day — 3rd Mon in Apr
Maine Small Business Week — 3rd week in May
Memorial Day — Last Mon in May
Garden Week — 1st full week in Jun
Maine Clean Water Week — 1st full week in Jun
Samantha Smith Day — 1st Mon in Jun
Seamen's Memorial Day — 2nd Sun in Jun
Maine Lighthouse Week — 3rd full week in Jun
R.B. Hall Day — Last Sat in Jun
Labor Day — 1st Mon in Sep
Colonel Freeman McGilvery Day — 1st Sat in Sep
Prisoners of War-Missing in Action Recognition
   Day — 3rd Fri in Sep
Landowner Recognition Day — 3rd Sat in Sep
Deaf Culture Week — Last full week in Sep
Children's Day — Last Fri in Sep
Firefighter's Recognition Day — 1st Sat in Oct
Columbus Day — 2nd Mon in Oct
Maine Business Women's Week — 3rd full week
   in Oct
Veterans' Week — Week including Nov 11
Alcohol Awareness Week — 1st full week in Dec

Fixed Dates:

New Year's Day — Jan 1
American History Month — Feb

Statehood Day — Mar 15
Edmund S. Muskie Day — Mar 28
Equal Pay Day — Apr 1
Former Prisoners of War Recognition Day — Apr 9
Maine Merchant Marine Day — May 22
Destroyer Escort Day — Jun 21
Saint Jean-Baptiste Day — Jun 24
Fourth of July — Jul 4
Major-General Henry Knox Day — Jul 25
Poetry Day — Oct 15
Veterans' Day — Nov 11
Organ Donor Awareness Day — Dec 3
Margaret Chase Smith Day — Dec 14
Chester Greenwood Day — Dec 21
Christmas Day — Dec 25

MARYLAND (MD)

Variable Dates:

Dr. Martin Luther King, Jr.'s Birthday — Jan 15
 or other day designated by the U.S. Congress
 (3rd Mon in Jan)
Washington's Birthday — 3rd Mon in Feb
Arbor Day — 1st Wed in Apr
Good Friday — Last Fri before Easter
Monday After Easter — Mon following Easter
Memorial Day — May 30 or other day designated
 by the U.S. Congress (last Mon in May)
Labor Day — 1st Mon in Sep
Columbus Day — Oct 12 or other day designated
 by the U.S. Congress (2nd Mon in Oct)
Thanksgiving Day — 4th Thu in Nov
Day After Thanksgiving — Fri after Thanksgiving
 Day

Fixed Dates:

New Year's Day — Jan 1
Lincoln's Birthday — Feb 12
Women's History Month — Mar
Maryland Day — Mar 25
John Hanson's Birthday — Apr 13
Law Day, U.S.A. — May 1
Independence Day — Jul 4
Defenders' Day — Sep 12
Poetry Day — Oct 15
Veterans' Day — Nov 11
Christmas Eve — Dec 24 (school holiday)
Unnamed School Holiday — Dec 24–Jan 1
Christmas Day — Dec 25

MASSACHUSETTS (MA)

Variable Dates:

Jaycee Week — 3rd week in Jan

Jaycee Day — Wed of Jaycee Week
Child Nutrition Week — 4th week in Jan
Tadeusz Kosciuszko Day — 1st Sun in Feb
Boy Scout Week — Week including Feb 8
Traffic Safety Week — 2nd week in Feb
Washington's Day — 3rd Mon in Feb
Homeless Awareness Week — Last week in Feb
Employ the Older Worker Week — 3rd week in
 Mar
Practical Nursing Education Week — Last full
 week in Mar
Earth Week — 1st week in Apr
Veterans of World War I Hospital Day — 1st Sun
 in Apr
Student Government Day — 1st Fri in Apr
Aunt's and Uncle's Day — 2nd Sun in Apr
Licensed Practical Nurse Week — 2nd last full
 week in Apr
Secretaries Week — Last full week in Apr
Secretaries Day — Wed in Secretaries Week
Workers' Memorial Day — 4th Fri in Apr
Arbor and Bird Day — Last Fri in Apr
Massachusetts Whale Awareness Day — 1st Thu in
 May
Massachusetts Emergency Responders Memorial
 Day — 2nd Sun in May
Mother's Day — 2nd Sun in May
Emergency Management Week — Week following
 2nd Sun in May
Massachusetts National Guard Week — Week end-
 ing with 3rd Sat of May
Police Officers' Week — Week including May 15
American Indian Heritage Week — 3rd week in
 May
National Family Week — 3rd week in May
Visiting Nurse Association Week — 3rd week in
 May
Joshua James Day — 3rd Sun in May
Massasoit Day — Wed of American Indian Her-
 itage Week
Massachusetts Art Week — Last week in May
Memorial Day — Last Mon in May
Public Employees Awareness Day — 1st Wed in Jun
Garden Week — Week beginning on the 1st Sat in
 Jun
Children's Day — 2nd Sun in Jun
Fire Fighters' Memorial Sunday — 2nd Sun in Jun
State Walking Sunday — 2nd Sun in Jun
Rabies Prevention Week — 2nd week in Jun
Father's Day — 3rd Sun in Jun
Destroyer Escort Day — 3rd Sat in Jun
John Carver Day — 4th Sun in Jun
Saint Jean de Baptiste Day — 4th Sun in Jun
Battleship Massachusetts Memorial Day — Last
 Sat in Jun

Lead Poisoning Prevention Week — Week beginning with 3rd Sun in Jul

Public Employees' Week —1st week in Aug

Youth in Government Day —1st Fri in Aug

Jamaican Independence Day —1st Mon in Aug

Caribbean Week — Last week in Aug

Labor Week —1st week in Sep

Grandparents' Day —1st Mon in Sep

Alzheimer's Awareness Week — Week following the Sun which follows the 1st Mon in Sep

Endangered Species Day — 2nd Sat in Sep

Cystic Fibrosis Week — 3rd full week in Sep

Native American Day — 3rd Fri in Sep

POW/MIA Day — 3rd Fri in Sep

National Hunting and Fishing Day — 4th Sat in Sep

Eddie Eagle Gun Safety Week —1st week in Oct

Employ Handicapped Persons Week —1st full week in Oct

Employee Involvement and Employee Ownership Week —1st week in Oct

Independent Living Center Day —1st Sun in Oct

Senior Citizens' Day —1st Sun in Oct

Social Justice for Ireland Day —1st Sat in Oct

Home Composting Recognition Week — 2nd week in Oct

Columbus Day — 2nd Mon in Oct

Robert Frost Day — 4th Sat in Oct

American Education Week — 2nd week in Nov

Geographic Education Awareness Week — 2nd week in Nov

Massachusetts Hospice Week — 2nd week in Nov

Silver-Haired Legislature Days — 3rd Wed-Fri in Nov

John F. Kennedy Day — Last Sun in Nov

Army and Navy Union Day —1st Sun in Dec

Disabled American Veteran's Hospital Day —1st Sun in Dec

Candle Safety Day — 2nd Mon in Dec

Veteran Firemen's Muster Day — Date not set by statute

Fixed Dates:

Anniversary of Battle of New Orleans — Jan 8

Albert Schweitzer's Reverence for Life Day — Jan 14

Martin Luther King, Jr. Day — Jan 15

American History Month — Feb

USO Appreciation Day — Feb 4

Lincoln Day — Feb 12

Maine Memorial Day — Feb 15

Spanish War Memorial Day — Feb 15

Lithuanian Independence Day — Feb 16

Iwo Jima Day — Feb 19

Homeless Unity Day — Feb 20

Kelevala Day — Feb 28

Irish-American Heritage Month — Mar 1

Anniversary of Boston Massacre — Mar 5

Lucy Stone Day — Mar 8

Slovak Independence Day — Mar 14

Peter Francisco Day — Mar 15

Robert Goddard Day — Mar 16

Evacuation Day — Mar 17

Greek Independence Day — Mar 25

Italian American War Veterans of the United States, Inc. Day — Mar 27

Vietnam Veterans Day — Mar 29

Parliamentary Law Month — Apr

Public Health Month — Apr

School Library Media Month — Apr

Bataan-Corregidor Day — Apr 9

Former Prisoner of War Recognition Day — Apr 9

Patriots' Day — Apr 19

Armenian Martyrs' Day — Apr 24

School Principals' Recognition Day — Apr 27

Exercise Tiger Day — Apr 28

Keep Massachusetts Beautiful Month — May

Law Enforcement Memorial Month — May

Loyalty Day — May 1

Senior Citizens Month — May

Polish Constitution Day — May 3

Horace Mann Day — May 4

Massachusetts Police Memorial Day — May 15

Anniversary of Death of Lafayette — May 20

Maritime Day — May 22

Deborah Samson Day — May 23

Special Needs Awareness Day — May 23

Presidents Day — May 29

Portuguese-American Heritage Month — Jun

Teachers' Day — Jun 1

Retired Members of Armed Forces Day — Jun 2

Flag Day — Jun 14

Anniversary of Battle of Bunker Hill — Jun 17

Korean War Veterans Day — Jun 25

Reflex Sympathetic Dystrophy Awareness Month — Jul

Independence Day — Jul 4

Rose Fitzgerald Kennedy Day — Jul 22

Purple Heart Day — Aug 7

Liberty Tree Day — Aug 14

Social Security Day — Aug 14

Susan B. Anthony Day — Aug 26

Literary Awareness Month — Sep

Sight-Saving Month — Sep

Commodore John Barry Day — Sep 13

Constitution Day — Sep 17

Head Injury Awareness Month — Oct

Italian-American Heritage Month — Oct

Lupus Awareness Month — Oct

Polish-American Heritage Month — Oct
Pro-Life Month — Oct
Town Meeting Day — Oct 8
Leif Ericson Day — Oct 9
Anniversary of Death of General Pulaski — Oct 11
White Cane Safety Day — Oct 15
United Nations Day — Oct 24
State Constitution Day — Oct 25
Statue of Liberty Awareness Day — Oct 26
Youth Honor Day — Oct 31
United States Marine Corps Day — Nov 10
Armistice Day — Nov 11
Veterans Day — Nov 11
Time for Survivors of Homicide Victims Awareness — Nov 20–Dec 20
Pearl Harbor Day — Dec 7
Civil Rights Week — Dec 8–15
Human Rights Day — Dec 10
Samuel Slater Day — Dec 20
Clara Barton Week — Week beginning with Dec 25

MICHIGAN (MI)

Variable Dates:

Saturdays (noon to midnight)
Martin Luther King, Jr. Day — 3rd Mon in Jan
Mrs. Rosa L. Parks Day — 1st Mon following Feb 4
Washington's Birthday — 3rd Mon in Feb
Arbor Day — 4th Fri in Apr
Memorial (Decoration) Day — Last Mon in May
Michigan Garden Week — 1st full week in Jun
Log Cabin Day — Last Sun in Jun
American Family Day — 1st Sun in Aug
Labor Day — 1st Mon in Sep
Michigan Indian Day — 4th Fri in Sep
Columbus Day — 2nd Mon in Oct
Thanksgiving Day — 4th Thu in Nov

Fixed Dates:

New Year's Day — Jan 1
Lincoln's Birthday — Feb 12
Grandparents' and Grandchildren's Day — Mar 18
John Fitzgerald Kennedy Day — May 29
Casimir Pulaski Day — Oct 11
Veterans' Day — Nov 11
Christmas Day — Dec 25

MINNESOTA (MN)

Variable Dates:

Martin Luther King's Birthday — 3rd Mon in Jan
Washington's and Lincoln's Birthday — 3rd Mon in Feb

Arbor Day — Last Fri in Apr
Take a Mom Fishing Weekend — Sat and Sun including Mother's Day
Memorial Day — Last Mon in May
Ethnic American Day — 1st Sun in Jun
Take a Kid Fishing Weekend — 1st weekend in Jun
American Family Day — 1st Sun in Aug
Labor Day — 1st Mon in Sep
Hunting Heritage Week — Week beginning with 3rd Mon in Sep
Take a Kid Hunting Weekend — 3rd weekend in Sep
Christopher Columbus Day — 2nd Mon in Oct
Thanksgiving Day — 4th Thu in Nov

Fixed Dates:

New Year's Day — Jan 1
Four Chaplains Day — Feb 3
Independence Day — Jul 4
Combat Wounded Veterans Purple Heart Day — Aug 7
Mighty Eighth Air Force Week — Oct 8–14
Veterans Day — Nov 11
Christmas Day — Dec 25

MISSISSIPPI (MS)

Variable Dates:

Dr. Martin Luther King, Jr.'s Birthday — 3rd Mon in Jan
Robert E. Lee's Birthday — 3rd Mon in Jan
Washington's Birthday — 3rd Mon in Feb
Mardi Gras Day — 40 days prior to Easter
Jefferson Davis' Birthday — Last Mon in May
National Memorial Day — Last Mon in May
Labor Day — 1st Mon in Sep
Thanksgiving Day — 4th Thu in Nov

Fixed Dates:

New Year's Day — Jan 1
Confederate Memorial Day — Apr 28
Hernando de Soto Day — May 8
Independence Day — Jul 4
Elvis Aaron Presley Day — Aug 16
Veterans' (Armistice) Day — Nov 11
Christmas Day — Dec 25

MISSOURI (MO)

Variable Dates:

Martin Luther King Day — 3rd Mon in Jan
Arbor Day — 1st Fri in Apr
Missouri Day — 1st Mon in Oct

Columbus Day — 2nd Mon in Oct
General State Election Day —1st Tue after 1st
 Mon in Nov
Thanksgiving Day — 4th Thu in Nov
General Primary Election Day — Date TBA

Fixed Dates:

New Year's Day — Jan 1
Missouri Lifelong Learning Month — Feb
Lincoln Day — Feb 12
Alzheimer's Awareness Month — Mar
Bird Appreciation Day — Mar 21
Prisoners of War Remembrance Day — Apr 9
Jefferson Day — Apr 13
Law Day — May 1
Truman Day — May 8
Peace Officers Memorial Day — May 15
Memorial Day — May 30
Flag Day — Jun 14
Korean War Veterans Day — Jul 27
Veterans' Day — Nov 11
Pearl Harbor Remembrance Day — Dec 7
Christmas Day — Dec 25

MONTANA (MT)

Variable Dates:

Sundays
Martin Luther King, Jr. Day — 3rd Mon in Jan
Lincoln's and Washington's Birthdays — 3rd Mon
 in Feb
Arbor Day — Last Fri in Apr
Memorial Day — Last Mon in May
Labor Day —1st Mon in Sep
Official Observance of Montana's Hunting Her-
 itage — Week beginning with 3rd Mon in Sep
Columbus Day — 2nd Mon in Oct
General Election Day —1st Tue after 1st Mon in
 Nov
Thanksgiving Day — 4th Thu in Nov

Fixed Dates:

New Year's Day — Jan 1
Independence Day — Jul 4
Veterans' Day — Nov 11
Christmas Day — Dec 25

NEBRASKA (NE)

Variable Dates:

Saturdays
Sundays

Birthday of Martin Luther King, Jr. — 3rd Mon
 in Jan
President's Day — 3rd Mon in Feb
Arbor Day — Last Fri in Apr
Memorial Day — Last Mon in May
Labor Day —1st Mon in Sep
American Indian Day — 4th Mon in Sep
Columbus Day — 2nd Mon in Oct
Thanksgiving Day — 4th Thu in Nov
Day After Thanksgiving Day — Fri after Thanks-
 giving Day

Fixed Dates:

New Year's Day — Jan 1
George W. Norris Day — Jan 5
State Day — Mar 1
Workers Memorial Day — Apr 28
Independence Day — Jul 4
Pulaski's Memorial Day — Oct 11
Veterans Day — Nov 11
Christmas Day — Dec 25

NEVADA (NV)

Variable Dates:

Martin Luther King, Jr.'s Birthday — 3rd Mon in
 Jan
Washington's Birthday — 3rd Mon in Feb
Arbor Day — Last Fri in Apr
Mother's Day — 2nd Sun in May
Osteoporosis Prevention and Awareness Week —
 Week beginning with Mother's Day
Memorial Day — Last Mon in May
Nevada All-Indian Stampede Days — 3rd week in
 Jul
Labor Day —1st Mon in Sep
Constitution Week — 3rd week in Sep
Columbus Day — 2nd Mon in Oct
Nevada Day — Last Fri in Oct
Thanksgiving Day — 4th Thu in Nov
Family Day — Fri following Thanksgiving Day

Fixed Dates:

New Year's Day — Jan 1
Tartan Day — Apr 6
Law Day, U.S.A. — May 1
Independence Day — Jul 4
Constitution Day — Sep 17
Nevada Indian Day — Sep 26
Veterans' Day — Nov 11
Pearl Harbor Remembrance Day — Dec 7
Christmas Day — Dec 25

NEW HAMPSHIRE (NH)

Variable Dates:

Martin Luther King, Jr. Civil Rights Day — 3rd Mon in Jan

Washington's Birthday — 3rd Mon in Feb

Gold Star Mother's Day — 1st Sun after Easter

Teacher Appreciation Day — 1st Tue in May

Law Enforcement Memorial Week — Week including May 15

Memorial Day — Last Mon in May

Labor Day — 1st Mon in Sep

Columbus Day — 2nd Mon in Oct

Election Day — 1st Tue after 1st Mon in Nov, biennially

Thanksgiving Day — 4th Thu in Nov

Fixed Dates:

New Year's Day — Jan 1

State Constitution Day — Jan 5

American History Month — Feb

Lafayette Day — May 20

Commemoration of Anniversary of Founding of the U.S. Army — Jun 14

Destroyer Escort Day — Jun 20

Independence Day — Jul 4

Commemoration of Anniversary of Founding of the U.S. Coast Guard — Aug 4

Federal Constitution Day — Sep 17

Commemoration of Anniversary of Founding of the U.S. Air Force — Sep 18

Commemoration of Anniversary of Founding of the U.S. Navy — Oct 13

Veterans Day — Nov 11

New Hampshire Pearl Harbor Remembrance Day — Dec 7

Christmas Day — Dec 25

NEW JERSEY (NJ)

Variable Dates:

Saturdays

Sundays

Volunteer Fireman's Day — 2nd Sun in Jan

Volunteer First Aid and Rescue Squad Day — 3rd Sun in Jan

Martin Luther King's Birthday — 3rd Mon in Jan

Washington's Birthday — 3rd Mon in Feb

Women's History Week — 2nd week in Mar

Good Friday — Last Fri before Easter

National Organ and Tissue Donor Awareness Week — 3rd full week in Apr

Take Our Daughters to Work Day — Last Thu in Apr

Holocaust Remembrance Day — The day corresponding to the 27th day of the month of Nisan on the Hebrew calendar

Loyal Heart Award Day — 1st Sun in May

Prayer Day — 1st Thu in May

First Aid Week — 2nd week in May

Human Potential Week — 2nd week in May

Long-Term Care Week — 2nd full week in May

Mother's Day — 2nd Sun in May

New Jersey Shore Celebration Day — 2nd Sat before the last Mon in May

Police, Firemen and First Aid Recognition Day — 3rd Sun in May

Memorial Day — Last Mon in May

Garden Week — 1st full week in Jun

Delaware Bay Day — 2nd Sat in Jun

Father's Day — 3rd Sun in Jun

Literary Awareness Week — 1st full week in Jul

Labor Day — 1st Mon in Sep

Grandparents' Day — 1st Sun after Labor Day

Grandparent Week — Week beginning with Grandparents' Day

New Jersey P.O.W.-M.I.A. Recognition Day — 3rd Fri in Sep

Native American Day — 4th Fri in Sep

Parents of Fallen Military Sons and Daughters Day — Last Sun in Sep

Columbus Day — 2nd Mon in Oct

New Jersey Retired Teachers Day — 1st Sun in Nov

Election Day — 1st Tue following the 1st Mon in Nov

Thanksgiving Day — 4th Thu in Nov

Fixed Dates:

New Year's Day — Jan 1

Lincoln's Birthday — Feb 12

Hepatitis C Awareness Month — Mar

Crispus Attucks Day — Mar 5

Irish-American History and Heritage Week — Mar 11–17

Thomas Mundy Peterson Day — Mar 31

Child Abuse Awareness Month — Apr

Parkinson's Disease Awareness Month — Apr

Women's Wellness Month — Apr

New Jersey Day — Apr 17

Kindness Awareness Month — May

Law Day — May 1

Women Veterans Awareness Month — May

Vietnam Veterans' Remembrance Day — May 7

Peace Officers Memorial Day — May 15

Senior Citizen's Day — May 15

Children's Memorial Day — May 25

Missing Persons Month — May 25–Jun 25

Prostate Cancer Awareness Month — Jun

American Flag Week — Jun 7–14
Lidice Memorial Day — Jun 10
Independence Day — Jul 4
Korean War Veterans' Day — Jul 27
National Airborne Day — Aug 16
Women's Equality Day — Aug 26
Toms River East Little League World Champions Day — Aug 29
New Jersey Care About Children with Cancer Month — Sep
New Jersey Seafood Promotion Month — Oct
Italian-American History and Heritage Week — Week ending with Oct 12
Alzheimer's Disease Awareness Month — Nov
Kristallnacht Memorial Night — Nov 9–10
Veterans' (Armistice) Day — Nov 11
Bill of Rights Day in New Jersey — Nov 20
Pearl Harbor Remembrance Day — Dec 7
Foster Children's Day — Dec 12
Christmas Day — Dec 25

NEW MEXICO (NM)

Variable Dates:

Martin Luther King, Jr.'s Birthday — 3rd Mon in Jan
Hispanic Culture Day — 2nd Tue in Feb
African-American Day — 2nd Fri in Feb
Washington and Lincoln's Birthday (Presidents' Day) — 3rd Mon in Feb
Arbor Day — 2nd Fri in Mar
Memorial Day — Last Mon in May
Onate Day — Jul TBA
Labor Day — 1st Mon in Sep
Family Day — 2nd Sun in Sep
Columbus Day — 2nd Mon in Oct
Thanksgiving Day — 4th Thu in Nov

Fixed Dates:

New Year's Day — Jan 1
American History Month — Feb
Guadalupe-Hidalgo Treaty Day — Feb 2
American Indian Day — Feb 4
Bataan Day — Apr 9
Independence Day — Jul 4
Ernie Pyle Day — Aug 3
Veterans' (Armistice) Day — Nov 11
Christmas Day — Dec 25

NEW YORK (NY)

Variable Dates:

Sundays
Dr. Martin Luther King, Jr. Day — 3rd Mon in Jan
Washington's Birthday — 3rd Mon in Feb
Memorial Day — Last Mon in May
Children's Day — 1st Sun in Jun
Flag Day — 2nd Sun in Jun
Labor Day — 1st Mon in Sep
Native-American Day — 4th Sat in Sep
War of 1812 Day — Last Sat in Sep
Columbus Day — 2nd Mon in Oct
Thanksgiving Day — 4th Thu in Nov

Fixed Dates:

New Year's Day — Jan 1
Haym Salomon Day — Jan 6
Lincoln's Birthday — Feb 12
Lithuanian Independence Day — Feb 16
Pulaski Day — Mar 4
POW Recognition Day — Apr 9
Workers' Memorial Day — Apr 28
Women Veterans Recognition Day — Jun 12
Korean War Veterans Day — Jun 25
Independence Day — Jul 4
Battle of Plattsburgh Day — Sep 11
John Barry Day — Sep 13
Uncle Sam Day in the State of New York — Sep 13
Freidrich Wilhelm von Steuben Memorial Day — Sep 17
Raoul Wallenberg Day — Oct 5
New Netherland Day in the State of New York — Oct 11
Theodore Roosevelt Day — Oct 27
Witness for Tolerance Day — Nov 9
Veterans' Day — Nov 11
Pearl Harbor Day — Dec 7
Bastogne Day — Dec 16
Christmas Day — Dec 25

NORTH CAROLINA (NC)

Variable Dates:

Martin Luther King, Jr.'s Birthday — 3rd Mon in Jan
Washington's Birthday — 3rd Mon in Feb
Arbor Week — Week including Mar 15
Good Friday — Fri before Easter
Memorial Day — Last Mon in May
American Family Day — 1st Sun in Aug
Labor Day — 1st Mon in Sep
Indian Solidarity Week — Last full week in Sep
Yom Kippur — Variable in Sep-Oct
Columbus Day — 2nd Mon in Oct
Election Day — 1st Tue after 1st Mon in Nov
Thanksgiving Day — 4th Thu in Nov
Indian Day — Date to be selected by Governor

Fixed Dates:

New Year's Day — Jan 1
Robert E. Lee's Birthday — Jan 17
Greek Independence Day — Mar 25
Prisoner of War Day — Apr 9
Anniversary of Signing of Halifax Resolves — Apr 12
Confederate Memorial Day — May 10
Anniversary of Mecklenburg Declaration of Independence — May 20
Independence Day — Jul 4
Veterans Day — Nov 11
Pearl Harbor Remembrance Day — Dec 7
Christmas Day — Dec 25

NORTH DAKOTA (ND)

Variable Dates:

Sundays
Martin Luther King Day — 3rd Mon in Jan
Four Chaplains Sunday — 1st Sun in Feb
George Washington's Birthday — 3rd Mon in Feb
Good Friday — Fri before Easter
Arbor Day — 1st Fri in May
Mothers' Day — 2nd Sun in May
Memorial Day — Last Mon in May
Labor Day — 1st Mon in Sep
Gold Star Mothers' Day — Last Sun in Sep
Thanksgiving Day — 4th Thu in Nov

Fixed Dates:

New Year's Day — Jan 1
Bird Day — Apr 26
Anniversary of the Declaration of Independence — Jul 4
Veterans' Day — Nov 11
Christmas Eve — Dec 24
Christmas Day — Dec 25

NORTHERN MARIANA ISLANDS (CM)

Variable Dates:

President's Day — 3rd Mon in Feb
Good Friday — Fri before Easter
Memorial Day — Last Mon in May
Labor Day — 1st Mon in Sep
Columbus Day — 2nd Mon in Oct
Thanksgiving Day — 4th Thu in Nov

Fixed Dates:

New Year's Day — Jan 1
Commonwealth Day — Jan 9
Covenant Day — Mar 24

Independence Day — Jul 4
Citizenship Day — Nov 4
Veteran's Day — Nov 11
Constitution Day — Dec 8
Christmas Day — Dec 25

OHIO (OH)

Variable Dates:

Saturdays (noon-midnight)
Ohio Braille Literacy Week — 1st week in Jan
Martin Luther King Day — 3rd Mon in Jan
Washington-Lincoln Day — 3rd Mon in Feb
School Energy Conservation Day in Ohio — 3rd Fri in Mar
Child Care Worker Appreciation Week — Week of Apr 19
Arbor Day — Last Fri in Apr
Memorial Day — Last Mon in May
Destroyer Escort Day in Ohio — 3rd Sat in Jun
Labor Day — 1st Mon in Sep
Native American Indian Day — 4th Sat in Sep
Gold Star Mothers Day — Last Sun in Sep
Columbus Day — 2nd Mon in Oct
Ohio Mammography Day — 3rd Thu in Oct
Election Day — 1st Tue after 1st Mon in Nov
Thanksgiving Day — 4th Thu in Nov
Ohio Aviation and Aerospace History Education Week — Week of Dec 17

Fixed Dates:

New Year's Day — Jan 1
Ohio Township Day — Feb 1
Lincoln's Birthday — Feb 12
Washington's Birthday — Feb 22
Ohio Statehood Day — Mar 1
World War I Day — Apr 6
Exemplary Adult Care Provider Day — Apr 18
Workers Memorial Day — Apr 28
Independence Day — Jul 4
Ohio National Guard Day — Jul 25
Ohio Breast Cancer Awareness Month — Oct
Ohio Hepatitis C Awareness Month — Oct
General Pulaski Memorial Day — Oct 11
Veterans Educate Today's Students (V.E.T.S.) Day — Nov 10
Veterans' Day — Nov 11
Christmas Day — Dec 25

OKLAHOMA (OK)

Variable Dates:

Saturdays
Sundays

Martin Luther King, Jr.'s Birthday — 3rd Mon in Jan

Arbor Day — Fri following the 2nd Mon in Feb

Presidents' Day — 3rd Mon in Feb

Vietnam Veterans Day — 3rd Thu of Mar

Arbor Week — Last full week in Mar

Senior Citizens' Week — Week beginning on the 1st Sun in May

Senior Citizens' Day — Wed of Senior Citizens' Week

Mother's Day — 2nd Sun in May

Purple Heart Week — Last week in May

Memorial Day — Last Mon in May

Shut-In Day — 1st Sun in Jun

Juneteenth National Freedom Day — 3rd Sat in Jun

Labor Day — 1st Mon in Sep

Grandparents' Week — 1st week in Sep

Indian Day — 1st Sat after full moon in Sep

POW/MIA Recognition Day — 3rd Fri in Sep

Election Day — 1st Tue following the 1st Mon of Nov

Oklahoma Heritage Week — Week including Nov 16

Oklahoma Native American Day — 3rd Mon in Nov

Thanksgiving Day — 4th Thu in Nov

Citizenship Recognition Day — Day selected by Governor

Official Day for each Indian Tribe — Day selected by each tribe

Fixed Dates:

New Year's Day — Jan 1

Youth Day — 3rd Sun in Mar

Prisoners of War Remembrance Day — Apr 9

Jefferson Day — Apr 13

Oklahoma City Bombing Remembrance Day — Apr 19

Oklahoma Day — Apr 22

Bird Day — May 1

Jim Thorpe Day — May 22

Flag Week — Jun 8–14

Independence Day — Jul 4

Cherokee Strip Day — Sep 16

Oklahoma Historical Day — Oct 10

Will Rogers Day — Nov 4

Oklahoma Week — Nov 11–16

Veterans' Day — Nov 11

Oklahoma State Flag Day — Nov 16

Oklahoma Statehood Day — Nov 16

Oklahoma Pearl Harbor Remembrance Day — Dec 7

Bill of Rights Day — Dec 15

Bill of Responsibilities Day — Dec 16

Christmas Day — Dec 25

Day After Christmas — Dec 26 in years Christmas is on a Thu; if Christmas is on a Tue, Dec 24 is a holiday

OREGON (OR)

Variable Dates:

Sundays

Martin Luther King, Jr.'s Birthday — 3rd Mon in Jan

Presidents Day — 3rd Mon in Feb

Women in History Week — 2nd week in Mar

Arbor Week — 1st full week in Apr

History of Oregon Statehood Week — Week of May 2

Armed Forces Day — 3rd Sat in May

Memorial Day — Last Mon in May

Garden Week — 1st full week in Jun

Labor Day — 1st Mon in Sep

Shut-In Day — 3rd Sun in Oct

Thanksgiving Day — 4th Thu in Nov

National POW/MIA Recognition Day — Date not specified by statute

Fixed Dates:

New Year's Day — Jan 1

Lincoln's Birthday — Feb 12

Admission of Oregon into the Union — Feb 14

Washington's Birthday — Feb 22

Asian-American Heritage Month — May

Flag Day — Jun 14

Independence Day — Jul 4

Columbus Day — Oct 12

Veterans Day — Nov 11

Christmas Day — Dec 25

PENNSYLVANIA (PA)

Variable Dates:

Saturdays

Dr. Martin Luther King, Jr. Day — 3rd Mon in Jan

Presidents' Day — 3rd Mon in Feb

Election Day — 3rd Tue in Feb

Good Friday — Fri before Easter

Rothrock Memorial Conservation Week — Week including last Fri in Apr

Arbor Day — Last Fri in Apr

Commonwealth Day of Prayer and Celebration of Religious Freedom — 1st Thu in May

Covered Bridges Week — 1st Sat after the 1st Sun in May, through and including the 3rd Sun in May

Police Week — Week including May 15
Memorial Day — Last Mon in May
Labor Day — 1st Mon in Sep
Pennsylvania POW/MIA Recognition Day — 3rd
  Fri in Sep
Columbus Day — 2nd Mon in Oct
Shut-In Day — 3rd Sun in Oct
Election Day — 1st Tue after 1st Mon in Nov
Thanksgiving Day — 4th Thu in Nov

Fixed Dates:

New Year's Day — Jan 1
Pennsylvanians with Disabilities Day — Jan 30
Lithuanian Independence Day — Feb 16
Charter Day — Mar 14
Bird Day — Mar 21
Local Government Day — Apr 15
Earth Day — Apr 22
American Loyalty Day — May 1
Peace Officers Memorial Day — May 15
Hubert H. Humphrey, Jr. Day — May 27
Rachel Carson Day — May 27
Flag Day — Jun 14
Pennsylvania German Day — Jun 28
Independence Day — Jul 4
Firefighters' Memorial Sunday — Jul 27
Commodore John Barry Day — Sep 13
National Anthem Day — Sep 14
Birthday of William Penn — Oct 24
Veterans' Day — Nov 11
Christmas Day — Dec 25

PUERTO RICO (PR)

Variable Dates:

Sundays
Eugenio Maria de Hostos Week — Week includ-
  ing Jan 11
Martin Luther King's Birthday — 3rd Mon in Jan
Educational Week Pro Tourism in Puerto Rico —
  1st week after last Sun in Jan
Week of Little League Baseball of Puerto Rico —
  1st week in Feb
Luis Munoz-Marin Week — Week including Feb
  18
Rotary Week — 3rd week in Feb
George Washington Day — 3rd Mon in Feb
Racial Equality Week — Week including Mar 22
Day of Homage to Old Age — A day in Apr se-
  lected by the Governor
Day of the Child — 2nd Sun in Apr
Cooperative Dialogue Day — 3rd Wed in Apr
Good Friday — Fri before Easter
Librarian's Day — Fri of the 2nd week in Apr

Jose de Diego Week — Week including 3rd Mon
  in Apr
Vaccination Day — Sun of the 3rd Week in Apr
Jose de Diego Day — 3rd Mon in Apr
Puerto Rico Land Week — Last week in Apr
Land Day — Sun of Puerto Rico Land Week
School Janitor Day — Last Fri in Apr
Teachers Week — Week beginning on the 1st Mon
  in May
Mothers' Day — 2nd Sun in May
Week of the Puerto Rican Danza — Week includ-
  ing May 16
Amateur Radio Operators Day — 2nd Tue in May
Accountant Week — 3rd week in May
Medical Records Transcribers Week — 3rd week
  in May
Glaucoma Day — 3rd Fri in May
Memorial Day — Last Mon in May
Gastronomical Week — 1st week in Jun
Puerto Rican Solidarity Week — 1st week in Jun
Oil Industry Week — 2nd week in Jun
Recreational Leaders Week — 3rd week in Jun
Youth Organizations Week — Week ending with
  4th Sun in Jun
Youth Day — 4th Sun in Jun
Young Blood Donors' Day — Last Fri in Jun
Municipal Assemblymen's Week — 1st week in Jul
Puerto Rico Domino Players Week — 1st week in Jul
Aibonito Flower Festival Day — 1st Sun in Jul (or
  1st Mon, if 1st Sun is Jul 4)
Transportation Week — 2nd week in Jul
Official Public Carrier's Day — 2nd Mon in Jul
Luis Munoz-Rivera Day — 3rd Mon in Jul
Abelardo Diaz Week — Week including Jul 24
Jose Celso Barbosa Week — Week including Jul 27
Press Week — Week including Jul 31
Small and Medium-Sized Retail Merchants
  Week — 3rd week in Aug
Television Non-Violence Day — 4th Thu in Aug
Labor Day — 1st Mon in Sep
National Guard Week — To be set by the Gover-
  nor in September
Santiago Iglesias Pantin Day — 1st Mon in Sep
Week Celebrating Manuel Corchado y Juarbe —
  Week including Sep 12
Housing Project Week — Week beginning 1st
  Mon in Oct
Government of Puerto Rico Pensioner's Week —
  2nd week in Oct
Nuclear Medicine Week — 2nd week in Oct
Columbus Day — 2nd Mon in Oct
Natural Resources Rangers Corps Week — 3rd
  week in Oct
Puerto Rico Business and Professional Women's
  Week — 3rd week in Oct

Quality of Life Week — Last week in Oct
Week of the Historian — 2nd week in Nov
Day of the Historian — Wed of Week of the Historian
Historical Archives Week — 3rd week in Nov
Historical Archivist's Day — Fri of Historical Archives Week
Thanksgiving Day — 4th Thu in Nov
Troubadour's Week — 1st week in Dec
Election Days throughout the Island — To be scheduled
Native Industries Week — To be set by the Governor
Natural and Environmental Resources and Environmental Quality and Health Education Term — To be set by a committee of four governmental departments
Women Devoted to the Religious Vocation Commemorative Week — To be set by the Governor
Also, each town has a Patronal Festival or Fiesta, usually lasting up to ten days

Fixed Dates:

Eye Care Month — Jan
New Year's Day — Jan 1
Three Kings Day — Jan 6
Day to Commemorate Felisa Rincon Vda. de Gautier's Birthday — Jan 9
Birthday of Eugenio Maria de Hostos — Jan 11
Birthday of Armando Sanchez Martinez — Jan 28
Month of Trio Music — Feb
Juan Boria Memorial Day — Feb 17
Day in Commemoration of the Birthday of Don Luis Munoz-Marin — Feb 18
Police Day — Feb 21
Roman Baldorioty de Castro Day — Feb 28
Advent of American Citizenship in Puerto Rico Day — Mar 2
International Women's Day — Mar 8
Emancipation Day — Mar 22
Puerto Rican Boxers' Day — Mar 23
Cancer Prevention and Control Month — Apr
Ramon Emeterio Betances Commemorative Day — Apr 8
Antonio R. Barcelo Day — Apr 13
Renowned Puerto Rican Statesmen's Day — Apr 18
Birthday of Rafael Martinez Nadal — Apr 22
Ernesto Ramos Antonini Day — Apr 24
Day in Honor of the Aged — Apr 30
Month of the Composer — May
International Red Cross Day — May 8
Nursing Personnel Day — May 12
Birthday of Juan Morel Campos and the Day of the Puerto Rican Danza Composers — May 16

Municipal Police Day — May 19
Municipal Police Week — May 19–26
United States of America Flag Day in Puerto Rico — Jun 14
Flag, Anthem and Coat of Arms Day — Jun 24
Puerto Rican Artisan's Month — Jul
Day of the Sports Reporter — Jul 2
Independence Day — Jul 4
Gilberto Concepcion de Gracia Memorial Day — Jul 9
Abelardo Diaz Day — Jul 24
Day of the Constitution — Jul 25
Birthday of Dr. Jose Celso Barbosa — Jul 27
National Journalist Day — Jul 31
Roberto Clemente Day of Remembrance — Aug 18
Bible Day — Sep 1
Day of Birth of Manuel Corchado y Juarbe — Sep 12
Lola Rodriguez de Tio's Birthday — Sep 14
Grito de Lares Day — Sep 23
Month of Mental Health — Oct
General Pulaski Memorial Day — Oct 11
Day of the Retired Educator — Oct 13
White Cane Day — Oct 15
World Rural Women's Day — Oct 15
School Lunchroom Employee Day — Oct 17
Day of Remembrance of Rafael Hernandez — Oct 24
Ramon Power y Giralt Day — Oct 27
Day of Peace — Nov 1
Month of Musical Arts — Nov
Pedrin Zorilla Memorial Day — Nov 9
Veterans Day — Nov 11
Day to Commemorate the Birth of Don Miguel Angel Garcia — Nov 17
Discovery of Puerto Rico Day — Nov 19
Day of No More Violence Against Women — Nov 25
Day of the Blind — Dec 13
Christmas Day — Dec 25

RHODE ISLAND (RI)

Variable Dates:

Sundays
Dr. Martin Luther King, Jr.'s Birthday — 3rd Mon in Jan
Washington's Birthday — 3rd Mon in Feb
National Women's History Week — Week including Mar 8
Rhode Island School Bus Safety Week — 2nd week in Mar
Social Workers' Day — 2nd Wed in Mar
Retired Teachers' Day — 1st Wed in Apr

Combat Veterans' Day — 3rd Sat in Apr
Arbor Day — Last Fri in Apr
Workers' Memorial Day — 4th Fri in Apr
Rhode Island Speech-Language-Hearing Aware-
    ness Week — 1st week in May
Nurses' Day — 1st Mon in May
Rhode Island Hero's Day — 2nd Thu in May
Friendship Day — 2nd Fri in May
National Police Week — Week including May
    15
Neighbor Day — Sun before Memorial Day
ITAM-Vets Daisy Day — 1st Sat in Jun
Gaspee Days — 2nd Sat in Jun, plus following
    Sun
Destroyer Escort Day — 3rd Sat in Jun
Old Home Week — Begins on the 1st Sun in Jul
Rhode Island Indian Day of the Narrangansett
    Tribe of Indians — Last Sat before the 2nd Sun
    in Aug
Victory Day — 2nd Mon in Aug
Labor Day — 1st Mon in Sep
POW-MIA's Day — 3rd Fri in Sep
Columbus Day — 2nd Mon in Oct
Election Day — 1st Tue after 1st Mon in Nov
Thanksgiving Day — 4th Thu in Nov
Veteran Firefighters' Muster Day — As proclaimed
    by the Governor

Fixed Dates:

New Year's Day — Jan 1
Dr. George Washington Carver Recognition
    Day — Jan 5
American History Month — Feb
Lithuanian Independence Day — Feb 16
Peter Francisco Day — Mar 15
Cesar Chavez Day — Mar 31
Dauphine Day — Apr 21
V.F.W. Loyalty Day — May 1
Rhode Island Independence Day — May 4
National Police Memorial Day — May 15
Viet Nam Veterans' Day — May 15
Saint Jean-Baptiste Day — Jun 24
Rhode Island Cape Verdian Recognition Week —
    Jul 2–9
Independence Day — Jul 4
Puerto Rican Recognition Week — Jul 23–29
Korean War Veterans Memorial Day — Jul 27
Disabled American Veterans (D.A.V.) Day — Jul
    31
American Indian Heritage Day — Sep 24
General Casimir Pulaski Day — Oct 11
White Cane Safety Day — Oct 15
Veterans Day — Nov 11
Christmas Day — Dec 25

SOUTH CAROLINA (SC)

Variable Dates:

Martin Luther King, Jr. Day — 3rd Mon in Jan
George Washington's Birthday/President's Day —
    3rd Mon in Feb
Purple Heart Day — 3rd Sat in Feb
Golf Week — Last week in Apr
Mother's Day — 2nd Sun in May
National Memorial Day — Last Mon in May
Garden Week — Begins 1st Sat in Jun
Family Week — Last week in Aug
Labor Day — 1st Mon in Sep
Grandmother's Day — 2nd Sun in Oct
Frances Willard Day — 4th Fri in Oct
Thanksgiving Day — 4th Thu in Nov
Day After Thanksgiving — Fri after Thanksgiving
Arbor Day — 1st Fri in Dec

Fixed Dates:

New Year's Day — Jan 1
South Carolina Day — Mar 18
Loyalty Day — May 1
Confederate Memorial Day — May 10
Jefferson Davis' Birthday — Jun 3
Carolina Day — Jun 28
Independence Day — Jul 4
General Pulaski's Memorial Day — Oct 11
Veterans' Day — Nov 11
Christmas Eve — Dec 24
Christmas Day — Dec 25
Day After Christmas — Dec 26

SOUTH DAKOTA (SD)

Variable Dates:

Sundays
Martin Luther King, Jr. Day — 3rd Mon in Jan
Lincoln's and Washington's Birthday — 3rd Mon
    in Feb
Arbor Day — Last Fri in Apr
Memorial Day — Last Mon in May
Labor Day — 1st Mon in Sep
Native Americans' Day — 2nd Mon in Oct
Thanksgiving Day — 4th Thu in Nov

Fixed Dates:

New Year's Day — Jan 1
Little Big Horn Remembrance Day — Jun 25
Independence Day — Jul 4
South Dakota Statehood Day — Nov 2
Veterans' Day — Nov 11
Bill of Rights Day — Dec 15

Christmas Day — Dec 25
Wounded Knee Day — Dec 29

TENNESSEE (TN)

Variable Dates:

Saturdays (noon to midnight)
Martin Luther King, Jr. Day — 3rd Mon in Jan
Washington Day — 3rd Mon in Feb
Good Friday — Fri before Easter
Mothers' Day — 2nd Sun in May
Memorial (Decoration) Day — Last Mon in May
Family Day — Last Sun in Aug
Labor Day — 1st Mon in Sep
Tennessee P.O.W.-M.I.A. Recognition Week —
    Begins 3rd Fri of Sep
American Indian Day — 4th Mon in Sep
Thanksgiving Day — 4th Thu in Nov

Fixed Dates:

New Year's Day — Jan 1
Robert E. Lee Day — Jan 19
Franklin D. Roosevelt Day — Jan 30
Abraham Lincoln Day — Feb 12
Andrew Jackson Day — Mar 15
Worker's Memorial Day — Apr 28
Statehood Day — Jun 1
Memorial or Confederate Decoration Day — Jun 3
John Sevier Day — Jun 23
Scottish, Scots-Irish Heritage Day — Jun 24
Nathan Bedford Forrest Day — Jul 13
Veterans' Day — Nov 11
Christmas Day — Dec 25

TEXAS (TX)

Variable Dates:

Martin Luther King, Jr. Day — 3rd Mon in Jan
Presidents' Day — 3rd Mon in Feb
Texas Conservation and Beautification Week —
    Week including Apr 21 and 24
Public School Paraprofessional Day — 2nd Wed
    in May
Memorial Day — Last Mon in May
Texas Parents Day — 2nd Sun in Aug
Labor Day — 1st Mon in Sep
Columbus Day — 2nd Mon in Oct
Thanksgiving Day — 4th Thu in Nov
Day After Thanksgiving Day — Fri after Thanks-
    giving Day

Fixed Dates:

New Year's Day — Jan 1

Sam Rayburn Day — Jan 6
Confederate Heroes Day — Jan 19
State of Texas Anniversary Remembrance (STAR)
    Day — Feb 19
Texas Flag Day — Mar 2
Texas Independence Day — Mar 2
Texas Week — Week including Mar 2
Former Prisoners of War Recognition Day — Apr 9
San Jacinto Day — Apr 21
National Wildflower Day — Apr 24
International Trade Awareness Week — May 22–26
Emancipation Day in Texas — Jun 19
Buffalo Soldiers Heritage Month — Jul
Independence Day — Jul 4
Lyndon Baines Johnson Day — Aug 27
Father of Texas Day — Nov 3
Veterans Day — Nov 11
Christmas Eve — Dec 24
Christmas Day — Dec 25
Day After Christmas — Dec 26

UNITED NATIONS (U.N.)

Variable Dates:

International Day of Cooperatives — 1st Sat in Jul
International Day of Peace — Day in Sep of open-
    ing of the U.N. General Assembly
World Maritime Day — During last week in Sep
World Habitat Day — 1st Mon in Oct
International Day for Natural Disaster Reduc-
    tion — 2nd Wed in Oct

Fixed Dates:

Asian and Pacific Decade of Disabled Persons
    (1993–2002)
Decade to Roll Back Malaria in Developing
    Countries, Particularly in Africa (2001–2010)
International Decade for a Culture of Peace and
    Non-Violence for the Children of the World
    (2001–2010)
International Decade of the World's Indigenous
    People (1994–2004)
International Year of Ecotourism (2002)
International Year of Freshwater (2003)
International Year of Microcredit (2005)
International Year of Mountains (2002)
Second Industrial Development Decade for
    Africa (1993–2002)
Second International Decade for the Eradication
    of Colonialism (2001–2010)
Third Decade to Combat Racism and Racial Dis-
    crimination (1993–2003)
United Nations Decade for Human Rights Edu-
    cation (1995–2004)

United Nations Decade for the Eradication of Poverty (1997–2006)

United Nations Literacy Decade: Education for All (2003–2012)

United Nations Year for Cultural Heritage (2002)

International Mother Language Day — Feb 21

United Nations Day for Women's Rights and International Peace — Mar 8

International Day for the Elimination of Racial Discrimination — Mar 21

Week of Solidarity with the Peoples Struggling Against Racism and Racial Discrimination — Mar 21–27

World Day for Water — Mar 22

World Meteorological Day — Mar 23

World Health Day — Apr 7

World Book and Copyright Day — Apr 23

World Press Freedom Day — May 3

International Day of Families — May 15

World Telecommunication Day — May 17

International Day for Biological Diversity — May 22

Week of Solidarity with the Peoples of Non-Self-Governing Territories — May 25–31

World No-Tobacco Day — May 31

International Day of Innocent Children Victims of Aggression — Jun 4

World Environment Day — Jun 5

World Day to Combat Desertification and Drought — Jun 17

World Refugee Day — Jun 20

International Day Against Drug Abuse and Illicit Trafficking — Jun 26

International Day in Support of Victims of Torture — Jun 26

World Population Day — Jul 11

International Day of the World's Indigenous People — Aug 9

International Youth Day — Aug 12

International Day for the Remembrance of the Slave Trade and its Abolition — Aug 23

International Literacy Day — Sep 8

International Day for the Preservation of the Ozone Layer — Sep 16

International Day of Older Persons — Oct 1

World Space Week — Oct 4–10

World Teachers' Day — Oct 5

World Post Day — Oct 9

World Mental Health Day — Oct 10

World Food Day — Oct 16

International Day for the Eradication of Poverty — Oct 17

Disarmament Week — Oct 24–30

United Nations Day — Oct 24

World Development Information Day — Oct 24

International Day for Tolerance — Nov 16

Africa Industrialization Day — Nov 20

Universal Children's Day — Nov 20

World Television Day — Nov 21

International Day for the Elimination of Violence Against Women — Nov 25

International Day of Solidarity with the Palestinian People — Nov 29

World AIDS Day — Dec 1

International Day for the Abolition of Slavery — Dec 2

International Day of Disabled Persons — Dec 3

Intentional Volunteer Day for Economic and Social Development — Dec 5

International Civil Aviation Day — Dec 7

Human Rights Day — Dec 10

International Migrants Day — Dec 18

U.S. VIRGIN ISLANDS (VI)

Variable Dates:

Sunday

Martin Luther King, Jr.'s Birthday — 3rd Mon in Jan

Midwives Week — 2nd week in Feb

Presidents Day — 3rd Mon in Feb

Holy Thursday — Thu before Easter

Good Friday — Fri before Easter

Easter Monday — Mon after Easter

Secretaries Week — Last week in Apr

Teachers' Day — 1st Fri in May

Virgin Islands Police Week — Week including May 15

Virgin Islands African Heritage Week — 3rd week in May

Memorial Day — Last Mon in May

Caribbean Friendship Week — 4th Fri in Aug and next 10 days

Virgin Islands Citizenship Day — TBA in Aug or Sep

Labor Day — 1st Mon in Sep

George Scott Day — Mon of 1st week in Oct

West Indies Solidarity Day — 1st Mon in Oct

Columbus Day — 2nd Mon in Oct

Puerto Rico Friendship Day — 2nd Mon in Oct

Virgin Islands Taxi Week — Last week in Oct

Thanksgiving Day — 4th Thu in Nov

Human Relations Day — 2nd week in Dec

Fixed Dates:

New Year's Day — Jan 1

Three Kings Day — Jan 6

Transfer Day — Mar 31

Cyril Emmanuel King Day — Apr 7

Earth Day — Apr 22
Timothy Theodore Duncan Day — Apr 25
Peace Officers Memorial Day — May 15
African Liberation Day — May 25
Ferry Boat Transportation Day — Jul 2
Emancipation Day — Jul 3
Independence Day — Jul 4
French Heritage Week — Jul 8–14
Nicole Robin Day — Aug 4
Melvin H. Evans Day — Aug 7
Support Our Public Schools Month — Sep
Rothschild Francis Day — Oct 5
D. Hamilton Jackson Day — Nov 1
Veterans Day — Nov 11
Virgin Islands Freedom Fighters Day — Nov 23
Christmas Day — Dec 25
Christmas Second Day — Dec 26

UTAH (UT)

Variable Dates:

Sundays
Dr. Martin Luther King, Jr. Day — 3rd Mon in Jan
Washington and Lincoln Day — 3rd Mon in Feb
Arbor Day — Last Fri in Apr
Memorial Day — Last Mon in May
Labor Day — 1st Mon in Sep
Columbus Day — 2nd Mon in Oct
Thanksgiving Day — 4th Thu in Nov

Fixed Dates:

New Year's Day — Jan 1
Independence Day — Jul 4
Pioneer Day — Jul 24
Constitution Day — Sep 17
Veterans Day — Nov 11
Bill of Rights Day — Dec 15
Christmas — Dec 25

VERMONT (VT)

Variable Dates:

Martin Luther King, Jr.'s Birthday — 3rd Mon in Jan
Washington's Birthday — 3rd Mon in Feb
Town Meeting Day — 1st Tue in Mar
Arbor Day — 1st Fri in May
Labor Day — 1st Mon in Sep
POW-MIA Recognition Day — 3rd Fri in Sep
Columbus Day — 2nd Mon in Oct
Thanksgiving Day — 4th Thu in Nov

Fixed Dates:

New Year's Day — Jan 1

American History Month — Feb
Lincoln's Birthday — Feb 12
Memorial Day — May 30
Independence Day — Jul 4
Bennington Battle Day — Aug 16
Veterans' Day — Nov 11
Christmas Day — Dec 25

VIRGINIA (VA)

Variable Dates:

Lee-Jackson Day — Fri preceding the 3rd Mon in Jan
Martin Luther King, Jr. Day — 3rd Mon in Jan
George Washington Day — 3rd Mon in Feb
Landscape Architecture Week in Virginia — 2nd full week in Apr
Arbor Day — 2nd Fri in Apr
Dogwood Day — 3rd Sat in Apr
Commonwealth Day of Prayer — 1st Thu in May
Mother's Day — 2nd Sun in May
Memorial Day — Last Mon in May
Virginia World War II Veterans Appreciation Week — 1st full week in Sep
Labor Day — 1st Mon in Sep
Virginia Championship Applebutter Making Contest — 3rd week in Sep
Columbus Day — 2nd Mon in Oct
Yorktown Victory Day — 2nd Mon in Oct
Virginia Drug-Free Day — Sat of the last week in Oct
Veterans' Recognition Day — 2nd Sat in Nov
Vietnam War Memorial Dedication Day — 2nd Sat in Nov
Day of Appreciation for American Indians — Wed before Thanksgiving Day
Thanksgiving Day — 4th Thu in Nov
Day After Thanksgiving Day — Fri after Thanksgiving Day

Fixed Dates:

New Year's Day — Jan 1
Virginia and American History Month — Jan 19–Feb 22
Day of Recognition for Bone Marrow Donor Programs — Apr 8
Month for Children — May
First Lady's Day in Virginia — Jun 2
Motherhood and Apple Pie Day — Jun 26
Independence Day — Jul 4
Citizenship Day — Sep 17
Constitution Week — Sep 17–23
Yorktown Day — Oct 19

Day of Recognition for Early Childhood and Day-Care Providers and Professionals — Oct 22
American Indian Month — Nov
Veterans Day — Nov 11
Pearl Harbor Remembrance Day — Dec 7
Bill of Rights Day — Dec 15
Christmas Day — Dec 25

Fixed Dates:

New Year's Day — Jan 1
Lincoln's Birthday — Feb 12
West Virginia Day — Jun 20
Independence Day — Jul 4
Veterans' Day — Nov 11
Christmas Day — Dec 25

WASHINGTON (WA)

Variable Dates:

Sundays
Anniversary of the Birth of Martin Luther King, Jr. — 3rd Mon in Jan
Presidents' Day — 3rd Mon in Feb
Arbor Day — 2nd Wed in Apr
Memorial Day — Last Mon in May
Labor Day — 1st Mon in Sep
Thanksgiving Day — 4th Thu in Nov
Day After Thanksgiving Day — Day following Thanksgiving Day

Fixed Dates:

New Year's Day — Jan 1
Temperance and Good Citizenship Day — Jan 16
Washington Army and Air National Guard Day — Jan 26
Former Prisoners of War Recognition Day — Apr 9
Mother Joseph Day — Apr 16
Anniversary of the Declaration of Independence — Jul 4
Purple Heart Recipient Recognition Day — Aug 7
Marcus Whitman Day — Sep 4
Columbus Day — Oct 12
Washington State Children's Day — Oct 12
Veterans' Day — Nov 11
Pearl Harbor Remembrance Day — Dec 7
Christmas Day — Dec 25

WEST VIRGINIA (WV)

Variable Dates:

Martin Luther King's Birthday — 3rd Mon in Jan
Washington's Birthday — 3rd Mon in Feb
Memorial Day — Last Mon in May
Labor Day — 1st Mon in Sep
Columbus Day — 2nd Mon in Oct
Election Day — 1st Tue after 1st Mon in Nov, plus dates of primary or special elections
Native Heritage Week — Week beginning Sun before Thanksgiving Day
Thanksgiving Day — 4th Thu in Nov

WISCONSIN (WI)

Variable Dates:

Presidents' Day — 3rd Mon in Feb
Good Friday — Fri before Easter
Memorial Day — Last Mon in May
Labor Day — 1st Mon in Sep
Primary Election Day — Sep TBA
Columbus Day — 2nd Mon in Oct
Family Sunday — 1st Sun in Nov
General Election Day — 1st Tue after 1st Mon in Nov
Thanksgiving Day — 4th Thu in Nov

Fixed Dates:

New Year's Day — Jan 1
Dr. Martin Luther King, Jr.'s Birthday — Jan 15
Independence Day — Jul 4
Indian Rights Day — Jul 4
Wisconsin Family Month — Nov
Wisconsin Family Week — Nov 1–7
Veterans' Day — Nov 11
Christmas Day — Dec 25

WYOMING (WY)

Variable Dates:

Martin Luther King, Jr., Wyoming Equality Day — 3rd Mon in Jan
Washington's and Lincoln's Birthdays — 3rd Mon in Feb
Arbor Day — Last Mon in Apr
Memorial Day — Last Mon in May
Labor Day — 1st Mon in Sep
Native American Day — 3rd Fri in Sep
Thanksgiving Day — 4th Thu in Nov

Fixed Dates:

New Year's Day — Jan 1
Independence Day — Jul 4
Veterans Day — Nov 11
Nellie Taylor Ross' Birthday — Nov 29
Pearl Harbor Recognition Day — Dec 7
Wyoming Day — Dec 10
Christmas Day — Dec 25

Subject Index

Africa: Africa Industrialization Day (U.N.) 117; African Liberation Day (VI) 62; Decade to Roll Back Malaria in Developing Countries, Particularly in Africa (U.N.) 7; International Day for the Elimination of Racial Discrimination (U.N.) 33; Second Industrial Development Decade for Africa (U.N.) 80; Virgin Islands African Heritage Week (VI) 54; Week of Solidarity with the Peoples of Non–Self-Governing Territories (U.N.) 62; World Refugee Day (U.N.) 71

African-Americans: African-American Day (NM) 16; Anniversary of Boston Massacre (MA) 29; Anniversary of the Birth of Martin Luther King, Jr. (WA) 6; Birthday of Dr. Jose Celso Barbosa (PR) 80; Birthday of Dr. Martin Luther King (CO) 6; Birthday of Martin Luther King, Jr. (FL) 11; (Fed, GA, NE) 11; Crispus Attucks Day (NJ) 29; Daisy Gatson Bates Day (AR) 17; Dr. George Washington Carver Recognition Day (RI) 9; Dr. Martin Luther King, Jr. Day (CA, HI, NY, PA, UT) 6; Dr. Martin Luther King, Jr.'s Birthday (WI) 11; (AR, DE, IA, LA, MD, MS, RI) 6; Jose Celso Barbosa Week (PR) 76; Juan Boria Memorial Day (PR) 21; Martin Luther King Day (CT, MO, ND, OH) 6; Martin Luther King, Jr. Civil Rights Day (NH) 6; Martin Luther King, Jr./Civil Rights Day (AZ) 6; Martin Luther King, Jr. Day (MA) 11; (DE,

ME, MI, MT, SC, SD, TN, TX, VA) 6; Martin Luther King, Jr.-Idaho Human Rights Day (ID) 6; Martin Luther King, Jr., Wyoming Equality Day (WY) 6; Martin Luther King, Jr.'s Birthday (AL, AK, IL, IN, KY, NV, NM, NC, OK, OR, VI, VT) 6; Martin Luther King's Birthday (MN, NJ, PR, WV) 6; Mrs. Rosa L. Parks Day (MI) 15; Thomas Mundy Peterson Day (NJ) 35; Virgin Islands African Heritage Week (VI) 54

Agriculture: Arkansas Agriculture Recognition Day (AR) 30; Farmers' Appreciation Days (GU) 28; Farmers' Day (FL) 102; International Day of Cooperatives (U.N.) 74; Kentucky Harvest Day (KY) 116; Land Day (PR) 41; Missouri Day (MO) 100; Puerto Rico Land Week (PR) 41; Washington Parish Free Fair (LA) 103

Alcohol and Drugs: Alcohol Awareness Week (ME) 119; Drunk Driving Victims Remembrance Day (AK) 77; Frances Willard Day (SC) 103; International Day Against Drug Abuse and Illicit Trafficking (U.N.) 72; Susan B. Anthony Day (CO) 20; Susan B. Anthony's Birthday (FL, IL) 20; Temperance and Good Citizenship Day (WA) 11; Virginia Drug-Free Day (VA) 104; Women in History Week (OR) 25; World No-Tobacco Day (U.N.) 63

Armed Forces: Armed Forces Day (OR) 55; Army and Navy Union

Day (MA) 119; Commemoration of Anniversary of Founding of the U.S. Air Force (NH) 96; Commemoration of Anniversary of Founding of the U.S. Army (NH) 70; Commemoration of Anniversary of Founding of the U.S. Coast Guard (NH) 83; Commemoration of Anniversary of Founding of the U.S. Navy (NH) 107; Joshua James Day (MA) 54; United States Marine Corps Day (MA) 115

Authors: Abelardo Diaz Day and Week (PR) 75, 79; Albert Schweitzer's Reverence for Life Day (MA) 11; Day and Week of Birth of Manuel Corchado y Juarbe (PR) 89, 94; Ernest Gruening Day (AK) 19; Jefferson Davis' Birthday (AL) 69; John Muir Day (CA) 47; Jose de Diego Week (PR) 40; Luis Munoz-Rivera Day (PR) 78; Maine Cultural Heritage Week (ME) 26; Missouri Day (MO) 100; National Journalist Day (PR) 80; Rachel Carson Day (PA) 62; World Book and Copyright Day (U.N.) 48

Aviation: International Civil Aviation Day (U.N.) 121; National Aviation Day (Fed) 85; Ohio Aviation and Aerospace History Education Week (OH) 120; Pan American Aviation Day (Fed) 122; Powered Flight Day (CT) 125; Wright Brothers Day (Fed) 122

Birds and Animals: Arbor and Bird Day (IL, MA) 41; Arkansas Bird Day (AR) 49; Bird Appreciation

151

Name Index